THE WORLD AT 10 MPH

THE
WORLD
AT
10 MPH

A MASTERFUL
PRENUP LEADS
TO A 3-YEAR
33,523-MILE
BICYCLE
ADVENTURE

WARD AND JACKY BUDWEG

LIONCREST
PUBLISHING

THE WORLD AT 10 MPH
A Masterful Prenup Leads to a 3-Year 33,523-Mile Bicycle Adventure

ISBN   978-1-5445-1539-7 *Hardcover*
       978-1-5445-1538-0 *Paperback*
       978-1-5445-1537-3 *Ebook*

We would like to thank all of our friends and families for supporting us on this grand adventure. We did not do this by ourselves, nor could we! I guess as they say, "It takes a village." Or, should we say, "a world." We had many people join us along the way, put us up for the night (or ten!), follow us through our website or the radio, talk to us through Skype, donate to our PayPal...and we THANK YOU. We also met so many great people along the way through the Rotary Club and the Elks Club who were so hospitable (and have since become lifelong friends). At other times, when we were desperate for a place to stay, strangers would put us up for the night either camping in their yard or welcoming us into their home. They gave us a whole new definition of trust and belief in humanity.

We would also like to thank Kathy Gundersen for taking care of our accounting, Travis Greentree for always being ready to lend a helping hand in getting and sending us needed bicycle parts, Kelly Reagan for helping distribute funds into our account, Sara and Dale Putnam for storing the heirlooms for us that we kept and Dale for taking care of our legal work. Also, thanks again to Dale Putnam and John Budweg for being our POAs.

This book is dedicated to Pat Tlusty, and Rose and John Budweg, who have passed away. They have played such an important role in our lives and have inspired us to go beyond. There is no end!

(Please see the list of family and friends, located at the back of the book who have joined us on this adventure or put us up for the night when we were in their region.)

CONTENTS

PROLOGUE

"Ward, we need a better map," said Jacky. "There are no roads. There are no towns on this map!"

"Welcome to Patagonia!" replied Ward.

We should have researched Patagonia, and Tierra del Fuego in particular, more thoroughly than we had. Yet, here we were, bicycling in the Andes Mountains, seeing no roads marked on the map, and facing the Patagonian winds. This phenomenally windy area should have been named Tierra del Viento!

We spent a week of fighting the winds in Argentina; we thought the windy condition would never change. Winds continued, ranging from 15 to 60 mph as we entered Chile. We struggled to haul ourselves and our bikes—Ward's weighed 130 pounds and Jacky's close to 75—through the Andes. The winds swirled around us constantly through gateways in the mountains, so we couldn't go very fast. The highest speed Jacky could muster was 5 or 6 mph, only to be stopped in her tracks by gusts of wind. Sometimes we were both blown sideways off the road. Big trucks passed us, whipping the wind around so we could barely steer. One gust actually blew Jacky over onto the road itself.

The harsh conditions affected us differently, though. Ward was in heaven, loving the survival-style ride we were on. He kept saying, "Isn't this great?! I just love this!" However, being at the mercy of the elements was frightening, especially for Jacky. The moment of reckoning came as we realized we were alone amidst the constant swirling winds with no hope of rescue should things go badly wrong. We had sort of stepped off the edge of the world. There was no 911 out there; we could only rely on ourselves.

After a while, you wonder, "Whose idea was this?!"

It was time to face the reality of what we had undertaken. We needed to decide: are we committed to this trip or are we turning back? We decided to ride on.

The next morning, things started to get better as we were able to get out of the wind thanks to a homesteader called Aquarius, who invited us in for coffee and fresh bread, cooked in his wood-fired stove. No bread will ever compare to his. It was prepared with such kindness. He had so little and gave so much. That's how our around-the-world trip began, with courage-testing trials followed by the welcoming, nurturing kindness of others.

Many memoirs proceed in chronological order, but that just didn't seem right for a journey as unusual as ours. Our three-year bicycle trip around the world launched unconventionally, after all, with Jacky writing a prenuptial agreement on the back of a bar napkin. That's where we—Ward and Jacky—first agreed to pedal the planet.

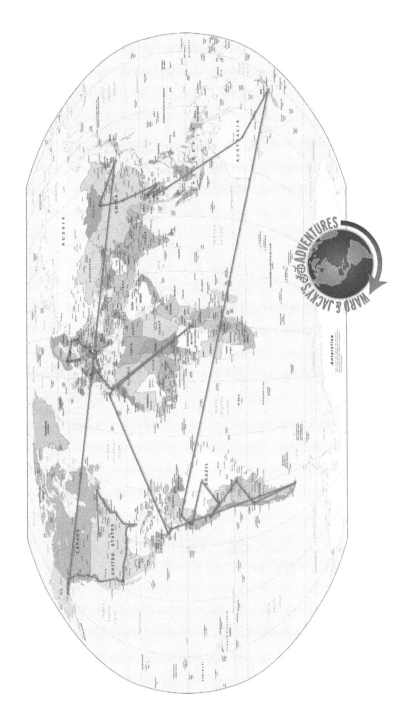

So much happened to us between 2007 and 2010 that we decided to organize our tale into thematic sections rather than plot out all the places we went in the order that we went to them. Several themes became clear over the course of the trip—the importance of staying dry, warm, and fed chief among them—but it always came down to the people we met and the warm, welcoming spirit we felt all over the world. That's what we want to share with our readers.

Writing a memoir is often a lonely experience, but we've done that differently, too. We've written it together, in much the same spirit that we give talks about our adventures. We tell the basics of the story as if we're reporting on this crazy couple who biked around the world, but each of us has a unique perspective on the experience, as well.

So you'll hear us bantering back and forth like the long-married couple we are. We'll take turns telling our story. Soon, you'll have no trouble telling who is talking about scooping up loose change at a busy intersection (Ward) and who is more concerned about making it through the traffic alive (Jacky).

Our mission statement at the outset was this:

From our bicycles, we want to explore the many cultural differences and hospitalities of the world, as we respond with open arms of friendship and service.

We wanted to learn as much as we could. Eat everything. See everything. Accept all the hospitality, be of service, and build friendships.

At times, our journey might seem like the most spontaneous

adventure ever, but this mission statement was at the heart of it all. We thought a lot about it and came up with a framework from which we would enjoy the world. Built into that framework was a lot of space for serendipity, which is just the way we wanted it.

Here we have chosen stories from the road that we hope will inspire, motivate, and entertain you, as well as reassure you that the human spirit is alive and well all over the globe. These are the tales that restored our belief in humanity.

Let's go for a ride.

CHAPTER ONE

THE PRENUP

What enticed us to take off on such a journey? It was that well thought-out prenuptial agreement signed on a bar napkin. (Actually, there were two prenups—one sealed the promise to bike around the world together and the other, perhaps more difficult commitment, specified that Ward was to become a Green Bay Packers fan after a lifetime of Chicago Bears allegiance.)

We met each other on a bike tour, the GRABAAWR (Great Annual Bicycling Adventure Along the Wisconsin River). This tour is a great way to meet people; everyone has the same goal—to make the weeklong, 500-mile journey from Northern Wisconsin to Southern Wisconsin. Biking is really a great equalizer. Everyone has to deal with the elements of wind, rain, and heat; the cost of one's bike makes no difference.

Jacky: Ward was Trek's Wrench Force bicycle mechanic on this ride. He pulled a Burley trailer behind his bike, equipped to fix people's tires and mechanical problems. As he repaired the bike, he told a joke or shared a piece of candy to make the rider's day a little sweeter. His charisma and true desire to help people captivated others.

Ward: Jacky was amazing on the GRABAAWR. I saw her spirit even in pouring rain. She was always looking for the break in the clouds, that little glimpse of light. That's really what I fell in love with. I thought, "Wow, that's just a real positive person even in the worst scenario."

Jacky: To this day, I often get asked why I wanted to go on this world trip. Was I crazy? But the journey was special to me. At the age of twenty, after losing my fiancé to cancer, I promised myself that I would live with no regrets. I was never going to say, "I wish I would have." In college, I had caught the biking bug. Once I graduated, a friend of mine and I biked from Seattle to Santa Barbara. Being self-contained gave me a complete sense of freedom. We weren't dependent on anyone. We had our tent, sleeping bags, clothes, bicycle tools, and daily food. I loved knowing we could stop when and where we wanted. When the trip was over, I knew I wanted to do more. I always wanted to go overseas and see other cultures and I thought, why not do it at 10 mph.

Ward: I was probably seven or eight years old when my friends and I regularly did a five-mile ride up the street from our house in New Hampton, Iowa. I could ride to my grandparents' farm six miles out of town. The only thing holding me back was my own energy. In high school, I rode my bike daily, going wherever I wanted. In college, my bicycle was my car. My love of the freedom to go wherever I wanted never subsided. Riding my bike always puts a smile on my face because of the freedom it gives me.

We're often asked how we chose our route. It took shape organically, growing from lists of places that we longed to see. Ward, for instance, remembered pictures from his fourth-grade geography book. He paged through it as a kid, thinking maybe someday he could see the Eiffel Tower, or the Great Wall of China. Maybe someday he could see the Panama Canal. That book just captivated him. Also, Ward had four uncles in the military, and when postcards arrived from them for his mother, he asked her, "Well, where are they?" The answers provided lessons on where a country like Australia or Argentina was located on the map. During the Vietnam War, Ward asked all sorts of questions when his uncles came home. "What's the food like? What's the temperature? What language do they speak?" His father had served in the United States Army during World War II as well, so he had heard stories about New Guinea, the Philippines, and Australia. The military connection created a sense of where people were from and gave him a connection to these places.

CHAPTER TWO

PLAN BECOMES REALITY

The prenuptial agreement specified taking the trip after ten years of marriage, but we ended up moving it up a few years. In 2007, the time was right. Our sons, John and Ross, (Ward's biological sons and Jacky's stepsons) had left the nest and were off exploring life on their own. Ward was turning fifty, his parents had both passed on, and Jacky's parents were in good health. It was time.

Meanwhile, though we had been living with the absolute intention of launching this trip, there was nothing whimsical about it. We had a plan we took seriously, right down to the timing. Jacky, who was working as a nutritionist, told her employer in the year 2000 that she would be quitting in seven years. Ward, a bike shop owner, let his employees know he would be selling the business.

Ward: It was all about setting a date and timeline. You put it on the calendar and pretty soon the calendar becomes reality. That's what we needed to do.

Jacky: There were people who thought we would never do it.

Ward: Some of our friends that like to gamble were betting the under on whether we'd really go or not.

We were simply determined to make the trip a reality. All practical efforts were made to increase the equity of the bicycle shop we owned prior to the sale, which provided our travel fund. We had to sacrifice and reprioritize how we were going to live. We lived simply and never bought anything new; we always knew we were going to get rid of everything. Our friends joked that we lived like Spartans. We thought it was imperative to sell the house, business, car, and all personal belongings (other than some family heirlooms), so we could totally immerse ourselves in the cultures that we would be visiting. Keeping these belongings back in Iowa would mentally distract us from our goal of learning about the world.

Jacky: It was so liberating when we had our yard sale and I watched the couch being hauled out of the house. Most people can't relate to this, but it was the best feeling.

Ward: I always tell people about my dad's farm. In 2004, an over-stoked fire burned the farmhouse down. A lifetime of memories was gone. But the reality is a good fire, flood, or tornado can take it all away. It's only stuff.

We both had a lot of confidence going into the trip, based on experience.

Jacky: My confidence probably came from when I was twenty-one, and two girlfriends and I quit our jobs and moved to Colorado. We had three old cars, and as we drove out there we'd have to stop on the side of the road and lift the hoods to let the engines cool off. We had no jobs and only about $500 to our names, but we made it happen. We applied for any job that we could and took the first ones that we were offered, in hopes of finding a better job down the road. That built a lot of confidence for me. Also, my bicycle trip from Seattle to Santa Barbara gave me a lot of confidence. I had to be the mechanic! (I don't even change a tire now. I have Ward.)

Ward: I've just always lived with a certain level of confidence. If I set my mind to it, I'm going to do it. I don't necessarily know how I'll do it, but it'll happen. There's just a "stick-to-it-iveness" that drives me. A lot of people say, "Well if he says he's going to do it, you better get out of the way!"

INSPIRED BY...

The travel bug infected both of us early on, and we knew frugality was key. In fact, it was a familiar habit for both of us. We are both from large broods where the family funds had to be stretched—Jacky is one of seven girls, and Ward has eight siblings.

Jacky: My mom was a big influence. She saved travel money in a rainy-day piggy bank hidden under a table and covered with a tablecloth. My dad didn't know anything about it. For three years, we pumped it full of change. When it came time to cash it in, there was $500 in there, which was a nice sum of cash back then. My mom wanted to go to Oregon to see her brother, so we loaded up the station wagon and went on my first trip ever. The $500 had to last our huge family three weeks, so we always stopped in the parks and made a picnic breakfast or lunch. At eight years old, this sparked my interest in seeing more of the United States and the world.

In addition to tracking his uncles in foreign lands, Ward always wanted to be an exchange student.

Ward: I wanted to live in Spain so I could understand that culture. Also, as one of nine kids, it wasn't that big a deal if one kid was missing, right? Really, though, being among so many siblings, it was sometimes important to set yourself apart and have different interests. Mine was about seeing things. In high school, I went to Mexico City twice with the Spanish class. It was the same trip both times, but I enjoyed it so much. I just immersed myself in it. Anytime there was anyone going anywhere, I always wanted to go along.

My mother was an important influence, too. Even with nine kids, she always had room for one more. When I was in second or third grade, she made an effort through the church to help out Cuban refugees. It was just part of the way my mother was, to want to drive us to learn about other people. We always had exchange students in our house and that sparked my interest in their home countries. In my first year of college, I went to a travel and transportation school so I could work for the airlines and travel the world.

WHO IS WARD BUDWEG?

Being from a farm family of nine children makes Ward a person who understands the values of family, hard work, sharing, and competing. With seven children in seven years, competing for food at the dinner table and the attention of parents was constant. Having minimal food made him appreciate what he did have.

Very simply put, Ward is a very kind, giving, strategic, inventive, resourceful, helpful, frugal, confident, and physically fit guy, but mostly he is one very driven son of a bitch. Get out of the way if something needs to get done. Do not tell him it can't be done.

He once signed up for an Ironman Triathlon without knowing how to swim. The first leg is a 2.4-mile swim. In another separate event, he bicycled 320 miles across the state of Iowa in less than twenty-four hours. One of his biggest accomplishments was graduating from college, as his high school counselor said he would not make it through. Hard work and perseverance have paid off over time.

WHO IS JACKY BUDWEG?

Jacky is number six in a lineup of seven girls. Brought up Catholic, Jacky and her sisters all developed the trait of "niceness." When it comes time to make a decision, it is hard for some of them. They worry, "What if I offend someone? What if the others don't like my choice? Will they tell me or keep quiet because they are 'nice' too?"

Being nice is a positive attribute, but it can be a fault if no decisions get made, or at least not efficiently.

Ward: I experienced this with Jacky on the bike trip. It drove me nuts if she couldn't make a decision. Even if I didn't agree when she finally did decide, I was just so thankful that she actually made one!

Jacky: My having no brothers meant my dad had no sons. Living in a house with eight estrogen-fueled women must have been challenging. Dad always said that he was happy having all girls, but at times, we did fill that son's role by stacking firewood, going fishing with him, etc. I don't consider myself a tomboy, but these outdoor activities with my dad did help me overall be more comfortable and adaptable to the outdoor challenges of this trip. I always believed that some of us younger daughters had names that could go either way, girl or boy (Jacqueline or Jack for instance). I knew I had my dad's respect when, after he diligently tried to talk me out of going on this trip, only to admit defeat, he took an active role in researching the upcoming countries to warn us about poisonous spiders, snakes, and other concerns. One of his most common questions was, "Do you have worms yet?" That was one question to which I was happy to say, "No!"

CHAPTER THREE

DETAILS IN THE PLAN

Having some basic ground rules helped guide our route planning. The top three:

1. It must be safe.
2. It should not be wet.
3. It can't be too cold (fifty degrees Fahrenheit).

Our around-the-world trip required a lot more planning than a three-week road trip to Oregon or a high school excursion to Mexico City, but we were up for the challenge. We didn't want to be bicycling during the rainy or monsoon season. We didn't want to be bicycling when the temperature was below fifty degrees. We didn't want to be bicycling in dangerous territories. However, there were times when we broke all three rules at once.

PLANNED HOW AND WHEN, BUT NOT WHAT

We planned the trip very, very carefully, though unconventionally. Where many travelers go by the guidebook and make hotel reservations in tourist towns, we did just the opposite.

We arrived in unknown towns and then looked around for a place to stay. We knew what countries we were going to explore and where and when we would enter and leave that continent, but the territory in between was up for grabs. We had to account for variations, always aiming to miss flood or monsoon season if possible. It required complex planning, but with so much taken care of ahead of time, we could then go where our bicycles took us within those parameters. Meticulous planning wasn't restrictive for us; it was freeing.

We developed a matrix that helped us answer the "how to, how much, and what if" questions. We answered the questions independently and found that we felt very similarly about these topics, which made the planning process easier. Everything was outlined in The Matrix.

THE MATRIX

- How often do you want to go to church?
- How many Rotary meetings do you want to go to?
- How many miles do you want to bike per day?
- What is our daily budget?
- What family events/occurrences will we come back for?
- How often do we want to stay with other people on the trip?
- How many days in a row will we bike before taking a break?
- How many museums do we want to go to?
- Do we want to ride with other people and, if so, how often?
- What other modes of transportation are we willing to take?
- What if someone in our family dies?
- What if one of us were to get sick or injured?
- What if either of us died?

This last question on The Matrix revealed a lot about our personalities. In the event of a death, we each intended to carry on with the trip, but Jacky was prepared to take a period of mourning first. Ward, on the other hand, thought he would maybe take a few days off and then carry Jacky's ashes with him for the remainder of the trip, sprinkling them as he went.

STAYING CONNECTED

As we were putting the trip together, we wanted to create a way for our family and friends to keep abreast of where we were. We also wanted to encourage a following of people to help support future trips. To that end, we created a website called "From the Benches of the World." The website name was a symbol for one way we would learn about the world. If we could not speak the language, we would just sit on a bench and watch how the society moved throughout the day.

It is amazing how cultures change in just fifty or sixty miles (a one-day ride). The deliberate study of people's daily routines opened our eyes to each culture. For instance, we witnessed the daily purchase of bread in France, the daily exercise regimen in China, the long lines for buying meat in Brazil, the morning scramble of dayworkers looking for a job in Rwanda, and the droves of children walking or riding their bikes to school in Laos.

Our website integrated email, a photo gallery, a blog, and e-group newsletters. The blog provided a snippet of what we were doing and the e-group newsletters gave much more detail in telling the stories. The website also offered PayPal options for those who wanted to help support our trip or buy Ward a beer in a certain country.

E-mail was our primary method of communicating with family and friends, but when it was important to talk to family "in person," we used Skype. It was hilarious when Jacky Skyped her parents, who live in Medford, Wisconsin. If we called from China, for instance, her dad, Elroy, who is quite a talker, always said, "This is costing you a fortune." Once Jacky reminded him, "It only costs 2.1 cents a minute," he talked on and on.

CHAPTER FOUR

NUTRITION: NOT ALWAYS BY THE BOOK

We don't have many regrets about our choices on this trip, but one thing we wish we had been able to do more of is sample the local cuisines. We tried to eat food that was culturally part of the country we were visiting, but with our tight budget, we missed many opportunities to enjoy culinary specialties, especially in Europe.

BURGERS AND PIZZA

Ward: On fifty dollars a day, you don't go out to eat in France. You don't go out to eat in Norway or Denmark either, where a Big Mac alone costs $12.50. Our budget largely prohibited eating in restaurants.

We used the Big Mac as an economic barometer of food costs around the world. While Big Macs cost $12.50 in Denmark, they were $1.38 in Panama.

Jacky: The Big Mac was something that we could count on

being the same no matter where we were. That was our gauge of what things were going to cost relative to our currency.

Fifty dollars a day seemed reasonable to us. We chose that amount because the return on the investments that we had in place at the time allowed us that amount per day. Other than in Europe, we did manage to stay within that budget. At the time, the Euro wasn't favorable, so that took a toll on our plan ($1.62 = 1 Euro). However, we were able to go to the bakeries in France, and other places in Europe, and sample their pastries.

Another food we tried to compare between countries was pizza. We allowed ourselves to splurge on pizza at local restaurants.

One of the best pizzas we had was in Slovenia. It was rich with tomatoes and cheese and the wood-fired pizza oven made it very flavorful. Italian pizza was exceptional, too, but the German version was less so.

Ward: The German pizza was not as good. They don't put much tomato on it, and they put slices of egg on top. As you're eating it, you go, "Gosh, this isn't right!"

Most of the time, though, we ate more simply. When we were carrying food with us, we brought only basic supplies. We lived mostly on rice, pasta, breads, cheese, and oatmeal.

NOODLES AND...MORE NOODLES

Ward: Our first meal on the road was in a campground in Germany. We found a store and bought noodles, cheese, and bread. We used ketchup to create a sauce and that was it. That was kind of our daily routine: buy some noodles, see if we can make a sauce, maybe find some cheese, and add salt and pepper as needed.

Meat was a rare treat, both because of the cost and the difficulty of carrying it with no refrigeration. There were times when we broke down and bought some meat to cook and add to our meal. We carried the leftovers with us and hoped we didn't get sick when we ate it later.

For the most part, this strategy worked well. We had a few bouts of dysentery, but Imodium took care of it. We were never plagued with E. coli or other food-borne illnesses. We were very practical about our decisions, so each day we considered the temperature and decided what perishable foods were safe to carry. If it was going to be in the nineties, we didn't carry hard-boiled eggs with us, but if it looked like it was going to be in the sixties and seventies then we did.

Jacky: We also did this with mayonnaise. We had a tube of mayonnaise that lasted over a week in the cooler temperatures. As a dietitian, I had to let go of many of the rules that I learned in school. If I had followed them all, we wouldn't have been able to eat hardly anything without refrigeration. Now, I think we have ironclad stomachs.

Breaking the rules meant taking some risks, though, and we did suffer from maintaining such a low-protein diet. Our fingernails started peeling while we were in Asia, and our hair took on a reddish tint; we often wondered if it was caused by not getting enough protein.

VEGGIE DELIGHTS

Still, some places offered fantastic, nutritious options. In Asia, we enjoyed great vegetables, though it was a little tricky ordering what we wanted. Most places had a luscious variety of broccoli, cauliflower, carrots, peppers, garlic, peapods, and onion greens to make a stir-fry. The challenge was that we had to tell them what we'd like in it. We resorted to pointing to other people's plates. When we went to small, local restaurants, the staff often took us back into the kitchen and encouraged us to point out the vegetables we liked, so they could stir-fry them for us. Our beautiful array of vegetables accompanied by an occasional plate of eggs and tomatoes hit the spot.

When we would buy fresh vegetables we would either have to cook them or soak them in a special solution to kill any bacteria that they might be carrying. Therefore, we would only eat cooked vegetables in the restaurants and well-cooked meats to decrease our chance of having GI problems.

In Peru, they eat a lot of potatoes. It makes sense because a high-carbohydrate diet requires less oxygen for metabolism. Everyone ate potatoes there. Hence, WE ate a lot of potatoes—2008 was the Year of the Potato—and learned that there are five thousand varieties of potato. The different types that we sampled did taste unique.

Most times, we found a place to buy food, although some spots in Chile were so remote, shipments were few and far between; by the time the truck arrived to make the deliveries, the vegetables would be old and full of mold. During those times, we supplemented with multivitamins as we didn't feel we were getting a good variety of food.

POTLUCK, OR NOT

We aimed for balance over time, but any given meal could be a total surprise. When we were in Southern Chile, for instance, the towns were so far apart that it was difficult to plan ahead. We simply bought whatever we could at any store or restaurant we could find and then took off again.

At one point, we thought we were approaching a good-sized town because we saw power lines—and it was actually on the map—but there was no town there. It was gone. We came to a farmhouse and asked the man there about the town. He shook his head and said "no mas" (no more). The man let us camp in his yard, but all we had to eat was rice as we were going to replenish our supply in the town. So, without any other choice, we put up our tent and had another dinner of rice! The next morning when we asked about filling our water bottles with drinking water the man pointed to a little canal behind the house. So, we went to the canal, bent down and filled our bottles right from the source. Pure mountain water. No filter needed.

We made a new rule at this point—"If you see food, buy it." We typically tried to have at least three or four days' worth of noodles or rice with us. You never knew where the next food source was going to be. When we were biking down through the Yukon from Alaska, the Mile Marker brochure indicated stores or restaurants at certain mile points, but frequently they were closed. The people who had owned them had retired or died and passed them down to their children who didn't want to move to that remote location and take them over. So, they sat vacant.

There were limits to the, "You see it, you buy it," rule. A hamburger in a restaurant in Alaska and the Yukon could cost twelve dollars, and we didn't have that kind of budget, so we passed up a lot of food opportunities. One day, Ward was so thirsty for milk that he paid eight dollars for a gallon and then shared it with other cyclists that we ran into. Sometimes, you just have to do what you have to do.

NOW WE'RE COOKING

Finding food was a constant battle, but we were very resourceful. We could cook anywhere, on just about anything.

> Ward: When I was in the Cub Scouts, my mother was the den leader. She taught us how to cook on a tuna can. You take cardboard and cut it to a thin strip the height of the tuna can, and then coil it into the can. Pour warm wax over it and you have a very large candle. The cardboard serves as the wick. Then you take a coffee can and put holes on the outer perimeter at the top and bottom, for air flow, and then cook your hamburger on top of the coffee can. I never thought I would actually have to use this method.

However, the tuna can method saved us when we were in survival mode in Chile. We had mailed our multi-fuel stove from Europe to South America because the airlines weren't allowing it on the planes. However, it never showed up and our replacement stove failed after less than a week.

We decided to solve the problem with the tuna can stove, which worked well. We could use our regular pots and pans on top of it. All we needed was wax. This we could sometimes get from a store, but as towns became scarcer, we were forced to improvise.

Ward: We ended up going into churches and cathedrals where all the vigil candles were, and there'd be pools of wax. We'd have our little Ziploc baggie and we'd fill it full of spent wax. Also, we thanked God for all the shrines along the route in Southern Chile and Argentina. They provided a plethora of spent wax!

We used that improvised camp stove for four months, since there were shrines everywhere. Many of these were shrines for Gaucho Gil, Argentina's patron saint for travelers and cowboys. People left whiskey and water along the route for Gaucho Gil. It's not clear that his provenance included candle wax, but we were definitely counted among the travelers protected by this cowboy figure.

Ward: We didn't take the whiskey, only the water, because we cooked a lot of beans.

Jacky: You can buy dried beans pretty much anywhere, so we would take one of our water bottles and we'd soak the beans in the water bottle. They'd jiggle and move around as we biked throughout the day, and by suppertime they had soaked up enough water that they would cook well with our tuna can stove.

CAMPGROUND CORNUCOPIA

Campgrounds proved to be an excellent source of a wide variety of foods. Many campers stayed only a few days and then left their unused food on a free table for others to take. Rather than pack up their extra bottles of beer, half-full jars of jam, or partial loaves of bread, departing campers left them on a free table or in the free refrigerator set up for this purpose.

The free tables and refrigerators were common in New Zealand, particularly in campgrounds near the Auckland Airport. If we were in one of these campgrounds, we tried to get to the free table and refrigerator early and often scored more than enough bread, butter, and jam. Frequently, people offered us the last beer they had, since they couldn't take it on the plane. We were happy to take it off their hands; it served nicely as our evening cocktail.

Down the west coast of Oregon and California there are hiker/biker campgrounds with food boxes for people to leave their extra food in when they have surplus or when their trip is over. In one campground, we checked out the food box and snapped up some rice, noodles, and dried vegetables that were left there.

> Ward: We met a couple from Connecticut, Skippy and Missy, who had care packages sent to the various post offices along their travel route. We happened to be at the same campground as them when they had just received a package. All the extra things they didn't want, they put in the free food box. We ended up taking a bunch of it.
>
> We didn't know where the food had come from until the next day when we were riding with them and we ended up sharing a meal in the evening. They took one look at our food and said, "Now, where did you get that?!"

GIFTS OF GLEANING

Depending on where we were during harvest season, farmers' fields and ditches could provide a variety of foods. Each country had a unique style of farming. In Norway, they were so thorough in the harvest that we were lucky to find a single two-inch carrot left in the ground, but in Italy, we had good luck gleaning onions, tomatoes, and garlic.

Ward: I always had great interest in farming equipment, so I would stop to take pictures of the harvesters working. I'm out running in the field, videotaping the harvesting of tomatoes, and I ask the foreman there, "Well, what about all the tomatoes behind the machine?" He says, "Oh, you can have all you want."

So here I am walking along with two plastic grocery bags, which I fill up and take back to Jacky. "Look it, we have a salad," I said. We chopped onions and added a little olive oil and vinegar and oh, my gosh, we ate like kings from the fields. It was really fun. For me, I was learning about agriculture, which was one of the things I wanted to do. Plus, vegetables were literally falling off the back of the truck for me to stuff into my bags. We looked like a couple of gypsies.

HOW SWEET IT IS

We did some wild foraging, too. In Southern Chile, there were blackberries growing beside the road. We took a little Tupperware container and filled it full of blackberries.

Ward: One hot day, we had just picked some blackberries and I said, "Gosh, if there was just a place we could get ice cream." We were in the middle of absolutely nowhere, but not even two miles later, at an intersection, there was an ice cream stand.

Jacky: It was the weirdest thing, because we were in no-man's-land. There was nothing. Not a town for many miles and all of a sudden, a little ice cream shop pops up. I typically don't care for ice cream but having cold ice cream with fresh berries, sitting under a shade tree was absolutely heavenly.

CASTING A LINE

Ward: I also went fishing. I tried to fish wherever I could, primarily in South America, New Zealand, and Australia. If I could catch a fish, then we added it to our protein consumption. Salmon run in the streams, so one time in Chaitan, Southern Chile, I went fishing. I didn't have any luck catching the salmon, but all the stores there sell salmon very inexpensively. I came back to our campground that day with this huge salmon and Jacky says, "Wow, you caught a fish." I had to admit I got it at the fish market. It was very reasonable at only four dollars for a full fish.

I also went fishing in Alaska and actually caught fish there... again, Jacky loves salmon, so whenever I could go fishing for salmon, it was going to be a treat for her.

Now, here's a fish story. When we were in Clammoth Falls, California, and the salmon were running, I went to the spit where all the Native Americans were fishing. They can use nets, while we had fishing poles. I didn't have any luck. It was a four-mile ride on the bicycle, on gravel. I didn't expect to stay as late as I did. It got dark.

As I was walking back on this mile-long spit, this young Native American man asked me, "Do you need a fish?" He had a cooler that was very, very large, and he said it again, "Do you need a fish?" I said sure, and I always carried a garbage bag with me to carry the fish in, so I could tie it onto my bicycle. He gave me a fish from the top of the pile, and it was a twenty-five-pound salmon; he couldn't sell it because the seals had bitten the belly out of it, so he gave me this huge salmon.

Well, this area of California has black bear all along it, and so I was a little worried when I got on my bicycle in the dark. I was riding with no lights, and all I could see were the edges of the road to guide me. I didn't know what was lurking in the dense woods on each side. Meanwhile, Jacky was waiting back at the camp.

Jacky: We had a little tiff and he took off with his fishing pole. When he never came back, I thought either he was mad and he was at a bar, or something happened to him, because I thought for sure he'd be back by dark. I ended up finding the ranger, and we drove his four-wheeler down the gravel road looking for Ward. We couldn't find him anywhere. Now I was really getting worried. The ranger said, "Well, let's just go back to camp, and wait and see if he comes back." In the meantime, I was thinking he either fell into the river or got eaten by a bear.

It was a scary time for both of us, and the adventure wasn't over when Ward returned to camp with his catch. Jacky was mad that he had been gone so long but thankful that he was safe. However, now what to do with such a huge fish? There was no refrigerator to store it in. A neighboring camper came to the rescue on that count. He offered to store it in his freezer, but first Ward had to clean the fish. We only wanted to keep one pound for ourselves. We were giving the rest of the fish to him for being willing to store the fish for us that night.

Ward: While we were cleaning the fish, there was a six-hundred-pound black bear sow at the edge of the woods. The fish-cleaning station in the campground was about fifty feet away. You could see the bear's teeth and eyes as it watched us clean the salmon. Within two seconds that bear could have pounced on us. I wasn't afraid as the guys helping me said the bear was a garbage eater. However, Jacky was pretty nervous. No bear attacks interrupted our proceedings. The next morning we retrieved our now frozen fish and wrapped it in towels to slow the thawing process as we traveled on bikes. That evening we enjoyed fish along the California coast with other campers. It tasted so good.

SURREAL SMORGASBORD

Restaurant eating was expensive, but when we did eat out, we were careful to go where the locals were eating. We knew they approved of the food and also that there was high food turnover. Most places had no refrigeration, so we learned to go to the busiest spots where we wouldn't risk eating leftover food and getting sick. We were never disappointed.

Some dishes were more exotic than others. We ate foods we had never tried before; in Vietnam, we ate dog and in China, we ate rat. It helped that we didn't always exactly know what we were eating at the time as we probably wouldn't have selected those animals. When we had something like rat, for instance, it was mixed in a sauce. We avoided it when it was obviously a rat, just skewered on the grill. The same went for dog; it was usually in a sauce and you weren't sure what you were eating at the time. It makes it a little easier.

Jacky: In Vietnam, we saw farmers' markets with stands that were piled high with roasted dogs. I mean, the head still on them and all. The whole dog! When I saw a dog on the street, I would jokingly say, "You better behave, or you know where you might end up." Eating dog meat is obviously not part of our culture, but we did try to understand how other cultures view their food sources.

Ward: Yeah, we met one young traveler from Western Europe who thought she was looking at a pet store and it ended up being a restaurant. You just chose your own animal and they kill it right there and prepare it for you.

When we were in Colombia, Ward went to a Rotary meeting and one of the Rotarians invited us over to their house for coffee. Four of us sat around the kitchen table drinking coffee and enjoying conversation with each other. Soon, they brought out a bag of large ants—fried. This was a delicacy for them, so we had to be polite and try them.

Ward: They're kind of crunchy on the front and gooey in the back.

Jacky: The legs got stuck in my teeth.

Eating unusual foods wasn't always difficult, though. We often fell in love with the fresh food served to us. In Costa Rica, for example, we had *pinto*, a blend of beans, rice, and egg. When we were tenting in the motherly Tomasita's yard, she made us pinto for breakfast every morning. She also made a hot pepper salsa to go with it. It was superb, and we would love to duplicate the taste here at home, but we just don't have the right spices for it. Maybe that food was good because of the situation as well.

In Peru, we encountered a homemade beer called *chicha*.

To make it, the women sit around in a circle and chew on unprocessed corn, which they then spit into a big pot where it ferments into a beer. When it's ready, they hang red plastic bags from a stick on it outside their house to let people know they have fresh chicha.

Chicha is also sold in pubs. Because we wanted to try the cultural favorites, we went to one of the pubs in Peru. The locals took an interest in us and bought us both a beer, which meant a lot as the Peruvians typically do not have much money. We felt obligated to accept this kind gesture, but it was not tasty, especially served warm. Unfortunately for Ward, the locals felt very generous and kept refilling his glass.

Beer was an ongoing theme in our travels, and Ward liked to try them all. There were, however, two beers he poured out. Banana beer, served in Rwanda, didn't make the grade, nor did a caramelized Peruvian brew.

> Ward: I tried beer from every country and every culture, so that was a tough day, pouring out a beer. The sweetness of both beers just did not work with my palate.

DAILY BREAD

Bread was another item, like beer, that we tried everywhere we went. German brotchen bread, made fresh every day, was excellent. Bread in Norway cost six dollars a loaf, so we had to buy less and conserve it. In France, however, we couldn't miss it.

When we went into the big grocery stores in France, we could smell the bread right away. They were bringing out fresh loaves, beignets, or baguettes for people to buy still warm from the oven. It was amazing. It tasted so good that whenever we visited a Carrefour Market and bought a couple of loaves of bread, one would already be gone before we got back to our bikes. We even bought butter to put on this very fresh bread. Ooh, la la.

One didn't even have to be human to get a fresh daily loaf in some countries. In Chile, we saw a dog who went to the bakery, picked up a sack of bread, and carried it home. The dog waited at the stoplight for traffic to clear and just trotted on home with his family's bread. (Now that is a great dog.)

French bread was the most flavorful, but almost everywhere we went, bread was just as important. When we were invited into an Italian home, we were astonished to watch them just tear a loaf of bread apart and throw it in the middle of the table. We all reached into the pile and grabbed a chunk. No breadbasket needed. It's just part of their daily life.

We thought we had seen it all, but when we got to Brazil, we learned a whole new technique for eating bread. In Brazil, because they believe the doughy part of the bread is what makes people fat, they pull out the center and just eat the crust.

Bread became the holy grail; we would do almost anything to have bread for the day. We got so used to having bread every day that we were in a bit of a panic when we couldn't find it. (Jacky especially could get a little whiney, per Ward.) Bread is not a big part of the Asian diet. They eat more noodles, rice, soup, and dumplings. In Vietnam, Jacky was so hungry for bread that she chased down a bicycle that had little baguettes on it just to get a taste. (Do not get in her way.)

HOT WATER ANYONE?

We learned in Asia that we could get hot water just about anywhere for our noodles. People carried little bowls and flavor-packaged noodles everywhere, whether on the train going to Mongolia, or in a hotel or hostel. There was always a hot water machine so you could cook your noodles.

We had never seen so many noodles. As we went through Thailand and Cambodia, we saw pallet after pallet of ramen noodles. We took a picture, because one pallet held about ten thousand ramen noodle packets. It stood over six feet tall and the pallet was three feet by three feet. In one restaurant, when we ordered soup, the waitress brought us a bowl of boiling water and a packet of ramen noodles.

LONGING FOR HOME

After so long on a local diet, we started dreaming of some foods we'd had back home. Strange things became special.

When we were in Cambodia, Jacky got so tired of soup and teriyaki flavor that she bought a box of Frosted Flakes cereal and ate it for every meal until it was gone. We never buy Frosted Flakes at home now and never did before, but at the time it seemed so right and tasted so good.

When we were in Asia, we didn't get much meat. We just craved it. We almost got our fix in China when we went to a hamburger place, but whatever they served us, it wasn't a hamburger. In Shanghai, however, we did find a McDonald's.

Jacky: I was so excited. I went in and ate a Big Mac. I don't even eat at McDonald's, but it was so special at the time. Ward's like, "I'm taking a picture of you eating a Big Mac." I said, "Go ahead." I didn't even care. (Remember, I'm a dietitian.)

Ward: Another time, we were riding in Cambodia. It was so hot and we were riding into a little town, trying to find something cool. Again, Jacky doesn't usually like ice cream, but when she heard the ice cream cart's bells ringing, she left me to track him down. She rode all around town and returned twenty minutes later.

Jacky: I did find him. He'll never be the same again.

Jacky: When you're on a trip like this, there are foods that you crave that you haven't had. I was missing foods like tater tot casserole, salsa and chips, and cake. I don't even like cake, but there were times I was desperately searching it out.

CALORIES VS. NUTRITION

With a fluctuating diet, we faced different types of health

issues depending on where we were and how long we were there. In South America, for instance, there is no fluoride in the water and they eat a high-carbohydrate diet, so it's very bad for the teeth.

> Jacky: Most people had a lot of missing, rotting teeth, if any at all. While we were there, I thought I had a filling fall out. I ignored it until I went home as it wasn't causing any pain. When I finally got to a dentist, he said, "You didn't lose a filling; it's all decayed." I ended up having to have it pulled and the whole inside was black with decay. That's after only eight or nine months of being in South America.

On the other end of the spectrum, meat was commonly served in Argentina. The Argentines bragged about the superior beef they frequently barbequed on outdoor grills called *asados*.

> Ward: Their meat isn't as good as ours in North America. Kind of tough, comparatively.

> Jacky: They have very skinny cows.

> Ward: People invited us over, while resting or camping at parks, and offered us meat. We'd try not to be rude, but we were fighting to even cut through it with our teeth. Our jaws would be sore from chewing.

> Jacky: If we were camping and somebody would be barbecuing at another campsite, they'd bring over a plate of meat for us. This was a common occurrence, a cultural norm for them.

CAN'T BUY ME...

It was a good thing so many people were so generous, because there were times when we simply couldn't pay the prices asked for food. Ward got so frustrated by high prices in British Columbia that even though he had money and found a store, he couldn't bring himself to pay for noodles and rice because the price was so ridiculously high.

> Ward: I don't even recall the price, but it was just too much. I was in kind of a funk; I don't know why. I just couldn't buy it. When I got back to the campground, Jacky was like, "Well, where are the noodles?" and I couldn't explain it.

> Jacky: It was lucky we had neighbors. They had extra food that night and brought it to our campsite.

The feeling that others along the way had our backs served us well in some of the more trying times that came our way, both physically and emotionally.

CHAPTER FIVE

RULE NUMBER ONE: IT MUST BE SAFE?

While we felt welcome and safe in most countries, there were times when we felt like we had narrowly escaped disaster. We weren't worried about having our bicycles, gear, or even our money stolen from us, but if something physically happened to one of us, it would have been devastating.

We probably felt most uncomfortable in South America, particularly between Brazil and Paraguay. As we crossed from Brazil into Paraguay, a third world country, there was a drastic change. The border city was "City of the East" and that day they were celebrating a holiday. Many people were aggressive and drunk. Some boys that were standing in the road ran out and started chasing us, grabbing at our bikes and trying to jump on them. We luckily found shelter for a short time at the border patrol station. After that, we headed to the closest convenience store to use their telephone, trying not to draw attention. Ward had a local Rotarian's phone number and wanted to call him for guidance on a safe place to stay. The closest store that we came across had an armed guard outside. That was extremely uncomfortable. It showed us how unsafe the area really was. While Ward was in the store calling the Rotarian, Jacky stayed outside in the shadow of the armed guard to keep an eye on the bikes. Younger boys would come around and check out our bikes and bags. It made us uncomfortable, but we just tried to stay between them and the bikes. Ward was able to contact the Rotarian and he met us at the store and led us to a safe hotel that was a few blocks away. The hotel also had an armed guard outside, but even so, we were told to lock all of our equipment in the luggage safe in our room. Normally, we were allowed to lock our bikes in the courtyard of a hotel, but here we were told to use our cable lock and lock our bikes in our locked room. This was even with an armed guard outside the front door! (Jacky was given a scapular for her first communion and this was the first and only time she felt she needed to wear it.)

The area was extremely poor. Families camped out, living under black tarps covered with sticks. Five or more people gathered under one tarp, trying to cook a meal. Kids ran around naked, even though it was chilly enough for us to wear fleece shirts and long pants. The area was filthy.

Jacky: We felt so sorry for them. It was one of the first times we realized how much our destiny depends on where we were born and how lucky we are to live in the United States. It made us feel sick to see their living conditions.

Even though we saw unbelievable poverty, we had those moments where our uniqueness brought out a kindness and acceptance throughout South America. Ward had learned about the Itaipu Dam. It is a binational dam on the Parana

River that separates the Brazilian and Paraguay borders. We had to check it out.

Ward: We were on one of the buses to the Itaipu Dam (just north of the City of the East, Paraguay). I'm always very interested to see structures that produce energy or process something. I'm always fascinated by the infrastructure of a country, just so that I can continue to learn about it. As we took a city bus to the dam, I was standing in the bus aisle, and this little girl looked up at me, and in Spanish said, "*Muy alto*," which is "very tall," because I had to bend my head to get into the bus. She just looked up at me, and her eyes were as big as silver dollars. Yes, at six feet, one inch, I was a giant in much of South America.

We wanted to bike to Asuncion, Paraguay, but we were warned by Rotarians and locals that it was very dangerous. They warned us that there was a high probability that we could be robbed or attacked along that route. Noticing that we were very vulnerable on bikes, we decided to take the bus to Caacupé, which was partway to Asuncion, to scope it out. The bus provided us personal safety, but we still needed to make sure our bikes were safe. They were stored in the under-carriage and Ward would get off the bus at every stop to make sure the bikes were not getting unloaded without us.

We ended up spending a lot of time on buses in Peru and Ecuador. We originally intended to ride our bicycles through this part of the world, but our plans didn't pan out. A friend, who became a marketing manager at Schwinn, offered us free bikes for helping with a marketing strategy. From our Schwinn bikes, we were to take pictures of what you can see traveling the world from a Schwinn and then send the images back to them. In return, we were hoping to get a stipend. With this plan in mind, we donated our own top-notch bikes to a Rotary Club in Brazil, to give to kids that needed them. Unfortunately, the Schwinn bikes never showed up. We needed to keep moving ahead due to visa requirements and because we had a flight out of Colombia in the next month or so. There was no time to stay stagnant. Therefore, we spent about a month moving around by bus and taxi. This wasn't by choice, but we did encounter experiences we wouldn't have had on the bike.

We had been given a lot of advice—wear your passport around your neck, place your money in different pockets, put your credit cards in the sole of your shoes, and so on—but nothing prepared us for having our equipment searched and our faces videotaped when we got on a bus in Lima, Peru. Everyone's face was videotaped. We never fully understood why, but we heard stories about entire busloads of people being robbed or individuals on the bus being drugged. Videotaping our faces was one way they knew who was on the bus to begin with.

On the buses, we were cautioned to sit right behind the bus driver because people got drunk and unruly in the back of the bus. You were also at greatest risk of being drugged in the back. Even behind the bus driver you still had to be careful.

> Jacky: One time I had my bag sitting on my lap, and the guy behind me told me to put it under the seat, where it would be safer. Of course, that guy went through my bag before he got off the bus. Later, when I picked it up, I noticed it was open. Surprisingly, the only thing missing was my apple.

Robbery is such a problem that the taxis in Lima have cages around the driver, so you can't rob the driver and the driver can't rob you. It's important to only get into registered taxis, because otherwise you are at risk of the driver driving around the block and picking up another rider, who will rob you instead. Yes, an accomplice. That was a challenging time, because we couldn't trust anyone.

We heard about all sorts of possible dangers, but thankfully, we encountered very few of them. We learned about a flower in Ecuador whose pollen was used like a date rape drug. People would put it on a map or a piece of paper and hand it to you like a gift, and once you touched it, and it was absorbed into your skin, you fell under their control. While you were out of commission, they could take you to an ATM machine and force you to draw out money for them, wiping out your accounts. So, we were cautious never to accept anything handed over to us in that way.

It sounds outlandish, but we did meet up with one gentleman in a hostel who felt that he had been drugged. He was ready to check out early the next day; he had his bags all packed and went to bed. While he was sleeping, in his private room, someone got in through his locked door. He vaguely remembers being patted down. In the morning, when he woke up, his bags were all torn apart and items were missing. This taught us we had to be on guard at all times.

Ecuador and Peru were beautiful, interesting places, but we always felt on edge there. Colombia was scary in a different way. The terrain was gorgeous, with narrow winding roads and canyons weaving through the mountains. But why were there military men protecting the bridges? Were the guerrilla terrorist groups we'd heard about lurking in the mountains? Yes, it was FARC (The Revolutionary Armed Forces of Colombia).

When we were in Colombia, there was a moto-taxi protest going on, with a roadblock, so we had to take an unusual route that was narrow, rocky, and full of potholes. Everybody had to take this route. We were in a small van with about eighteen people. We were warned that the vans go very fast, speeding around the tight corners and passing on the curves.

At one point, we were following a truck that wasn't going very fast. Other vehicles wanted to pass it, but they didn't wait for a clear chance to pass. Instead, everybody tried to go around at once. Four vehicles were passing this slow-moving truck when a car started coming straight at us. The passing vehicles all tried to move over. The bus next to us came within inches of our van. While our van driver tried to maneuver out of the way, he saw a bicyclist on the right side of the road and barely missed him.

Jacky: I was so scared. I had to keep my eyes closed for most of the ride. I couldn't take it! The steep canyons that lay below were too unsettling to look at. Some people were getting sick and having to use puke bags. I knew I had a reason to be scared when the Colombian woman sitting next to me started praying with her rosary. It was super, super scary.

Ward: That's Jacky's take on it. I was sitting in the front seat where I could see all of this happening, and I thought it was a hoot. We actually didn't see many accidents. I probably should have been scared, but I was sitting there going, "Yeah!" It seemed like I was at a rodeo.

Jacky: He was having a great time. He asked to sit in the front and was getting the thrill of his life!

That day, we got to the city of Cali in the mid-afternoon. It was alive with people. It felt friendly, and we didn't feel any uneasiness at all. In fact, we decided to take a nap because we had been on the bus so late. When we woke up at seven o'clock in the evening and went out to get something to eat, the streets that had been overflowing at three o'clock were totally empty. The only guy on the street was the hot dog vendor, and it didn't seem like a stretch to think that he had a gun. The entire area had an indescribable eeriness. Where did all the people go? Why was there no traffic? What was going on? A couple of weeks later, we heard that there were car bombings in this area. Spooky.

We had the same feeling multiple times in Armenia, Colombia; only we saw actual riot police on the corners. We heard stories about people getting robbed at knife point. When we got off our bus there, we tried to take in as much as we could very quickly as we only had a few hours of daylight. We made a stop at a pub right next to our hotel room. We started visiting with the Colombians. They came across as being very friendly, asking what we were doing and offering to take us to the national park that we wanted to visit the next day. One man invited us over to his house for supper and a man claiming to be with the police asked if we wanted to stay at his house that night. Unfortunately, we couldn't accept any of these invitations because we had been warned that they can befriend you and then rob you. How did we know if he was actually with the police?

> Jacky: I could just see it in the news. "American couple goes to a man's house who is pretending to be with the police, and they are killed." People would say, "Boy, that was sure stupid of them!"

For the first time, people were guessing us as Americans. Over the previous year, no one ever guessed us as Americans. They normally thought we were Germans; we told people we were Canadians We knew groups like FARC like to kidnap Americans and hold them for ransom.

Around four or five o'clock that afternoon, though, the friendly tone of the bar changed. People started telling us we needed to leave. We couldn't figure out why, but they wanted us to be off the street before darkness fell. So, we listened to them and we returned to our room.

The view from our second-story hotel room told the real story. It was haunting. We watched merchants hurriedly closing their shops, people rushing to get home, locking their doors, and pulling down their shades. We were prisoners in our own room until dawn. We couldn't go to the store or do anything as the streets were just too dangerous. We only had the food in our room. I know some travelers venture out in this environment, but then you hear the horror stories.

While we were in Colombia, we took more precautions than usual. We took off our wedding bands. We hid our credit cards in the soles of our shoes (which turned out not to be a great strategy, because the sand wears off the magnetic strip). We luckily stayed safe, but we did hear some stories of robberies with one of them being surprisingly amusing.

At the hostel in Bogotá, Colombia, we met a man from Sweden who had been robbed at knifepoint on the beach. The thieves wanted all his money, but he only had 3,000 pesos ($1.70) in his pockets. When he pulled it out, the thieves wanted to know where the rest of the money was, but there wasn't any more. They gave the $1.70 back to the man because he had so little, they figured he needed it worse than they did. (Maybe they had robbed a rich American earlier that day, so they were good.)

Luck was with us through most of our travels, though. We were very seldom victimized and never seriously. We didn't carry anything like pepper spray for protection, even. We prayed to God that we would be safe, and we learned to listen to the locals. In Panama City, for instance, we asked the hostel manager for advice. He told us that up until three o'clock in the afternoon we were fine to walk anywhere. But after five o'clock in the evening we shouldn't go beyond Eighth Street and after seven o'clock in the evening, we shouldn't venture past Fifth Street. He warned us to be sure to take a taxi after dark, and to make sure it was a good taxi. We listened, and we were fine. We didn't pay much attention to the safety alerts put out by the US government because if we did, we wouldn't have visited many of the countries such as the Baltic region and Rwanda, for example. The state department would issue warnings for the entire country when, in fact, the area of concern was very isolated. It would be similar to saying all of the United States is dangerous, but maybe just one small neighborhood in Los Angeles or Miami or New York has problems.

South America was a great experience, but we were glad to stand on United States soil again after that.

> Jacky: On our way to New Zealand, we stopped back in the United States to see one of our sons before he was deployed. I remember the feeling I had as I walked into a grocery store in North Carolina, with my money pouch hanging from my shoulder. At that moment, I realized how good it felt to feel so safe and free.

CHAPTER SIX

NAVIGATION 101: DETAILED MAPS NOT NECESSARY

If you don't know where you're going, it's tough to get truly lost, but it is unsettling to find yourselves in literally uncharted territory. It may have happened first when we bought that barely marked map in Patagonia.

Leaving Argentina to go into Chile was even more ominous, when we came to a sign that said *Fin de Pavimento*. End of the paved road. We took a picture of Jacky standing near the sign, shrugging, like, "What's up with that? No more pavement?" We spent the next four months on gravel roads, the ungraded, wash-boarded, potholed type, the ones we try to avoid at all costs when we are on our bicycles in the US.

Having a map was itself a luxury, as we found out when we crossed from Vietnam into China and spent about a week with nothing to guide us. Remember, we did not have any navigational devices such as GPS. It was all up to us. Luckily, Ward remembered survival strategies from his Boy Scout days like looking at trees to see which side the moss grew on—north in the northern hemisphere and south in the southern. If we were in a city, there were other clues to study, such as the angle of the satellite dishes. We had a compass, but we never needed to consult it. Our method was to take the things we knew and apply them to whatever environment we were in, whether it was primitive or high tech.

Armed with as much information as we could glean from the environment, we headed north until we could find some sort of map. It turned out to be an atlas of all of China, with only a few words of English written on the front page. We couldn't read Chinese, so we turned to the internet for help. From an internet café, we typed in "Shanghai" and looked at the Chinese script that turned up. We painstakingly tried to match shapes of the characters to something on the atlas. We had four destination goals in China—the Three Gorges Dam, Shanghai, Beijing, and the Great Wall of China. Essentially, we just headed in that general direction in hopes of seeing signs for them.

A good percentage of the people in China cannot read or write, so when we showed them our map, they didn't know the characters or the names of the towns, so no matter how helpful they tried to be, they couldn't really assist us. Many did not let on that they couldn't read the map and directed us anyway, so we started out thinking we were on the right path, only to find out we weren't. We soon learned that we couldn't rely on any particular person's answer; we sought a consensus before moving on.

We realized that most people never traveled more than twenty miles from home, so they couldn't give directions more than twenty miles away. They just didn't know the route. (This is true in most parts of the world.) So, we learned to ask for a nearby town, and then when we arrived there, we asked for the next segment, and so on until we made it to our destination.

Many people do not have an accurate sense of distance. They might know local landmarks but not road names or the length of the route. They weren't sure how far it was between landmarks. People would say, vaguely, that the next town was half an hour away. They seldom meant by bike.

No matter what country we were in, it seemed that if a local said something was five kilometers away, we could pretty much figure it to be ten kilometers. We just doubled the distance.

The lily pad approach—hopping from one landing to the next until we crossed the proverbial pond—worked well almost everywhere, though in France it could be a challenge to get a definitive opinion. When we asked one person, he would give us his proposed route, and then someone else would suggest another route. The ensuing discussion included comments about traffic, road quality, scenic beauty, hilliness, and possible restaurants and accommodations. Before long, our helpers were arguing about which way was the best route. Sometimes, we just left two Frenchmen to their argument because it seemed like the debate could go on forever without reaching a satisfying conclusion.

That's when we developed the consensus method, where we asked a bunch of people for directions and then went with the most common answer. As we headed in our desired direction, we stopped and asked more locals if we were still on the proper route and how many kilometers remained. This worked fairly well, though because of our language barrier, we sometimes misunderstood the directions and had to turn around.

China presented a lot of challenges. One day we found a new four-lane highway without any traffic. We decided to take it. The quiet route seemed heavenly compared to China's typical snarl of traffic and chaos on the roads. It seemed strange to us, though, that in two hours of bicycling we only saw four cars. The road was so quiet, Ward felt perfectly comfortable lying down in the middle of the pavement for a picture. We had no idea where this highway went.

Around lunchtime, we decided to get off the four-lane road to go into a little village, assuming we could get back on the highway and continue on our way after eating. Only we could not figure out how to get back onto this highway. Again, we asked many locals who pointed us in every which direction. Soon, we were on a paved road again. Then that turned into a gravel road, which became a tractor path, and finally a narrow walking path. We were trying to get to Shanghai, but here we were at the top of a hill, looking at a little farmhouse.

> Jacky: I was getting a little nervous. We had been biking all day. Now it was getting close to dusk and we still had no idea where we were. Knowing we had a tent with us gave me some comfort; at least we could make our own shelter.

When you travel the way we did, you can't be in too much of a hurry, and it's a good thing we knew that. We went into the house, where we found a group of four or five men playing *mahjong*. We had our map, and we pointed to Shanghai, but they invited us in for tea while they continued their game. In their own good time, they pointed toward the east, and we were on our way once more.

Now the footpath grew back into a tractor path, a gravel road, and finally pavement again. After about five miles, we came to a small town where we could ask for more directions. A young man who could speak English was very helpful. We gave him the map and asked, "Where on the map are we?" He pointed to the city we were in, which turned out to be only eighteen miles from the town we had started in that morning. We had spent seven hours on the bikes, pedaled eighty-five miles of trails and tracks, but on the map, we had only covered eighteen miles. We were very frustrated during the ride that day, but now we laugh at how we saw parts of China that no one ever sees.

After that, we learned to write the phrase for "Where on the map are we?" in Chinese characters so we could show it to other people if we didn't know where we were.

> Jacky: One of the questions we get asked a lot is, "Did you ever get lost?" How would we know? We never had a route plotted out. We just saw parts of the world we didn't plan on seeing, sometimes places almost nobody sees. So, what if we turned down a dead end? We'd just see what was there.

Big maps like the atlas of China got us in all sorts of trouble, but a simple map of Austria afforded us the chance to cycle in several countries very quickly. Because of Austria's irregular shape, we could use the same map in the Czech Republic, Austria, Hungary, Croatia, Northern Italy, part of France, and Switzerland.

At other times, we had to get off the bikes and take completely unexpected modes of transportation. In Paraguay, we expected to have no problem crossing the bridge over the Rio Negro into Argentina. We saw people crossing the border freely, carrying bags and commercial goods and luggage, so we arrived expecting an open border. When we presented our passports, though, the agent denied us because we were not citizens of Paraguay.

Apparently, this was a common occurrence, though, because we were quickly approached by a man on a scooter who beckoned us to follow him. We had to have some kind of trust, so we let him lead us down a back alley onto a little path to the edge of the river, where there sat a man with a rowboat. For fifty cents, he would row us across the river with our bikes. It could have been a sketchy situation, but the boat saved us from having to ride twenty extra miles and cross the border in the dark, which we had just decided not to do.

We looked like George Washington crossing the Delaware, standing in that little boat with our bicycles. We never expected this kind of situation to crop up, but we just had to go with it. (Border crossings after dark are never fun and usually scary.)

CHAPTER SEVEN

ROADSIDE GUARDIAN ANGELS NUMBER ONE

We were incredibly lucky throughout our trip, but some moments stuck out as almost miraculous. One of these happened in Brazil, riding among the many trucks that travel the poorly maintained and overused roads. Trucks transport corn, cotton, and soybeans across the country and to the shipping ports because the Brazilian legislature has vetoed the construction of a rail system. Double-trailer semis dominate, filled with grain and covered with tarps held in place by metal hoops.

Ward: I'm always noticing things along the side of the road and just trying to understand how things work. One day, I noticed an exploded brake drum lying on the side of the road. The overloaded trucks are hard on the brakes. I wanted to have a picture of it, but Jacky, who had the camera, had already climbed the hill. I yelled up anyway. She didn't want to come back down and have to climb it a second time. Finally, she agreed to come down to take a picture of me holding the brake drum.

While I was standing there, an empty semi went by with the metal hoops stored in the undercarriage. One hoop had vibrated out and was sticking four feet out on the right side of the truck. When these trucks pass you, they give you less than two feet of room. The hoop was facing forward, so if Jacky had not come down and taken the picture, the tube might have gone right through her back, because the driver didn't know the hoop had vibrated out. I said, "Jacky, did you see that?" She went, "Oh my God, I would be dead." Somewhere along the line, someone, a guardian angel, was looking out for Jacky, and it took the form of my insistence that she take a picture of this blown-up brake drum.

MOTHERLY LOVE

Our guardian angels were looking out for us again when we were heading into the city of Setubal, Portugal. It was mid-December, a few days before Christmas, and people were roasting chestnuts on the streets. We were thinking about Christmas, religion, and family a little more than normal, talking about Ward's parents and how he thinks of his mother during this time of the year.

Jacky: That morning I had asked Ward, "Do you pray to your mother?" He said, "Yes, I do. All the time."

When we got to our hostel, we found out it was under construction, so we asked for recommendations for another inexpensive place to stay, which we got. When we arrived in the suggested neighborhood, though, we had an eerie feeling about the hotel. Our standards weren't particularly high, but this place was dark and very unnerving. It looked as though drug deals were going down in the alleys and prostitutes would be hanging out on the corners. We did not want knocks at the door or yelling in the hallways that night.

We had no place to stay, so we went to the center of the city, to a big square, and Jacky sat with the bikes while Ward scouted for a hotel. He had no luck. The sun had set by now and we were in the dark in a new city with no place to stay. Back at the bikes, Jacky noticed a woman walking toward her. She walked across the entire square, right up to Jacky, and started speaking. The entire time she spoke in Portuguese, which we don't understand. The woman appeared to know no English.

> Jacky: Sometimes people aren't always that receptive to us on bikes, so I thought she was telling us we had to leave, that we weren't welcome there. But she was telling us that it was very dangerous, with lots of drug deals going on in the area.

The woman indicated that we should follow her. We were a bit nervous, although she was not imposing or aggressive. She was probably in her late sixties, and fairly small. As we went down the narrow dark streets after her, we wondered if it was the smartest thing to do, but then we came to a little corner hotel. Our escort asked the young lady at the counter if there was a room available, and the attendant said there wasn't. Our fearless leader would have none of that, however, and just kept pushing, telling the girl to find another room somewhere in the city, to give us a map, to quote us a price. So, she did. This went on for thirty minutes. During this time, Ward saw the personality traits of his deceased mother coming through in this lady. Our new friend was persistent, insistent, exacting, and yet very kind. Again, all this conversation was in Portuguese.

Ward: I thought, "Oh, my God, that's my mother. God sent my mother to help us find a room." It was just like her.

Having set us up with a map and a price quote for a room, the lady gave a smile and left. When the mystery woman walked out of the hotel, she passed Jacky with the bikes, and said, in English, "Merry Christmas."

Jacky: That was really strange. The woman never spoke a word of English to us before and now, she smiled and wished me a Merry Christmas. That was all she said to me.

When Ward came out of the hotel, he said to me, "That was my mother!" He was almost in a trance or state of shock. We both had shivers and a state of comfort.

At the beginning of the evening, we never dreamed our day would turn out this way. It was a very nice hotel, affordable and cozy, with a warm feeling to it. Our Christmas gift was the gift of safety and comfort.

Our belief in God was strong going into this trip, and it's only stronger now. It wasn't a faith-based trip, but faith helped us manage it. We simply had to believe in each other and believe in God that we'd get to where we needed to be. Plus, we had plenty of time for reflection and contemplation while biking; we had lots of opportunities for prayer. We were often praying for our safety and praying our thanks for how safe we had been.

CHAPTER EIGHT

PRIDE IN THE AMERICAN FLAG

Traveling so extensively outside of the United States gave us a unique perspective on our home country's politics and the way people from other countries see us. We left in 2007, when George W. Bush was president and very unpopular because of the Iraq War. We weren't looked on very favorably, particularly in Europe, so instead of telling people right away that we were Americans, we posed as Canadians. We wore Canadian patches and Canadian fanny packs to make people think that's where we were from. Once we got to know someone, we came clean, but we didn't want to be automatically judged because we were Americans.

> Ward: There was a lot of animosity toward Americans. Most every other country knows our politics better than we know them, and they just weren't in agreement with us. We wanted to be judged for who we were, not where we came from, or who our leaders were.

It got tricky navigating the political conversations that some people insisted on having with us. One man in Australia went on a tirade about things that happened historically between Australia and the United States, how John Howard and George Bush were friends and not well liked, as if we were representatives of that decision. Another man in Australia hounded us about the presidential election process (the Electoral College most particularly) in the United States. He stated that Obama won by a landslide. That may have been true of the electoral votes, but not by the popular vote. When Ward tried to explain it to this man, he was not interested in learning how our system worked.

> Jacky: One night after we set up camp, an Australian man walked by. He stopped and asked me where we were from. This was right after Obama became president. When I told him "the United States," he said, "Now, you can finally be proud to be an American." I replied, "I have always been proud to be an American!"

It could get contentious at the most unexpected times. When we were in Latvia, looking for a campsite, Jacky went into a café that served coffee and pastries and offered internet access. When she walked in to scope it out, the woman there shooed her out, telling her to get on down the road. A little further along, we stopped at a campsite where the attendant asked where we were from. When we said, "America," he said, "No, you're Germans." We again said, "We are Americans," and he again quite firmly let us know that this was the wrong answer. If we wanted anything to go our way, we needed to say we were German. For his own safety and ours, he had us register as Germans.

It was kind of funny, because we were so far removed from

life in the United States, and we were so out of touch with our politics. We made an effort to connect with family via email and internet, but we didn't have access to daily papers or television. Our daily lives were consumed with riding and finding safe places to lay our heads at night, safe drinking water, and something to eat. However, people really wanted to discuss American politics with us.

> Jacky: It was so strange, before the election in 2008, we were riding in a very desolate and isolated area in Patagonia, South America. We hadn't seen a person or car for hours. Then, we saw another cyclist coming toward us. It is customary to stop and inquire where each of us has been and to exchange information about what is up ahead. He asked us, "Have you guys seen the news?" We replied, "No, why?" He said, "Well, Hillary took Nevada and Obama took Colorado." This guy wasn't even from the States! Ward and I looked at each and commented, "I bet a lot of Americans back home don't even know that!"

As much as we got criticized for American politics, we were always proud to be American. We were probably more proud as we saw more of the world. Looking at the roads to nowhere in China, or dealing with bribery in so many countries, we knew we didn't want to live anywhere else but the United States.

CHAPTER NINE

THE BOSS

Let's set the stage for the next story. Lithuania was the third of the three Baltic countries that we visited. The Russian influences were evident. Buildings weren't being maintained. Vodka and beer flowed freely, with alcohol content ranging from 8 percent to 14 percent. Overall, the people seemed more closed natured. The Baltic countries (Estonia, Latvia, and Lithuania) opened our eyes to a very different cultural way of life.

We arrived in the small village of Babtai, Lithuania, with a plan to travel another fifteen miles down the road. We noticed a little kiosk with many locals hanging around drinking beer. It was spirited and full of energy. After all, it was Friday afternoon, so we decided to call it a day and share a beer with them. We started asking them where we could put up our tent. A young man came up and told us he knew of a hotel that was being renovated. We needed to follow him and go talk to The Boss. Apparently, this boss owned the hotel. The hotel wasn't officially open, but for us, they'd certainly make an exception, he told us. So, Ward followed him while Jacky stayed behind.

The Boss, who looked something like Yul Brynner, showed

Ward around the partially renovated hotel. It was majestic with marble floors, a great room, and a beautiful staircase. There was one room that was finished that we could stay in. Ward asked the young man what the cost was. He asked, "What did you pay last night?" When Ward told him, he said, "You will have to pay more than that." But Ward still wasn't quoted a price and then went back to get Jacky and bring her to the hotel. Once we returned, The Boss was eager to show us around and serve us. "Would you like a sauna?" he asked. Sure! He came back to stoke the fire and, in his commanding tone, told us that we would be having dinner with him and his family at six o'clock in the evening. He would be back to get us.

> Ward: The Boss lived kitty-corner to the hotel where he could see everything that went on. When we had a moment alone in our room, I said to Jacky, "I think he's mafia. Just the way he talks, and all of this. I think he's mafia."

They called this man The Boss, he clearly had lots of money in a town that wasn't very affluent, he owned a hotel...The more we thought about it, the more we worked up a mobster scenario in our minds. They were treating us so well, we had to wonder what sort of favor we owed in return.

> Jacky: I kept watching him from our hotel room window. What's he doing now? Oh, he's mowing the lawn. That seems to be okay. All the time thinking, "Oh no, he's going to make us carry a package across the border!"

The evening meal did little to ease our suspicions. Vodka and champagne flowed freely, glass after glass lifted to honor the "Canadians" at the table. We eventually revealed that we were Americans, and The Boss (his name was Yannis) was a bit confused at first and offered a toast to the Canadian Americans. Once it was clear we were Americans, he brought out an American flag he had brought back from a trip to Las Vegas. Next thing we knew, they called over a couple of friends who were in town but lived in Las Vegas. The family had done business there and in Russia. Between vodka shots, Yannis confided to us the secret to doing business in Russia: "The one who drinks the most gets the business."

Yannis tossed back the most shots that night, Ward was good for five shots. We knew Ward was in trouble since he hardly ever drinks hard alcohol. As the shots were taking effect, he knew it was time for him to lie down. Yannis had him sleep in a reclining lawn chair by the swimming pool, because it was simply impossible for him to navigate the forty yards to the hotel room at that point. They covered him with a blanket. The family dog took a liking to Ward and sat there and licked his face. Ward was oblivious to it. At midnight, Jacky decided it was time to go. Yannis wanted Ward to remain sleeping in the lawn chair that night, but Jacky still wasn't sure what was going on. She thought there might be hell to pay, by Ward, if she left him there.

Ward: They tried to get me up and I got sick four or five times. All over everything. In the morning, I felt terrible that I was such a poor guest, so I went over to try to wash down the stone wall and the driveway. Yannis was already there with the hose. I apologized to him and he had no worries with what had occurred the night before. When I asked how much we owed for our room. He replied, "No charge amongst friends. Stay another night."

We had that Hotel California feeling, like we might never leave this place if we stayed another moment, so we didn't take him up on his offer. We seriously wondered what we owed him for his extravagant hospitality, but our stay at Hotel Yannis has never come back to haunt us. It has actually enlightened us.

Jacky: It puts a smile on my face as I think of how genuinely nice he was to us. He wished us a safe journey and sent us off with a bag of apples that he picked from his tree. This was a reminder to me to not prejudge people.

CHAPTER TEN

YOU DON'T EXPERIENCE THIS ON A TOUR BUS— EUROPE EDITION

One of the rewards of traveling by bicycle instead of boarding a tour bus was that we got to meet real people living their everyday lives. We got to live the cultures of the countries we visited.

TIME TRAVEL IN LITHUANIA

When we got to Joniškis, Lithuania, for instance, we thought we were entering a well-populated area. There was a big dot on the map, but when we arrived, the town was small. We rode around trying to find a lawn to camp on. We started talking to some people outside of their house. It happened to be next to a bar. The people took great interest in what we were doing. Soon, the bar owner came out with two complimentary mugs of beer. Only one of the locals there could speak English so, through fun gestures, we continued to ask where we could camp. Everybody kept pointing to the forest. It was clear we were going to have to camp in the woods.

As we pedaled down a small dirt path towards the woods, we passed an elderly man and his grandson tending a cow in a field. They smiled and waved. Jacky said, "Maybe we should stop and ask if we can camp in their yard." We pulled up and talked a while—the grandson, Mingus, knew a little English—and soon we were on our way to camp out in their farmyard. It was the most pastoral scene imaginable. The farmhouse was unoccupied (the grandfather's parents once lived there, but he himself lived closer to town) and the lawn un-mowed. They offered to get out the lawnmower, but we told them we'd rather sleep on the long grass. It's softer.

We were happy just to be there, but after sharing a few beers with the grandfather, called Antonis, we saw an elderly woman come rolling up on a rickety old bike. This was Aldona, the grandmother. Using sign language and Mingus's English translating skills, she asked us if we would like some milk and potatoes. We gladly accepted the hospitality.

Of course, milk and potatoes aren't a simple thing when there's no store or storage for miles. Instead, Grandma took Ward to the field to milk the cow. Then she started the milk boiling on a single-burner hotplate and took Ward back out to dig the potatoes. To wash the spuds, we used a bucket to bring up water from a well. It was as though we had stepped back in time.

Meanwhile, Aldona and Antonis's son (Mingus's father) and his daughter (Mingus's sister) came walking down the path with sausages in hand. The daughter got right to work helping Jacky peel potatoes, Ward fixed Mingus's and Aldona's bikes, cucumbers and tomatoes were picked, we dug out whatever food we had available, and we had a nice picnic in the yard. While our bread and cheese served as appetizers and the skewers of sausages sizzled on a little barbecue grill, the family tried to teach us Lithuanian folk songs. The grandfather upon learning how much Ward liked beer, went to their nearby apartment, which is close to the family homestead, for a two-liter bottle of his home brew, and next thing we knew, Aldona had called one of her friends to bring over her accordion and play us a song. Soon, everyone was singing and dancing around a bonfire.

> Ward: I thought, "Oh, my gosh how can this even happen? You can't organize this on a bus trip." It was amazing.

The hospitality did not end here. The next day, Aldona came to the farmstead with coffee, milk, bread, and homemade cheese. She made a nice table for us in the far house and the three of us enjoyed a lovely breakfast. It was interesting to see everyone smiling at each other with coffee grounds in their teeth as they don't filter their coffee. Soon, Antonis, Mingus, and his sister showed up to drive us to the Hill of Crosses.

The story behind the Hill of Crosses, that we were told by the locals, dates back to around the sixteenth century when an ill man said that if he got well, he would place a cross on the hill. He did get well and placed the cross on the hillside. Soon, others started placing crosses on the hill. When the Russians took over, they did not like the religion and power that this cross-filled hillside represented and in the 1960s destroyed it. This didn't stop the believers. They snuck back under the coverage of darkness and replaced their crosses. The Russians destroyed it two more times. Currently, there are hundreds of thousands, if not millions, of crosses on this hillside and Pope John Paul II even said mass there.

> Jacky: I like this version. However, if you Google it, there wasn't an ill man and the hill represents Christian devotion and is a memorial to Lithuanian National Identity. The Russians did flatten it three times, though, because they didn't like the power that it resembled.

Now, people can bring or buy a cross and place it on the hillside and make a wish or say a prayer. We bought a cross and placed it by the Virgin Mary and asked for our safe travels. What a moving experience this was.

"PEEK" EXPERIENCE IN ITALY

We couldn't always predict the social norms in any given society; some situations worked out great like in Lithuania, but others were a bit trickier to negotiate. Sometimes, something as simple as taking a shower can lead to unexpected interactions, as Jacky discovered in Italy.

We were on the road in Italy, planning to set up camp at a

campsite like we often did. At the campsite, though, the man running the place asked if we would rather rent one of their bungalows. A rainstorm was approaching, and the bungalow didn't cost much more than the campsite, so we agreed. We were grateful, as it rained the next day as well. Jacky decided it was time to clean up and headed to the showers. There was a single men's shower and a single women's shower. Each had their own entry from the outside.

Jacky: As I was gathering my shower attire, Ward said, "It looks like you have to use coins." I took a coin of their currency with me. As I put it into the machine to start the shower, the machine jammed. So, I put my clothes back on and I went back to the restaurant area for help. Using sign language, I indicated what had happened. The manager understood and quickly showed me the shower token that was needed. He followed me to the shower. He unjammed the box, put a token in and, I thought, went on his way.

So, I took my clothes off for a second time, and all of a sudden, he was pulling and pulling at the door. I was yelling, "*Uno momento,*" (one moment in Italian). I threw on my fleece top and my shorts. He was yelling that he had to, "Check the water." I let him in. He showed me how to work the hot and cold dials and then proceeded to try to unzip my fleece top! I was shouting, "No, no!" but he kept trying it. It got kind of scary because it was only the two of us in there. I had nothing on underneath. I pushed him out the door, but he protested all the while, "Just a peek! Just a peek!"

He finally went away, and I apprehensively finished my shower. I went back to the bungalow and told Ward that he wouldn't believe what had just happened. That a guy tried to get down my top in the shower! Ward just looked at me and said, "Why didn't you let him? Maybe he would have given us a discount on the bungalow!"

ROADSIDE CRICKET

Because Ward was knowledgeable and curious about so many different things—agriculture, architecture, industry, sports, and so on—we were drawn into unusual, and rewarding interactions everywhere we went. Often, Ward would be talking about his interest in whatever was going on, whether we were watching rope-makers in China or touring a curling stone factory in Canada, and the locals picked up on his inquisitiveness.

One afternoon in Slovenia, we were riding past a field and noticed a group of men playing cricket. Ward asked Jacky, "Do you know what they are playing?" He then started explaining the game. Soon, we heard shouts from the field. The cricket players heard us speaking English and yelled for us to come over and join them. It was a three-day tournament between an English team and a team from Lijubjana, Slovenia (actually ex-patriots of England). They were all friends and would get together once a year for three days of fun and camaraderie. Apparently, there was room for one more, because they asked Ward to join in.

Ward: I said, "Sure! Well, I don't know how to play this game, but I've played some baseball. It's like baseball, isn't it?"

They put a helmet on me, along with all the protective gear, and meanwhile I was thinking I knew how to swing and connect with the ball, but after that I would be lost. I didn't know whether to run or not run. So I hit the ball, and everyone was yelling, "Run! No, stay!" while I went back and forth, jumping this way and that.

The game ended shortly after that, but the English team gave me the thumbs up.

Jacky: They all said he scored a couple of points. He was quite surprised.

We enjoyed pizza and beer with the players afterward; we had a great time. One English player asked, "What am I going to see next? I've never seen an American get off his bike and join in a game of cricket before."

It was one of those things that astonished us on this trip. We never expected to be joining a cricket game in Slovenia, but we wanted to get immersed in the culture wherever we were. We were never in a big hurry, so we never had any regrets about missing an opportunity to try new things.

As we moved south from the Baltic countries, people became friendlier and friendlier. One morning in Slovenia, we asked a woman standing at the end of her driveway how to get to a certain road. Before we knew it, we were sitting at her picnic table with her family, sharing drinks and cookies. We didn't even know their language.

CHAPTER ELEVEN

IN PRAISE OF DOING THINGS UNPLANNED

We didn't do a lot of the usual touristy things on our trip, but we did prioritize visiting the Great Wall of China. On the other hand, we took a different approach than most.

Biking the Great Wall was one possibility, but we had heard from people who had done it that it wasn't the best experience. We didn't want to get stuck in the crowds that traveled half an hour by bus from Beijing to visit the Great Wall, either. Instead, we chose a longer bus ride that took us to a different section of the Wall, where we could take a two-hour hike. During that time, we saw only a couple dozen other people. The path wasn't filled with vendors like at the main entry; there was only one lady selling water.

> Jacky: We have a picture with the Great Wall winding behind us and there's not one person in the picture other than us. This was a really remote and neat part of the Wall to see. The steps were not rebuilt for tourists. It was authentic.

Ward: Yeah, and nobody could photo bomb your shot, so that was good.

We saw so few people on our hike, civilization seemed very remote. We were quite surprised to find a zip line waiting for us at the end of our hike. It was so strange to discover you could take a zip line off the Great Wall! The line spanned four hundred to five hundred meters over *Yuanyang Lake*. There was nobody there to cheer you on, just the man that ran it. You just had to muster your individual courage and strength and step off.

Jacky took the plunge, while Ward carried everyone's bags and hiked to the end.

Jacky: I had not zip-lined before. I'm normally afraid of heights, but being strapped in made this different, plus it's the GREAT WALL OF CHINA! Now, when someone asks me if I've ever zip-lined, I say, "Oh, yeah, I went off the Great Wall of China" like it's no big deal! You can imagine their response.

CLIMBING HIGH

When we went through Peru and Bolivia, we had no plans to do any mountain climbing, but once again, plans changed midstream. We were in a restaurant on the Peruvian border when we overheard a couple of women talking about climbing Huayna Potosi, a nearly twenty-thousand-foot mountain near La Paz. Apparently, one woman really wanted to go, but her hiking partner had backed out on her. Her name was Stacey McClain, and she was from New Brunswick.

Ward: When I heard that, I raised my hand and said, "Well, I'd hike with you." I looked at Jacky to see if it would be okay and she said, "Sure. I don't have to go, do I?" The hike would give her a few days to herself.

About a week later, Jacky and I rode our bicycles into La Paz. Shortly after, Stacey met up with us. Stacey and I found a guide, packed up three days' worth of rented gear—sleeping bags, ice axes, crampons, etc.—and caught a taxi ride to the mountain, all for $185.

The city of La Paz is located at twelve thousand feet, and the taxi took us up to fourteen thousand feet. The first day we hiked over to an ice wall and our guide taught us how to use the ice axe and the crampons. We practiced climbing straight up a wall of ice and repelling back down. For me, it was a hoot! The next night, we slept at the *refugio* (shelter) and the following day we climbed to over seventeen thousand feet. That's the same height as the base camp on Mt. Everest. Once there, we were advised to just rest and acclimatize.

We went to bed early, because we planned to start out again at 1:45 in the morning, but above seventeen thousand feet it's cold at night, so you don't sleep well. By 2 o'clock in the morning, though, we were strapping on our headlamps and starting to climb. Stacey had a bit of a cold, nothing big at first, but it grew into a severe headache and stomach problems. At 18,500 feet, she started to get delirious and I could tell she was getting altitude sickness. Stacey asked me to tell her stories to keep her awake. She moved very slowly, taking a step every two seconds or so. She didn't speak Spanish, so I had to use my Spanish skills to communicate to the guide that she was getting seriously sick. It wasn't easy, but I got the message across. We left her alone for maybe twenty minutes while our guide led me up to join another guide and climber. By the time he came back to her, she was vomiting blood. She had to get down the mountain immediately.

Stacey and I had made a pact that if one of us got sick, the other would turn around and go back down with them. I would have been happy to go back down with Stacey, but since there was this opportunity to join this other guide, I continued on to the summit while our original guide helped Stacey to safety.

Now with my new team, I proceeded to the ascent. We moved very slowly as everyone was struggling to breathe. My hands were going numb from the lack of oxygen and the bitterly cold temperatures did not help any either. The final section to the ascent got very, very steep going up the ridge. It was like climbing stairs, only very, very steep stairs. At times, we were climbing a sixty-degree incline. We had to use our ice axes and crampons to climb.

I don't get scared easily, but each time I dug in with my ice axe, I felt about two inches of purchase and then just a void. The mountain had corniced over and one foot away from me there was nothing but air under the snow. I was very glad I was tied to a guide. It was so dark and snowy I couldn't see well, but that may have been a blessing because when it got to be daylight, I could take in the actual situation: we had exposure on both sides for thousands of feet and a ten-inch piece of ice as our trail. The only thing that could stop us from sliding from here to tomorrow were our ice axes.

When we got to the top and looked north and south along the Cordillera Mountains, it was amazing. We could see the Amazon jungle in the east, the sun was just coming up, and it was gorgeous. The sunrise cast a shadow of the mountain on Lake Titicaca. We were spellbound.

Our guide saw the large number of climbers coming up the steep ridge and asked if we wanted to descend on the French route. He indicated it was steeper but less crowded and that we would not have to fight the advancing climbers. On the way back down, I could see that the only footprints in the snow were ours, and I thought, "Wow, this is something nobody else sees." When we arrived at base camp Stacey had already gone down to the first staging area. She turned out fine, but it was scary. You hear of people dying from altitude sickness. Also, as stated, once the sun rose, I became aware of how the snow had corniced over and how dangerous the climb actually was. In the dark, you are oblivious to this.

As I reflect back, I think about how this was all very unplanned. Meeting Stacey and climbing a mountain were never on the agenda, yet here I was having this singular experience. Amazing.

PB&J: LUNCH OF CHAMPIONS

In Argentina, the typically mundane task of finding a campground led to more adventures for us. We stopped into a sports shop to ask for directions, and while we were standing there learning about this campground, which was five or six miles away, a man named Alejandro came out of the office next door and asked what we were doing. The office turned out to be a radio station, and Alejandro wanted to put our story on the air.

Suddenly, we were live on the radio, patching together enough Spanish to be understood. People were calling in to wish us luck on our journey. We were surprised anybody could understand Ward's "gringo" Spanish, and we were touched by how many people reached out. It was the sort of event we never would have planned.

Alejandro had more surprises for us, in fact. He kindly offered to bike with us to the campground, to show us the way. Not only did he escort us, but it turned out he was planning a mountain biking trip with some friends the next day and wondered if Ward wanted to join the group.

Ward: I only had my tour bike, so I wasn't set up with the right suspension and tire width. My bike had fenders and racks, so I didn't look like much of a mountain biker, but of course I said yes. This would just be a friendly ride, right?

When I showed up the next morning, about twenty-five Argentinians were raring to go.

Jacky: I got food ready for him, packed him peanut butter and jelly sandwiches to take along.

Ward: It was an all-day trip, so I needed to have food and water. They had an epic mountain biking route set up, and I was keeping up, but they were all kidding around about the gringo in their midst. I was awarded grudging respect; I might have been a skinny white guy on an unimpressive bike for mountain biking, but I kept up. I didn't know exactly what they were saying, but the gist of it was, "Well, okay, this gringo can ride!"

We were riding along a dried-up riverbed when everybody stopped. It was lunchtime. I sat down to eat my peanut butter and jelly sandwiches, while everyone else pulled out their backpacks. Out came bottles of wine and steaks on skewers, ready to cook. The Argentinians made a fire and were having a barbecue of meat in the middle of this old waterway. They laughingly called over to me with my PB&J, "What are you eating? Here, have some meat!"

It turned out we needed the energy from that steak for the next leg of the trip. The only way to get down this riverbed was over a waterfall, twelve feet straight down. We handed our bikes down and crawled down a rope into the pool of waist deep water at the bottom.

By the end of the day, we had done over sixty miles of mountain biking. I tell my buddies here, "Yeah, I went mountain biking in Argentina and Chile," and they wonder, "How do you wind up doing these things?"

FLYING HIGH

Our flexibility was the key to being able to do all sorts of adventurous things.

In New Zealand, for instance, we took ten days off from our bikes to check out the north and south islands with our friends Ben and Christina. We went mountain biking, which was enjoyable, but they really wanted to try skydiving. We said, "Yes, let's do it!"

All four of us got tickets to skydive, but once we arrived at the location, we were told we couldn't jump that day due to the overcast sky. They told us to come back the next day. In the meantime, Jacky noticed an overnight cruise in Milford Sound. We couldn't afford both skydiving tickets and cruise tickets, so Jacky sacrificed her skydiving day to make the Milford Sound tour possible, leaving Ward to make the big leap with Ben and Christina.

Ward: They took us up to around thirteen thousand feet. You do it in tandem, with a diver who snaps all the points of the parachute together around both of you. As you're leaving the plane, he tells you to cross your arms and put your head back. You sit on a small bench looking right out the door. The reason for crossing your arms and looking up is to thwart your natural reactions at this point. You can't look out the door and panic, and you're less likely to reach out and try to stop yourself, which would be dangerous.

Then you just flop right out into midair. We jumped out above a beautiful lake with snow-capped mountains surrounding us. Mt. Cook was just peeking through the clouds. We fell through a cloud and the ground opened up below us. After free-falling for about ninety seconds, the parachute deployed and we had a beautiful three-minute descent of beauty and quietness, and then a soft landing.

Again, something we hadn't planned on doing, but I'd do it again in a second. It was a rush.

CHAPTER TWELVE

MOTHER NATURE IS NOT ALWAYS ON OUR SIDE: GUARDIAN ANGELS NUMBER TWO

Deciding when to push on and when to stay put was often tricky. When we were in Poland, heading for Ward's grandparents' roots in Zlotow, searching for traces of his family in places tourists never go, we faced a storm that required good judgment and a little bit of good luck.

We got off the bikes around noon, because we could see a storm brewing up ahead. Ominous green and black clouds filled the sky. We stopped at a gas station restaurant and took temporary refuge; we expected to stay less than an hour to wait out the storm, but it was over two hours before the howling winds died down, leaving the temperature outside a good thirty degrees cooler.

We knew something had happened. When we got on our bikes

and headed down the road, we came across all these branches and trees in the road. When we finally got to our overnight spot, you could tell they were recovering from a big storm. Emergency vehicles were out all over the place and people were running around trying to help each other. We realized we had just missed being in a tornado. We were so thankful we had made it to the truck stop when we did and decided to wait it out.

We were in such a remote area that there weren't a lot of choices of towns to stay in; we just timed it right when we landed in our overnight destination, Kujang.

> Jacky: In this town, they obviously don't get many tourists. One girl came up to me and asked me where I was from. When I said "America," she said I was the first American she had ever met.

All of the electricity in town was out. Candles lit the restaurants and bars, and the shower rooms, too. There was still a little hot water left for showers. Later, we learned that three people were killed in that storm, and eight had been missing.

Even in the wake of the destruction, the townspeople were welcoming when we rode into town. They were very kind and still tried to serve us, help us find a place to camp. It should have been us serving them.

It helped that we had vivid memories of riding in the rain in the Czech Republic, where it poured for three days with temperatures in the thirties (Fahrenheit), leaving us wet, cold, and miserable. At that time, we made a new rule then, "No riding in the rain," which may have been what saved us this time in Poland.

Ward: Another factor we had to consider was the roads in Poland. Due to the indention in the roads that can fill with water, it can be very dangerous to bike through. The trucks are heavy and the roads aren't built that well. Where the trucks travel, they leave an indentation in the road. That builds the shoulder of the road up to five to six inches high in places. Riding your bike, you either ride in the depression or up on the shoulder; both choices were risky at best. We didn't need to be out there when the roads/depressions were full of water.

GOING DOWNHILL FAST

We were lucky to have had so few truly close calls on our trip, but there were a few heart-stoppers. One of the scariest happened in the Andes. We started the day pleasantly enough, watching trains rolling through the hills, going fishing, and studying Spanish as we biked up the Andes, preparing to cross to Argentina.

Soon, though, the weather turned miserable. It started to rain and the temperature dropped from a high of eighty-three degrees down into the forties. We were soaked after the four-hour bike ride to the top, but we were looking forward to the relative ease of the downhill ride.

Little did we know it would be metal-to-metal braking all the way down. The rain came even harder, and we passed a truck that had been in an accident.

Ward: On the way down, the rubber of my brakes wore right through. I thought, "Oh, my gosh, this is not good." It wasn't slowing me down. As I squeezed the brake lever, it was going all the way back to the handlebars and it was not slowing me down at all. There were no guardrails on this descent. I was freewheeling. I was praying the whole half hour it took me to make it to the bottom.

The road was curvy, with a five hundred foot drop off the side. It wasn't a sheer cliff, but if you went off the road, it would take you a long time to pick yourself up. I was behind Jacky, who still had some brake control. Mine were shot, because I had the heavier load on my bike. I kept thinking, "If the rim explodes..."

Jacky: The downhill was very windy, and it was scary. And it was so cold. I had to stop to put all my socks on my hands because I couldn't feel my fingers. It seemed like forever before we made it to the border. When we reached the bottom, I said to Ward, "When we get to the border, we are going to get a hotel room. Even if it costs us one hundred dollars." We didn't have one hundred dollars to spend on a hotel, but that didn't matter at the time.

When we arrived at the border, though, there was no hotel in sight. No town, even. It was just a crossing spot. We were drenched and frozen solid. Hot coffee in hand, we waited in line, and Ward asked a bus driver if we could have a ride.

Ward: It was the best twenty dollars I ever spent. When we got on the bus, Jacky's lips were the same color as her dark blue jacket. She was shaking and shivering. I was afraid she was going hypothermic.

Jacky: I would've slept at that border crossing. I couldn't have gone any further that day. I was both mentally and physically whipped.

However, it was no small feat to negotiate a bus ride. We had to find someone who could take us with the bicycles who was also going to Bariloche. Fortunately, we got one that stowed our bikes in the luggage compartment. They also turned on the heat for us, though we never got warm until we got to the hostel where we could change clothes and turn the heat up to toast ourselves.

Unbelievably, the day ended on a high note. Once warmed up in Bariloche, we found a lively bar at our hostel and took immediate advantage of an all-you-can-eat pizza party and two-for-one beers. It was a blast. People were there from Poland, Ireland, Germany, and the United States. A band played and then they had karaoke.

> Jacky: It was my dad's eighty-first birthday, so I got up on stage with the band and we did a video with everyone singing Happy Birthday to my dad. It was a horrible day, but it ended up really awesome.

> Ward: The warmth and security of the place brought a new energy to us. It revitalized us, because there was electricity and there were other people. We embraced it, even though we were dead tired. If we had been staying in a cold wet tent, we would've been sleeping by seven o'clock in the evening, but here with the people in this place, we were energized.

It was always satisfying to be immersed and talk with the locals wherever we went, but it was also fun to share stories with other people traveling. Other folks at the hostel could relate to how we felt as travelers. They understood the whole lifestyle of not being sure where you were going to stay next or what you were going to experience.

We often traded war stories at campgrounds at the end of the day. Our stories usually made the biggest splash. Some of them complained about the two-hour bus delay they dealt with earlier in the day, while we told a story about descending the Andes with no brakes. They may have been late to their destination, but we had just defied gravity!

CHAPTER THIRTEEN

SERVING OTHERS ALONG THE WAY: RWANDA

Our Rotary Club connections made us aware of projects and needs we never would have known about otherwise. Our friend, Frank Pollari, for instance, was working with the Thunder Bay, Ontario Rotary Club, so that's how we found out about a mission trip to Rwanda, Africa. The goal of the trip was to build a usable library in a new school that was being built in Kabuga, Rwanda. Thunder Bay Rotary had ties to Kigali Rotary through an Ontario-trained ophthalmologist, Martin Ruzzangga, who had set up an eye clinic in his hometown of Kigali. After the genocide, Martin returned to Rwanda to check on his family. After he saw the awful conditions in his home country, he returned to Thunder Bay and asked for help. Thunder Bay was sending library books and shelving to the facility to assist in building this library.

As we were cycling in Europe, Frank contacted us with hopes of meeting up in Spain during his travel to Africa. He told us about the mission and then said, "You never know unless you ask. Do you guys want to go to Rwanda?" We looked at each other and said, "Why not?"

So, in November of 2007, we met up with Frank and his friend in Seville, Spain and we all headed to Africa. As we understood it, we were just to assemble the shelving units and Dewey Decimal the books being sent. It sounded straightforward, but of course, it was not.

> Ward: The shelving units they sent were old, rickety metal ones that you wouldn't want to put anything on. Books are heavy, and we had six thousand books. I basically said the metal shelves were junk and decided we'd build our own. There are so few libraries in Rwanda, I wanted to make this one last.

We set to work getting materials and building the shelves, but it was nothing like any building project we ever undertook in the United States. The library was about twenty-five miles outside of Kigali on a dusty dirt road over which we made many trips with materials for the library.

> Ward: With the help of an interpreter, I purchased sixty sheets of plywood for sixty shelving units. The catch was we had to get these stacks of wood back to the school site over miles of hilly, rocky roads. The Rwandans were unfazed, however, and just loaded a single pickup truck sky high with wood. The plywood was strapped down, but the pile reached higher than the cab of the truck. The front wheels barely touched the ground. Even so, we headed off down the road. Only when we were coming down hill to a stop light did I realize that the brakes weren't working right under the heavy load. The driver pumped the brakes like crazy. I have never seen anyone

pump brakes that fast. I thought maybe that was the day I was going to die.

Plywood in Rwanda is a tricky thing, because it is made of two layers with flat sticks in between. If you cut it the wrong way, it folds up like an accordion. We wanted to do it right, because each sheet cost fifty dollars! Unfortunately, we wouldn't be doing the cutting ourselves; we had to take the full sheets of plywood to a shared tool area. It looked like a farmer's market of tools and services. The men there were dressed in different colored jumpsuits according to their specialty. The men in blue ran the saw, while the men in orange served as handlers. Then there were people to unload the truck and foremen and cutters in other colors, all clamoring to be chosen for a job. When we drove in, at least ten people rushed the truck, vying for the job of unloading it. People in Rwanda who had jobs worked like crazy to keep those jobs. The haggling was intense as they worked through an interpreter, eager to work for a white man because they associated that with money and reliable payment.

Ward: My interpreter helped me hire the right people, but he didn't understand the importance of cutting the lumber the right way, so I had to stand there for hours while they cut, just making sure they didn't take a shortcut that would harm the integrity of the wood.

None of the workers had any safety gear or protection. They just ran the saws without guards on the blades, while little kids were running around underneath grabbing the scraps for cooking wood. There were no electrical outlets, just wires running from a central junction box, connected here and there with wire nuts or electrical tape, and lying on the ground. We expected someone to get electrocuted. No OSHA here!

We knew, however, that whatever was left undone at the library when we left in three weeks would stay undone, so we pushed to finish the work. We worked long hours, sometimes hauling wood back and forth using local transportation, which consisted of a Toyota Hiace minivan. Twenty or so people were packed into these minivans—plus, you paid extra for the wood to ride with you. Poor Ward, by far the tallest of all of us, got smashed into the corner. The rounded roof line forced him to ride the whole way with his neck bent.

> Jacky: Luckily, most of the windows were open to help dissipate the odors from other riders' infrequent showers and the high outside temperatures.

It was never miserable for long, though. Frank and Ward told stories on the bus, and Frank played the harmonica. The locals taught us to say *amakuru,* a greeting in Kinyarwanda along with some other words. When we tried to repeat them back, the locals would laugh as we were clearly not doing them justice with our pronunciations.

What was truly amazing about this kind of camaraderie was that it existed at all after the horrible things these people had been through. We knew about the genocide, but the reality of it hit home when we were actually there with the people.

One thing that was very different in Rwanda was that we didn't take a lot of pictures. People in Rwanda were wary of having their photographs taken, because during the genocide that was one way people were marked for killing. There were photo albums documenting all the people to be killed; nobody wanted their picture in those albums.

Rwandan fabrics made the most colorful clothes we had seen throughout our trip, so we tried to get some shots of the clothing on the women and children, but people almost always turned away in fear. Taking a photograph seemed so innocent to us, but to them, it felt like a threat.

We finished the library, complete with heavy-duty shelving. We strength-tested the shelving by asking 175-pound Frank to climb to the top shelf and take a seat. We numbered and shelved thousands of encyclopedias, science books, history texts, art books, and more. We even wrote policies and procedures for running the library. We truly tried to make a positive difference.

RWANDA REFLECTIONS

We didn't understand a lot about Rwanda's history when we started. We had read about the genocide and we knew that the Rotary Club of Kigali had lost half of its members, with members killing other members. It was just unbelievable.

Our understanding was that the Rwandese had been colonized by the English, the French, and the Belgians. Before the outsiders came, the tribes of Rwanda lived peacefully in the lush hills. They spoke one language and practiced subsistence farming. Working side by side is key to their entire history.

During their time of colonization, though, certain tribes got special preference, leading to a split. Because the Tutsis looked more European, with their fairer features, Belgium started to give them more rights and benefits. Special favors led to better education and higher prominence in society.

In the early 1990s, the rift between Tutsi and Hutu grew into a civil war of one faction over the other. The Hutus planned the elimination of the Tutsis, with help from China, which supplied them with things like machetes. Between April 1994 and July 1994, about eight hundred thousand people were killed, and most of them within arm's length of the others.

We were in Rwanda thirteen years after the massacres ended. We felt like we had stepped into the pages of a living history book. What seemed most amazing to us was that a country that had been so badly traumatized so recently was already working toward togetherness again. There's a new culture there, led by the current president, Paul Kagame, who outlawed retribution, and we found ourselves during its unfolding.

We went to the fiftieth anniversary celebration of independence while we were there. We were at Martin's and we saw the celebration on television and decided to go; the gathering was just a fifteen-minute walk away, though we weren't sure we could even get into the stadium. But, as white people, we were immediately granted entrance and ushered into nice seats. Modern Rwandans associate white people with the non-governmental organizations (NGOs) that have helped them in their recovery. It felt strange to be singled out that way, but we were excited to be part of the celebration, which included lots of dancing and music.

On the other hand, the walk back to the compound revealed the effects of war and poverty. Infrastructural change comes slowly to a poor country that depends so heavily on foreign aid. We saw broken-down machinery—road graders and dump trucks—just left where they were when they were last used. The roads were so rough that a four-wheel-drive truck with good clearance was a must. Electricity was only on part of the time, so walking after dark was rough. As we walked around the city, we always had to have a light with us.

We saw roads that had not been worked on since 1985, water being hauled in five-gallon cans on bicycles, and a public transit system based on motorcycle taxis, bicycle taxis, and Toyota vans used as buses. The airport had one runway for landing and takeoff; passengers walked across it from the terminal to board.

Poverty cut so deep there. When we got up early to go for a walk, we found men sitting on the corner at half past four in the morning, shovels in hand, waiting to see if they'd be picked for a two-dollar-a-day job. If you needed two workers, you drove by and put up two fingers and the first two people to hop on the back of your truck were the ones who got hired.

People were eager to work everywhere we went. At the lumber yard, men rushed the trucks to get the job. At the school, we saw many workers like gardeners. Their wages, if they could get work, didn't amount to much in terms of buying food or clothing, or anything really. People were so poor they ate the sandwich scraps we had leftover, even when they had sat in the sun for days. Food that we threw away always got eaten.

The country's violent history hung over everything. We saw fields full of prisoners wearing pink jumpsuits to denote their murderous role in the genocide. We heard stories about neighbors torturing and killing each other.

Jacky: Every single person that we talked to had their own story about family members who had been killed. Our main host told us two of his uncles were taken and tied to trees. Their mother was made to witness them as their torturers cut off one limb each day. They used tourniquets so the men—who until recently were neighbors they had bought milk and eggs from—wouldn't die right away. They wanted it to be a slow death for the men, and for their mother, who would no doubt die without their support.

If a wife was a Hutu and her husband was a Tutsi, she had to kill him. Otherwise, she and any of the children who looked like Tutsis would be killed by others.

It was almost impossible to believe, because the Rwandans seemed like such peaceable people in our everyday interactions. We saw them sharing gardens and goats, and yet just over a decade earlier, the devil was inside them. We struggled with reconciling the stories we heard with the peaceable people we saw around us. How can a people turn and do such torture? Emotionally, this was a hard time for us.

In an effort to understand the history better, we visited one genocide site, in Butare, where fifty thousand people died and only four survived. We met one of the survivors at the site. He had lost his wife and five children.

Because of the lime on the bodies at Butare, they are partially preserved, so we could see where skulls were cracked, limbs were amputated, or tendons were severed to stop people from running away.

> Jacky: I remember this one little boy lying on one of the tables. He still had half his hair and he had a little orange sweatshirt on. It's not just the bones you see; you actually see a person.

We did see some results of President Kagame's "no retribution" policy; he has worked hard to eliminate corruption and violence. He was trying to turn the country around to being a loving, peaceful country, and we felt that.

One day, we helped the mission deliver some goats to a village. Twenty-eight goats got loaded into our truck. In the market where we picked them up, children and adult women touched our arms and giggled, having never touched a white person before. On the way back to Kigali, we picked up three reporters and another truck with more goats. We had forty-eight goats to deliver to a community of 110 families, many of them orphans and widows from the genocide.

You might expect the survivors here to resist an arrangement where they shared livestock with their neighbors, but these folks were delighted. Theirs was a cooperative community, where they all worked together. The understanding is that when a goat has a kid, you give it to your neighbor. It was remarkable, because they did not behave like trauma victims. The community spirit was alive and well after all.

Ward: I never saw any scuffles between anyone. Even in traffic, we didn't see aggression or anything like that. The only time anyone got aggressive was if they wanted to get a job.

BREAK TIME

It sounds like we were always serious in Rwanda, but we had some lighthearted moments, too. When we were staying at a place called The Jamba House, for instance, the water for the hotel was rationed, because the city of Kigali only had water in certain sectors of town on certain days. Hotels had water tanks on the roof to serve as the ready supply of water. When the tanks are empty, you are out of water. All rooms had a five-gallon pail to accommodate for those unexpected shortages.

Ward: One time Jacky was halfway through taking her shower and her hair was full of soap when the water from the shower just quit. She yelled, "Ward, I need some more water!" Well, I went down to the main desk and grabbed a five-gallon pail. When I got back to the room, I got to pour the five gallons of water over her head.

Jacky: Refreshing.

Ward: Well, it was air temperature water, but it was always ninety degrees. But it was kind of funny. I got to pour water over her head, oh man. Prior we had not kept our five-gallon pail full of water, but we did after that.

The Jamba House was about three miles from the airport,

so many businessmen stayed there. It had a little bar, and at night we met people from all over Africa who were in Kigali doing business. It was an interesting part of our trip, coming to understand the different cultures coming together there.

Ward: One thing I learned was that men from Rwanda found slim-hipped women like Jacky not very attractive. And Ugandans found bigger women with wide hips more attractive because they could bear children and they could work harder.

Jacky: Just the opposite from here.

MOTHERS AND CHILDREN

We ate a lot of rice and potatoes in Rwanda, along with everyone else. We also had fish, bananas and more bananas, and some vegetables, but rice and potatoes were the staples because they went a long way. We bought five hundred pounds of rice to take to an orphanage, and they were very grateful.

When we visited an orphanage or a maternity hospital, we brought big bags of rice, corn meal, sugar, and soap. The people there always greeted us kindly. The extra food was helpful in the maternity hospital because the families of patients were responsible for bringing in food and linens for them and they could always use more.

Jacky: If you don't have any insurance, the family is responsible for bringing you food and washing you up and doing all the laundry. If you do have insurance, you get to pay a thousand francs and get the "Red Cross" treatment. Services were still minimal but a little more than if you didn't have any insurance at all. We also brought them soap; a lot of families didn't have soap.

The hospitals and orphanages were linked in a way; it wasn't uncommon for mothers to give birth in the hospital and leave the babies there. It was horribly sad, but at least they had the babies in the hospital where they received care before going to the orphanage.

> Jacky: There were two baby girls born at the hospital when we were there. Their mothers took off. The hospital asked Frank to name them. One was called Tatiana and the other Sarah.

> Ward: When I was there, the hospital didn't have a sterile smell. The baby was in bed with the mother, and everyone was sweating in the heat, so there was a smell. Not a locker-room smell, but a unique baby-mother smell. Things seemed to be peaceful, though there wasn't much for nursing staff or any staff for that matter. I don't recall ever seeing a doctor in the maternity hospital.

We visited one orphanage that was in poor condition and housed 186 kids, from infants to twenty-five-year-olds. Some of the residents were born with AIDS. Some kids lost their parents to the genocide and others to illness.

> Jacky: The only inviting element was the smell of burning wood. The kitchen was a small room with a dirt floor and three huge barrels holding kettles. One had cabbage, one had water to boil for drinking, and one had greens. The bathrooms and showers were very dirty.

It didn't seem like the children would necessarily be leaving the orphanage. Some were adults with no place to go. The unemployment rate was around seventy percent, so there were no jobs. Rwanda has few natural resources to capitalize on, so the economy needs to rely on human resources, yet there was no education available.

The urgent need for education is what spurred our efforts to make a library.

CHAPTER FOURTEEN

LANGUAGE BARRIERS

Smiles are the universal language, and it's a good thing, because we were constantly searching for ways to be understood all over the globe. The first thing people ask us when we tell them about our travels is: "How did you handle all the different languages?" We tried to communicate verbally, but facial expressions and emphatic gestures were often the most effective methods of communication.

We started out carrying a translator, a gadget that let us type in a word and pick the language. It didn't work very well; the machine's pronunciation was not adequate for all the different dialects. Besides, it was heavy and needed batteries, so we decided not to lug it along.

Picture books helped a lot. We said a word and pointed to a picture to show people what we were asking about. While the picture method worked better than the translator, the book was still large and awkward, so we sent that back, too.

The best option turned out to be a rotating supply of translation dictionaries. We could look up the English version of a word, find the proper word in the other language, and point to that. People looked at what we'd selected and then they could understand what we meant to be saying. When we left one region, we sent that dictionary back home and got another one for the next country.

> Ward: I studied Spanish all through high school, and then a couple of years of college. It was coming back to me, and it was a good basis for understanding many languages. It worked well enough that we could read French, Italian, and Spanish. That was a good fundamental base that let us read signs and understand them.

It was fairly easy for a good portion of the trip, at least in Europe, Central America, and South America, where they used the same alphabet as us. When we got to Asia, though, we didn't even understand their alphabet. The spoken language was also tonal, so a single word, like "Ma" could have four different meanings depending on how it was inflected.

Written words were always easier than spoken sentences, especially in some of the less common dialects. Spanish was very helpful in South America, if we saw it written down, but we couldn't understand everything that was being said.

> Jacky: It got frustrating, because we would think we were close to the right pronunciation, but people couldn't get what we were saying. "internet" is pretty much the same word everywhere, and yet when we said, "Where's the internet?" people would be like, "Huh?"

We did come up with a list of the most valuable languages to know if you are going to travel the world. If you can, learn

English, Spanish, French, and Chinese. With the first three alone, you can go to many places with a strong foundation for communicating.

Most people around the world speak more than one language. When we were in a campground in France, we met a group of young couples that highlighted this for us. When we all got together, they always asked which language everyone wanted to speak in. One couple was from Denmark, but they could speak four or five languages. "Should we speak in English, German, Danish, French, or Italian?" they asked. We voted for English.

> Jacky: Lots of times we asked in another language, "Do you speak English?" Often, people said no, so we would try to speak their language instead. We'd be pronouncing words so badly that then they would try to use their English, which was always pretty good.

France was fascinating. We heard a lot about how the French could be snobby, but we found that if you at least attempted to speak French, they tried to help you out. Still, even very close to the border with Italy, the French only spoke French. Crossing from Italy to France was astonishing. When we ventured over the border—only one mile into France—nobody there could speak Italian.

> Ward: I could have spoken some abbreviated Italian, but the guy we asked for directions didn't know any. He didn't speak any Spanish or English either. He spoke only in French. He was very kind and patient while we did our best to speak French.

Pictures were often worth a thousand words for us, so we frequently took photos of things we saw and the signs that went with them. If we saw a sign for a hotel, we took a picture of that word so if we needed to ask someone where a hotel was, we could show them the picture. *Voila*, instant understanding.

Ward: We did get snafued a few times in France, because we thought we were getting pretty good at procuring food for ourselves. We wanted some oatmeal for a nice warm breakfast, so I went to the store. I got this bag and came back to the campground, where Jacky asked me why I bought a bag of flour. I thought it said "oatmeal" on the bag.

Jacky: It said "farina."

Ward: Another night, I went looking for cottage cheese. It was cool enough out that we could carry it with us. I go into the store, thinking that I knew fromage was the word for cheese, so when I saw a package marked fresca fromage, I figured that was fresh cheese, like cottage cheese. I came back to the room and found out I had bought a pound of sour cream.

Jacky: I was like, "What are we going to do with a pound of sour cream?"

Because we traveled outside the usual tourist areas, we found ourselves in communities where the locals weren't used to accommodating English speakers. Early on, in Germany, we went along side roads that took us to tiny villages where there was no way they knew any English.

Ward: You couldn't predict what people would speak. In Poland, when we came to Diersburg, we saw a little lake and a bar, and there were people playing volleyball. We stopped and asked the bar owner if we could set up our tent, and he understood us well enough but kept asking us if we wanted to speak German.

He ended up bringing in someone who did speak English. But really, sports were our common language. They saw my willingness to join in the game even when I couldn't speak their language. We spent the entire evening playing volleyball.

Certain words were valuable to know anywhere. We made a list:

WORLDWIDE WORDS TO KNOW

- hello
- goodbye
- please
- thank you
- excuse me
- sorry
- the cost
- beer
- wine
- you're welcome
- your name
- right
- left
- food
- water
- hotel
- internet
- yes
- no
- big
- small
- money
- good
- bad
- ...and the key phrase: "Where on the map are we?"

As soon as we entered a country, if we saw anybody who spoke any English, we asked them how to say those words. "Where on the map are we?" We wrote the words down phonetically—we weren't interested in how to spell the words, we just needed to know how to pronounce them.

One truly universal word, though, was "hello."

Ward: In Asia especially, young kids all want to say hello to you. In Thailand, Cambodia, Laos, and Vietnam, kids ran to the edge of the road—many of them naked—just to shout "hello!" Sometimes the only word a person said to us was "hello."

Communication could quickly get confusing, as we found out while camping in Germany. Our campsite was right off a walking trail, so, not surprisingly, a couple came walking past our spot. We invited them to share a beer with us. While we were chatting, the man got a phone call, and a hush fell over the group.

Jacky: We could tell, "Oh, okay. That's the wife on the phone. This girl must be his mistress." They left after that, but the girl came back later, all distraught. She was crying, waving her hands around and everything. Ward just kept replying to what she was saying with, "Yeah, yeah. Okay, yeah." Finally, at 10:30, we headed for bed. And she walks up to the tent and starts unzipping it. I was saying, "No, no!" And she's like, "Yeah, yeah!"

Apparently in the conversation, she must have asked if she could share our tent, and Ward kept saying yes!

Finally, Ward came over and said "Nein! Nein! Nein!" The

girl finally left. After that, we made the rule that if you don't know what the other person is saying, admit it; don't keep acting like you know.

Ward: It's a good rule for any kind of living. If you don't know what you're agreeing to, don't.

GRAND GESTURES

When we didn't speak the language, gestures could help. There was a stop in Estonia where Jacky took sign language to a whole new level in procuring a campsite.

Jacky: It was just a little road out in the country, it was getting dusk, and Ward wanted to set up the tent in the woods. I said, "Give me a few minutes to see if I can find a place where we can camp." I sleep very lightly, and out in the woods, you hear every animal and every sound. So, I wanted a good place.

As we were biking, I all of a sudden heard these voices behind some apple trees. Ward and I pulled in and saw a couple picking apples in their front yard. I decided to go ask them if we could put our tent up in their yard—it's less intimidating for a female to go—so I went up to them, showed them my wedding ring and pointed to Ward. I made a triangle with my fingers for "tent," then put my hands up by my tilted face for "sleep" and so on. They welcomed us in. When I brought Ward over, they showed us this beautiful spot in a flower garden where we could camp.

They picked up the hand gestures at this point, using their hands over their heads to indicate showers, also showing us the sauna.

As we were walking back to our tent, Ward saw a pile of wood that needed splitting. He said, "Jacky, they are being so nice to us, I would like to chop some wood for them." So, I brought the woman over and picked up the axe, and indicated the axe makes a big piece of wood into little pieces of wood. I then pointed to Ward and he's all smiles. She says, "Yah!" I say to Ward, "See how easy that is? You just have to use a little charades!"

Apparently, our communications hadn't been a complete success, though, because a little while later, the woman came running out of the house with a phone in her hand. She handed the phone to Jacky. There was a female voice on the other end, speaking English. She asked, "What seems to be the problem?" We told her there was no problem. Everyone was being so nice to us we wanted to help out by splitting wood, maybe mowing the lawn.

Jacky returned the phone to the homeowner and after a short consultation, she handed it back to us. The voice on the phone said, "She wants to know, HOW long do you plan on staying?"

Jacky: She must have thought we were moving in! We were able to explain that we were leaving the next day. The next morning, she was yelling, "Coffee! Coffee!" from her kitchen door. We grabbed our cups and headed over. We had given her our business card the day before and she must have looked us up as she had a big grin on her face and was pointing to her Michigan T-shirt.

She sent us off with a bunch of apples and vegetables from her garden. We were surprised and pleased to get a Christmas card from them later on.

It was amazing how hospitable everyone was to us. However, early on when we returned to North America for the final leg of our trip we had asked if we could camp in someone's lawn and we were turned down. He was even a bike shop owner and even knew that we used to own a shop. At that time, we realized we needed to change our techniques when asking or searching for hospitality. We found we couldn't approach people and ask them if we could stay as their defenses went up. "Who are they? What is their motive? Can I trust them?" We quickly found out that if we let people approach us and offer help or a place to stay, they were just as friendly as people in other countries. Here in the United States, they needed time to get comfortable with us. So, one of our strategies was to go to an Elks Club (if available) or a local pub. We sat at the bar with the locals. They always asked us where we were from and what we were doing. After some stories and laughs, we asked them if they knew where we could put up our tent for the night. Nine out of ten times one of them offered to have us stay at their house or camp in their yard.

The sensational way the news is presented in the media here in the United States makes people wary. When we do our talks, we ask the audience how many of them would open their yard to a stranger, and most people say they would not. We've found that once people here have a chance to scope you out, they are extraordinarily kind, but the wrong approach can make for a different outcome.

MISSED CONNECTIONS

A few times, the language barrier was truly frustrating and we felt we were not getting through to people. One incident happened when we were flying out of Panama. We needed a taxi van that could haul our bikes for the forty-minute ride to the airport. We had a five o'clock in the morning departure. We went so far as having the hostel receptionist order the taxi van for us to ensure that the vehicle was large enough to accommodate our bike boxes. When the taxi showed up at three o'clock in the morning, it was a car and not a van. We were very disappointed that our efforts to communicate with the receptionist were not understood.

At this hour, getting a van taxi would have been almost impossible for us to still meet our flight departure time. So, we decided to make the boxes fit in the back seat. The back seat was wide enough, but the curvature of the car prohibited us from closing the doors. Our solution was to roll the windows down. The boxes then fit and doors could be shut.

> Ward: Jacky had to ride on my lap in the front. When we got to the airport, the taxi driver asked for an extra fifty dollars for luggage handling. He never even touched the bikes! I was furious. I wanted to punch the guy in the face, but Jacky kept saying no, don't, they'll call the police and we'll miss our flight.

China was probably the most difficult, because a good portion of the Chinese people couldn't read. Even if we had a picture of the word for hotel, they couldn't read the characters. Also, the dialects changed quickly across China. Every day we had to learn a different way to say the word for beer. Once we understood the tone used where we were, we could get a beer.

Surprisingly, nobody seriously took advantage of us because of our lack of language skills. The only real drawback for us was that it was hard to dig deeply into a culture except through observation, because we couldn't carry on serious conversations much of the time.

One way we got around the language barrier was through pictures Ward took along the way.

Ward: I'd take photos of light poles, farming, sewer systems, whatever I could. Then I would show the picture to people and hopefully learn something from what they told me about it.

Rotary clubs provided some respite from the constantly changing languages, because there were always members there who spoke English. We might attend a Rotary meeting held in Polish or Swedish, but after the meeting, people conversed with us in our native tongue. It was nice to have an easy conversation once in a while.

We noticed we changed our delivery of the English language. We spoke slower and enunciated every word more clearly. We were in Lithuania, standing at an intersection waiting for the light to change, and we asked a young guy standing next to us where a certain hostel was. He looked at us and asked, "Why do you talk so slowly?" Here the guy was from California.

CHAPTER FIFTEEN

SPECIAL NEW FRIENDS MADE ALONG THE WAY NUMBER ONE: RALPH AND LOUISE

Very early in our travels, we met a Swedish couple who became lifelong friends. Ralph and Louise camped next to us on one of our first stops in Germany. We gave them our business card, which led us to email each other. When they saw our planned route, they invited us to spend some time with them in Vasteras, Sweden, to experience the Swedish culture from their perspective. We gladly accepted the opportunity.

Again, we were welcomed with open arms. We had a sauna, ate Swedish food like caviar on eggs, drank Akavit, and sang to Swedish folk songs. The next day, they took us on an extensive tour of the area, including historical sites, a round of miniature golf, and a fresh fish lunch. We wrapped up the day with some extra-creamy ice cream that was popular in all the Scandinavian countries. Ward wanted to pay back the hospitality offered to us. Luckily, he spied a stack of uncut firewood calling his name, so he was able to put some time into ensuring their warm and cozy winter.

Ward: Well, if I saw a pile of wood, then I'd ask, "Can I split the wood for you?" That's how I put myself through college, selling firewood. It gives me some exercise, and I feel as though I am contributing to the household.

Ralph and Louise own a taxi company. As a parting gift, Ralph gave us a bottle opener shaped like a little man, with his taxi company's name written on it. We referred to this little taxi man bottle opener as "Ralph." The taxi man traveled with us and helped us open bottles of brew in each new country. We always sent photos back to Ralph with the taxi man opener standing up next to the bottle. Ralph received pictures of the taxi man next to a beer in Thailand, a beer in China, and so on, so it was a little like he was traveling with us.

In 2010, in our last year of the trip, we were bicycling the perimeter of the continental United States, touching the four corners: Seattle, Washington; San Diego, California; Key West, Florida; and Portland, Maine. When Ralph saw that we were going to be going to Key West, he sent us fifty dollars through PayPal to have dinner and drinks on him. He especially wanted us to stop at a place called Sloppy Joes. We emailed him back a thank you and asked, "Why don't you come and join us?"

Ward: The next email we got from him was their flight itinerary.

Jacky: We were so surprised. They flew into Miami. Rented a car and followed us down to Key West.

Ward: I had joked with Ralph that the bottle opener he'd given us was wearing out. It had a metal tip but otherwise was plastic. I said, "Well, Ralph, I don't want to be mean, but the Swedes don't know how to make a very good bottle opener, because it's breaking." (Ralph thought it was from overuse and not a quality issue.)

Upon their arrival in the Florida Keys, he handed me a new bottle opener made of stainless steel, saying, "This one won't break!" Either the original opener that we call "Ralph" or the new upgraded stainless steel opener is used at our home to this day.

Jacky: The original Ralph taxicab opener still travels with us on all our trips.

In Key West, we had talked about buying or building a house when we returned to Decorah. If it was going to be a brick house, Ralph wanted to be the one to buy the first brick. In 2013, when Ralph and Louise came to the United States to visit us in Decorah, Iowa, they bought us a brick with a little placard put on the side, saying "Buy Ward a brick. Love to you in your new home, from Ralph and Louise, Sweden." It's in our dining room hutch now, in our brick house (that we bought).

Gifts from Ralph and Louise were always fun, but some were more interesting than others. They knew we had enjoyed things like caviar when we visited them, so we were very surprised to receive a care package back in Decorah with tubes of caviar and other treats in it. We also found a can of fish tucked in the box. The can was bulging, and it came with very strange and precise instructions.

Ward: It's a sixteenth century Swedish tradition, the eating of fermented herring called *Surströmming*. It comes in a can that's deformed, almost ball-like. You're instructed to open the can under water so it doesn't explode. But even the smell coming out of the water was just...

Jacky: It was putrid. My mom couldn't even be outside with us; she had to go in the house because of the intense smell. The worst thing was then you had to eat it.

We said, "All right, if this is their tradition and he sent it all the way from Sweden, we have to try it." I took a little bit on a cracker and it was horrible. Ward took a little on a cracker, same thing. My cousin, he had two crackers of it, and the next day he called me and asked, "Do you have really bad gas?"

We poured it out at the far end of our lot by some trees, and you could still smell it way up at the house. We said, "Ralph, we thought you liked us!"

The relationship that developed from a chance meeting on the second or third day of our trip was just amazing. We did visit them again on our most recent biking adventure in Malaga, Spain. I'm sure we'll meet up with them again somewhere in the world.

CHAPTER SIXTEEN

A ZOO WITH NO FENCES

We learned that meeting new people could lead not only to heartwarming friendships, but to some exhilarating adventures, too. This was especially true of another couple we met, Fabio and Larissa. In October of 2007, we were staying in a hostel in Geneva, Switzerland that had three couples to a room. One of the couples was from Brazil. During our short time there, we enjoyed each other's company and exchanged contact information.

When they found out we were traveling to South America, they kept emailing us, asking, "When are you going to come to Brazil?"

We planned to be in Sao Paulo in February of 2008 to take in Carnival, so Fabio and Larissa met us at the airport and put us up in their home in Sao Carlos. We enjoyed Carnival, but the big attraction, as far as Fabio was concerned, was fishing. We did a little kayak fishing on this visit, but only enough to whet our appetite. We were then off to Argentina.

The following months Fabio stayed in contact and kept asking us about coming fishing. So, we agreed to meet them in July of 2008 in Cocalinho, Brazil.

> Jacky: As we were trying to plan it, we were trying to figure out how much food and drinks to bring, so I emailed Fabio, asking, "Will there be a store at the campground?" He just said, "No," but he must have been laughing to himself, since he knew we were going to be in the middle of nowhere.

It quickly became clear that where we were going, there were definitely no stores. Fabio and Larissa picked us up in their car, packed with fishing poles, reels, licenses, and all the food we needed for the trip. We crammed everything in the car and we headed off down a dirt road.

The powdered dirt was five or six inches deep. We drove right through a stream, which was deep enough to swamp the engine, so we had to stop and put the hood up to let it dry out. Monkeys ran by us while we waited. Engine restored, we drove through pastures, opening and closing gates and finally following a grassy path to a little cleared area by the water. That was where we were going to be camping. There was nothing else there; we were out in the middle of nowhere.

> Ward: We were a good thirty miles from any town, right on the edge of this stream that goes into the Amazon. That first night, we made a fire, because Fabio told us, "You have to make a fire, because otherwise the jaguars will come around."

> Jacky: It was a real big fire the first night, to let the jaguars know we were there. To make them afraid.

The big cats were definitely out there. One day, we went for a walk and saw a jaguar's paw print less than a quarter of a mile from the tent. It was bigger than a man's hand.

Surprisingly, we slept well. Fabio and Larissa are very calm people, so we took our cues from them. They didn't seem afraid. We later found out maybe they were, a little, but they never let on.

We saw monkeys, crocodiles, toucans, ariranha (river otters), and countless exotic birds. In the river, we caught barracuda, tyranena (wolf fish) pio, and piranha, in addition to the tucunare (peacock bass) we ate every day.

What little contact we had with civilization during our fishing trip came unexpectedly from the owners of the property we were camping on. We went over to visit—Fabio and Larissa knew the couple—and the woman was thrilled because she had seen us on television a few days earlier. We had done an interview in Campo Verde, so she was over the top to meet "the ones from the TV!" We tried to say we were just normal people, we were just there to fish, but she treated us like celebrities, offering us coffee and apologizing for the dirt floor in her home. We thought we were the lucky ones to get to share time with her and her family.

Most of the time, though, we were in or on the river. We went fishing three times a day, we got our drinking water from the river, and we bathed in the river. Fabio taught us tricks like sliding our feet to nudge sea urchins out of the way when we were bathing, to scare them off so we wouldn't get stung.

Sea urchins weren't the only concern. There were also piranhas in the water. We knew it for sure, because Ward and

Fabio took one of the fish they caught and hung it out on a stick in the water overnight. In the morning, the fish was shredded; only a skeleton was left.

Jacky: When we were there, I just happened to have my menstrual cycle. They were all yelling, "Come in the water!" I said, "No, I don't think that's a good idea."

We caught and ate piranha, but the tucunare (known as the Peacock Bass to us) was the fish we were looking for. The tucunare was delicious cooked over an open fire with salt, garlic, olives, and tomatoes in the belly of the fish. We used a palm leaf to sew the belly back up to hold in all the vegetables and the juices. We turned the fish on a stick over the fire, and then pulled back the skin to find nice fillets of fresh fish.

Animals surrounded us. Every kind of snake imaginable lived in the river, and each morning, we heard the parrots and toucans singing.

Ward: You'd go, "Geez, right off a box of Froot Loops, here's a toucan with all the colors!"

Jacky: In the morning, you would also hear this roaring and moaning sound. I remember the first day, we asked, "What is that sound?" It came from across the river. Fabio and Larissa said, "Oh, those are the gorillas." Oh, okay.

Going to the bathroom was interesting. You had to walk into the woods carrying a machete in case there were jaguars or snakes. Thank goodness I never had to use it. I'm not sure what I would have done if I had seen either of them.

ON THE RIVER

We were planning to stay three or four days, although Fabio hoped for seven to ten days. We ended up staying five. Each day, we went out fishing. Fishing different parts of the river was sometimes a real challenge with the dense canopy and encroaching jungle. At those times, we sat very low in the boat and were told to use our paddles to move along, but it was tempting to reach out and grab the trees just above our heads. You could pull yourself along this way but risked coming in contact with snakes and biting insects that lived in the trees. We really were in the jungle.

> Ward: Whatever the height of the boat was, that's how low we were going below the trees, trying not to pull ourselves through. We were thinking, "Don't grab the trees. Snakes. Don't grab the trees." You didn't know what would drop in on you, with monkeys just overhead and everything. I am thinking to myself, "Okay, this is an adventure."

One stream led to another, bigger waterway, where we got in a tough spot. Larissa grabbed a limb to pull us through, even though she had warned us against it. The tree had a hornet's nest in it. The hornets swarmed and stung Larissa thirteen times. Luckily, we were far enough away. In her panic, she threw her paddle into the water. Fabio jumped in after it.

> Jacky: In that area, you don't want to be in the water because there's crocodiles, there's snakes, there's everything.

> Ward: It was pretty terrifying, because we were going, "Okay, she's stirred this hornet's nest up. Are they going to come to us? What do we do? Do we get in the water? Don't get in the water?"

Luckily, Fabio retrieved the paddle and got back in his kayak. Things calmed down for a bit, but as we were moving downstream, fishing, we heard a sound like a horse nickering. The sound was coming from the water.

> Ward: We could see heads in the water swimming at us, and it's like "Oh, these creatures are big."

> Jacky: They were swimming at us aggressively. They were not happy. Their heads were the size of volleyballs.

The creatures were the ariranha—giant, carnivorous river otters very different from their cute and cuddly North American cousins—defending their dens. The seal-like creatures will attack the boat you're in to protect their young. Fabio told us to stay calm, but it wasn't easy with Larissa sitting there covered with hornet stings and giant otters stalking us from all sides. As if there weren't enough threats at that point, a crocodile also surfaced.

We were surely the only humans out there. Deep vegetation encroached from all sides. It's not at all like being on the Mississippi River, for instance, where you see the human signs of boat docks on the shore. Here, there were no beaches, just a river full of water lilies and vegetation that had not been disturbed by anyone other than us.

We quickly paddled out of there, as far from the otters and crocodiles as we could.

Unfortunately, we came away with very few pictures from our Amazon excursion. We got a virus on our Scan Disk, so most of our South America pictures were lost.

Ward: We have just a few, but not a lot. We think we need to go do it again, right?!

Jacky: Maybe not.

Ward: Yeah, maybe not.

CHAPTER SEVENTEEN

DO YOU KNOW WHERE YOU'RE GOING TO STAY TONIGHT?

A lot of people don't see right away what was different with the way we traveled. The main day-to-day difference was that, unlike many travelers, we didn't plan ahead of time where to stay each night. The freeform approach allowed plenty of room for serendipitous adventures. However, it also left us scrambling for shelter on more than one occasion.

Each morning, we looked at where we were on the map and set a goal for our destination at the end of the day. We had a rough idea of our route, but we didn't have any hotels lined up. We didn't know if there were campgrounds where we were going. We didn't even know if there was a town where one was marked on the map.

HOTEL CHINA: YOU CAN LEAVE BUT YOU CAN NEVER STAY

We knew China posed a challenge, because there weren't

likely to be any campgrounds as it is highly populated. If we had found a place to camp, we risked waking up to twenty people standing around our tent in the morning.

We looked for a hotel without much luck. We didn't understand until we got closer to Shanghai that Chinese hotels have strict rules against Western guests. In the larger cities, the government licenses certain hotels to accept Western tourists. We were riding in rural areas, though, where it was tough to even find a hotel, let alone a licensed one.

As mentioned earlier, we used our camera to take pictures of the different Chinese characters necessary to convey our need for something. The character for hotel was on our camera and it helped us find hotels, but they were not always legal ones. Recognizing a sign that indicated a hotel, we stopped there and befriended the locals. When we went in to get a room, though, they said no, we couldn't stay there. We couldn't understand why. Maybe it was because we had just come in from riding in the rain and were all wet and messy. Maybe they just didn't want to deal with that.

When we did find a place, it could be grim. In one small town, we got a room for five dollars a night that just had a rusty metal frame bed with a thin mattress on it. There was no running water, no bathroom for our room, and no lights to show us the way to the basement bathroom. It was very dark and dirty, too. We huddled in our sleeping bags that night. We were just happy to be inside and not outside in the ever-curious population. The room was not worth the five dollars, but our options were few.

It happened again and again, though. We thought we might

be getting shunned because we were white people. Finally, we got some clarity at one hotel, when a very kind young lady used her computer to translate and explain the legal situation to us. Once it was established that we couldn't stay there, her grandfather called the police to ask permission. The answer was no and we had to go to another city to stay.

There was a crowd gathering outside, watching us, and it was getting dark. We couldn't stay. We wound up taking a truck ride thirty kilometers to another town with the help of the grandfather because we didn't want to be on the Chinese roads at night. The driver took us to a licensed hotel. The cost of the truck ride was greater than the cost of staying in the first hotel of the evening and the cost of the new hotel was at least double.

Trying to find a room felt like being in the movie Groundhog Day; it was the same story day in and day out. There was no way to be inconspicuous and just stop somewhere for a while. Once we rolled in on our bikes, everyone in town knew we were there. Because we went to places that travelers rarely venture into, we were rarities to the local people, so they noticed us right away.

Eventually, we found registered hotels, but even there, nothing was assured. Hotel managers and even police officers sent us on wild goose chases where we were apparently expected to offer bribes in return for registering. At one hotel, a police officer indicated that we had to come to the police station to register. When we refused, the hotel manager called him off and let us stay.

China's hotel rules dogged us everywhere, even in more populated areas (a small city is three to five million people). We had to leave a hotel we found just a short way outside of Beijing, on a day when we really needed the break.

Jacky: It was a super smoggy day and it was making us feel nauseous. I just felt really punky. It was a very hard day to bike. We were on the right road, but then ended up on another, because the roads are signed so poorly. We never turned off, so how could we be on a different road? I was hoping to only do sixty kilometers that day and one hundred the next, after some good rest. However, this didn't happen.

We stopped in one very small town and they indicated there was a hotel in a bigger town just a short distance away. We biked there. It was a much bigger city and Ward worried that the price might be a lot higher because we were so close to Tianjin, a tourist spot.

At this point, I didn't care. I needed to stop. My glycogen reserves were empty. As soon as my beverage and food wore off, I felt like I was going to faint. My biking speed dropped considerably.

When we reached the city, we instantly started asking where the hotel was. We got a lot of different answers. One very aggressive woman tried to charge us one hundred yuan—about sixteen dollars—for a small, dirty room with no shower. This room was worth about twenty yuan—about three dollars. Even if we couldn't have found another place, we wouldn't have gone back there.

At that point, people pointed us in every direction—east, west, north, and south—even though there was supposedly only one hotel in town. We finally found it down a long driveway. The woman there gave us a small, pleasant room with lots of windows and a bathroom for fifty yuan a night. This was more like it. We were happy, ready to relax, shower, and go to bed.

Jacky: While Ward went out to get food, what did I see out the window, but a policeman walking up to our door with the hotel owner. He walked right in without knocking, a Chinese custom we never got used to. The officer could speak little English and was quite annoyed that I couldn't speak Chinese. They got a translator, which probably saved us, because the last thing you wanted to do was make one of these guys mad.

He wanted to know where we were going, where we had been, how many of us were there, and why were we there.

Friendship saved the day when a young man Ward had shared a beer with while getting food showed up and invited us to stay at his house. He had to get permission from the policeman. Permission granted, we went with this guy, who was so drunk we feared for our bicycles when he offered to help us walk them. He led us to a house with lots of his friends in it; we sat outside in the courtyard and enjoyed numerous plates of great food and more beer. We assumed this was his house.

We tried to pay for this wonderful food and beer, but they wouldn't let us. What they wanted was for us to party with them. We tried—Ward arm wrestled with the guys and jumped around with the kids—but by half past eight in the evening we had to go to bed. And the only verbal communication was the word hello.

Once again, it was not so simple. It turned out we weren't

staying there but somewhere else. The young man's house was down a couple of alleys, and his parents were certainly surprised to see a couple of foreigners and their bikes arrive on their doorstep. Still, hospitality reigned supreme. They set us up in a storage room, where the mother quickly made up a bed and started mopping the floor. We tried to tell her it was fine, but she wanted it clean.

We were so tired we didn't even shower. It seemed to take forever to get ourselves alone in our room, but at last we locked the door and turned out the light. Ah, peace at last. Or maybe not. In the next forty-five minutes or so, there were at least six different knocks on the door.

On the first knock, the young man brought ice cream for us. On the second, he brought watermelon. Then hot tea. Then water. Then a pee bucket. On visit number six, he wanted to show us where we could watch TV. Ward, being the gracious guest, got up and watched TV with him. We didn't think we were ever going to get to sleep.

We got up early the next day, hoping to put together a gift basket for these nice people and tuck some money in it, when we heard a knock on our bedroom door. It was the chief of police making sure we were leaving as soon as possible. Not only did the chief check our documents, he made it clear he wanted money.

> Jacky: He pulled some money out of his top pocket, where we could see it, and then he rubbed his fingers together in a gesture used around the world meaning "Show me the money." I said, "Ward, just ignore him."

We played dumb and smiled and told him we did not speak Chinese. We didn't want to pay this guy off, but we also didn't want the family to get into trouble.

> Ward: The mother was standing there and the look on her face, it was one of despair. It was so full of fear and I felt so bad that her kind gesture had brought the police into her home. It made me so angry—and I don't get angry very often—but this bribery-driven society infuriated me.

We got out of there. We were so afraid the police were going to follow us out of town and then demand the money. Luckily, they didn't, but we don't know what happened to our new friends.

> Jacky: Other travelers don't know what we're talking about when we tell about our China stories, because they stayed in tourist areas. They state, "That never happened to us," but that's because they either traveled with a tour group, which automatically stays in licensed hotels, or they only visit the major cities, which have the licensed hotels. Rural areas don't usually host foreigners, so their hotels aren't licensed and most hotel owners in these remote areas don't even know of that rule.

It was tough all over China. We had talked to a lot of cyclists before our trip, but only one who had ridden through China, so we didn't really know what to expect. In our conversation, they never brought up hotels. We didn't expect them to be a problem. We just assumed it would be easy like in Vietnam and Cambodia. However, even to go to the licensed hotels in China required our passports and visas, which did create another problem for us.

Jacky: The inside pages of my passport split away from the cover so it was in two parts. I got a new passport in Shanghai, but my Chinese visa was in the old one. Each passport had its own number. The police come to the hotels each morning to check the hotel registration of foreigners. Needless to say, I had to answer a lot of questions about why I had two passport numbers. We were never nervous about this, but it just got annoying. It was like, "Oh, no, not this again."

SWEDEN: THE GREAT OUTDOORS

In Scandinavian countries, we had a lot more freedom to stay where we liked—we were free to camp wherever as long as we were not a bother to anyone else—but it wasn't without its hazards.

We realized hotels, and even hostels, were expensive in Denmark, so as we rode into Sweden we opted to camp as much as possible to save money. One day, we set up our tent on a slope and behind a school that wasn't in session. Our dark green tent blended in nicely with the landscape. We saw a woman across a fence picking cherries. We asked if it was all right to camp behind the school. She indicated "yes" and also to help ourselves to some cherries. So, we picked cherries, had dinner, and laid down for the night.

It was very peaceful until four o'clock in the morning.

Jacky: I heard a car revving its engine. I thought to myself, "Oh, it's some kids drag racing on the street above us." Soon tires were spinning and we saw car lights coming straight at us! We both sat up in the tent, not knowing what to do. Reactionless. It was pretty scary.

Fortunately, the car swerved around us, but it ended up going right through a nearby hedge. We then heard them revving the engine again and the lights were facing our direction. We thought, "Oh, no, they're coming back to get us." Fortunately, the car engine then died.

The next morning when we examined the tracks, we could see the car missed the tent by only about two feet before crashing through the hedge. The car was still sitting in the parking lot. We took the license plate number and went to the police station. No one was at the station, so we never were able to report it, but we think it was a stolen car that someone had taken for a joy ride, almost through our bedroom!

SLOVENIA: MISSED CUES

We thought we knew how to choose a campsite, but obviously, we had a lot to learn. The importance of vetting a site completely was never so clear to us as it was in Slovenia. Slovenia is a very hilly country. Biking there, we climbed hills up to a 14 percent grade, compared to a maximum 7-to-8 percent grade in Iowa. About ten miles from the Italian border, we noticed that the tiled roofs had rocks on them. We couldn't figure out why there were rocks on top of the tile, which was already so heavy.

We stopped in a little town with a campground rated one star on the European campground rating system. We later joked it should have been a half star. The campground was essentially a farmyard with internet access. One-half of the farmhouse held hogs, while the other half served as a winery.

The camping was modest at best, but the area was popular

with hang gliders. There are cliffs that they can walk right off and just sit in the thermals, gliding for hours. From the campground, we could see hang gliders swooping around. It was beautiful to watch. We envisioned the free feeling they were experiencing and envied them.

Because it had rained the day before, our tent was soaked, so we decided to stay an extra day to dry it off and catch up on our website. We set up our tent on a cement slab in the barnyard; the slab was covered so rain wouldn't be an issue. Because of the cement we could not stake our tent. That night just as we settled in to cook dinner, the winds came up very, very quickly. No thunder in the distance or anything to let us know it was coming. Our cooking pan blew off the stove and everything just went helter-skelter.

Because our tent wasn't staked, we had to figure out how to hold the tent down and keep our backs to the wind to make sure the poles didn't snap. For two and a half hours, we just sat there and prayed for the winds to stop.

Jacky: I seriously thought we were going to die that night. Part of it was all the junk that was in the farmyard that we heard flying just past our tent.

Ward: We thought a piece of metal or a barrel or something was going to fly at us and hit us in the back of the head. Just when we thought it might calm down, around four o'clock in the morning, the winds started up again. Luckily, we had survived round two of ninety-plus mph winds. In the morning, we went to talk to the camp manager.

Ward: He said, "Oh, yeah, we lose three or four tents every

time the Bora winds come up." He never said to us, "Maybe you should put your tent a little bit out of the wind," or, "Maybe your tent should be staked."

Jacky: He knew the winds were coming that night and never warned us! He said those winds get up to 100 mph.

We were just a couple of months into the trip at this point, so we didn't know much. We had completely missed the cues from the rooftops strewn with rocks. Of course, they were reinforced because of the winds, but we had no idea when we first arrived.

The wind was still strong the next day when we headed west. We could barely hold our bikes on the road, but we knew we had to get away from the valley that channeled those winds. When we crossed from Slovenia into Italy (only about ten miles away) there were no more rocks on the roofs, and the winds died down. Relief!

BACK IN THE U.S. OF A.
DARK DESERT HIGHWAY

You might think finding a place to stay in the United States would be more predictable, but locating overnight accommodations back home came with its own surprises. For instance, in New Mexico, we traveled Route 40 (as this is one of the few east to west roads in New Mexico), wondering where we could safely set up a tent. We were moving alongside the interstate, so we were somewhat wary of transients and others who might rob us during the night.

We found an unlikely temporary home at the Navajo Truck

Stop in Arizona. We asked the truck stop manager if we could camp close to a picnic table in the yard. He said we could if we did not mind the sound of semitrucks idling. The sound of idling engines offered the comforting knowledge that we weren't alone. It was chilly—twenty degrees by morning as this was in November (2009)—so the trucks idled all night.

Truckers weren't our only company, however. From the truck stop, we sent an email out to friends and family with a clue to our whereabouts—the lyrics from the Eagles' song, *Take it Easy*. The next morning it turned out that Ward's Aunt Chrissy and Uncle Larry were twenty minutes away, heading to visit his uncle Maury in San Diego going the other direction on Route 40, so we got to have coffee with them at the truck stop as they passed through. We just never knew how any one day might begin.

YUKON TERRITORIES

Spots to camp were seldom farther apart than when we rode the Alaskan Highway through the Yukon and British Columbia.

Over four hundred miles could pass between cities, with no campgrounds in between. We camped on the side of the road, like a lot of other cyclists did. Most people set up their tents downhill, out of view of the road, but we hoped a spot up at the top meant more winds and fewer mosquitoes, so we stayed close to the road.

Even being that close to the highway, we had to be cautious about wildlife. We cooked away from our tent and were careful to never bring food back into the tent with us. Any food we stored had to be hung up in trees far from the tent as well as any garbage.

We tried to sleep, but it was impossible to not hear the forest's sounds all around us. We had seen a lot of animals on our way, so we knew what was out there. A pack of wolves had passed us on the road, and we had biked through a herd of bison.

Jacky: They were spooky! The bisons' heads are so big and they just stared at us. We were told how to behave around bear and moose, but nobody told us about the bison and their heads.

We saw eleven black bears during the trip. We were told to talk a lot and make a lot of noise. I sang songs all along the road just to make sure I didn't spook any bear. They'd rather eat berries than us, so as long as they had their food, we just had to make sure we didn't scare them or go near their cubs.

There were so many scenic spots we camped at on our trip, but when people ask us where we camped in Alaska, the only way we could respond was "Mile marker 1,534" or whatever mile marker it was. Sometimes, we'd get to camp at an intersection, and then we could at least give it a name, like "Jake's Corner."

With four hundred-plus miles between towns, we had to stock up on food just to make it to the next village. We couldn't buy anything perishable, so we loaded up on pasta and rice.

Jacky: I had a big smile on my face whenever I saw power lines because then I knew a town was not that far away. When we finally hit a town, we were ready for our "civilization rejuvenation." We would take a day off and enjoy walking the city streets, going into the stores, doing laundry at a laundromat, and taking a shower! A trip like this makes you appreciate those things.

While we traveled long distances each day in many cases, the chance for a little fun could stop us in our tracks early in the day, too. When we came out of San Diego, we were riding right next to the Mexican border on Highway 2, where every third or fourth car we saw was US Border Patrol. We weren't sure how safe we would be there, but when we came through Campo, we saw signs for a Veterans of Foreign War (VFW) pig roast we couldn't resist.

> Jacky: Ward was actually ahead of me, and I saw the sign, and I'm like, "Aw, wouldn't that be fun to go to?" But we'd only gone ten miles. I was sure Ward wouldn't do it. When I got up over the hill, though, I saw him standing at an intersection pointing toward the pig roast. I was like, "Yay!"

> Ward: It was something I had never seen before, a deep pit pig roast. It was a fundraiser for the VFW, with dollar glasses of wine and fifty cent beer. I thought, "Oh, well, we could have a beer or two."

We ended up staying for the barbecue, and after lunch we realized we either had to get back on the bikes right then, or ask the commander where we could stay in this small town.

> Ward: I went to the commander of the post and he said, "Well, you're welcome to stay. Put your tent up under the American flag in the front lawn." He told me that if we heard people running by us during the night, not to worry; they're trying to get into the United States. They wouldn't bother us.

The number of people getting across was not insignificant. We talked to a number of locals who had worked for the border patrol, and they told us they "catch" about four hundred people a night right in Campo, California. We wondered how many actually made it each night.

Jacky: I believe I heard them running by during the night. But it's hard to discern if it was reality or a dream.

Ward: I didn't hear anybody because I sleep very soundly, even under a flood-lit American flag.

VFWs and Elks clubs always welcomed us. It's part of the Elks' creed to help other lodge members who need a place to stay, so we stopped at lodges and let them know we were members. Often, we could help out around the lodge and earn our breakfast. They appreciated our willingness to pitch in on less-than-desirable tasks like scrubbing floors and washing walls.

One time, we walked into an Elks Lodge on a Friday evening and someone offered to buy us dinner. Another time, a member invited us over to her house for breakfast and a shower. Yet another day found us accepting prime rib dinners at a lodge in Gallup, New Mexico. We never did learn who our benefactor was that night.

When we visited Elks and shared our story of what we were doing, nine times out of ten somebody asked us to stay at their house. Once, two people wanted us to stay with them in the same town. What an embarrassment of riches for us!

Jacky: One said, "Well, I asked them first!"

Ward: We stayed at one gentleman's house, but the other guy negotiated to take us out to breakfast the next day.

We frequently went to the police station or the fire station looking for someone who could grant us the authority to camp in a park. We found these people to be public servants who were truly ready to serve. In Breckenridge, Texas, for instance, the whole network of city administration went into high gear to give us a good, safe experience in their city. The city manager and the city park superintendent said we could stay in the park, the police got us set up with showers at the local hospital, and on top of that, the police circled the park during the night, so we felt very protected as well.

Rotary clubs were a big help all over the world. The Rotary Club in Cedar Falls, for instance, asked Ward to meet with Barry Williams when we were in New Zealand. We ended up emailing ahead and Barry helped set up schools for us to do our Pedaling for Pencils project, which we'll talk more about in later chapters. Several different Rotarians hosted us while we were there, many we had never met before. The highlight was probably when we got to stay at the district governor's place on the ocean. We deeply appreciated all the hospitality, even if it could get a little overwhelming at times. The Rotarians were so eager to help us out, it was tough to get much time to ourselves!

One memorable stay was with Rotarian Mark Morton, a big game trophy hunter. He had a room added on to his house devoted to his international trophies. From rhinoceros to kudu to zebra, it was all there. All the floor coverings were animal skins. Even the place mats were made from skins. He made us the most delicious chili that night, and then revealed that the meat was from many different animals he had shot. He figured the price was about seventy dollars a pound.

Even hotels sometimes let us camp out back and just come

in to use their bathroom. All we had to do was ask the hotel manager. When it got to be under twenty degrees, though, we splurged and stayed in the hotel. We got stuck in a three-day snowstorm in Albuquerque, New Mexico. That didn't work well for our budget.

Not knowing where we were staying each night was sometimes unnerving, but our open-ended plans led us to meet fascinating people. More than that, though, depending on others for shelter taught us how generous, welcoming, and caring people are all over the world, and made us glad to do others favors when we could. We knew when we took the opportunity to help others, it would lead to other things down the road.

CHAPTER EIGHTEEN

SPECIAL NEW FRIENDS MADE ALONG THE WAY NUMBER TWO: THOMASI

We met so many fascinating folks along our route. One of the least likely came our way in Italy.

Leaving Vicenza, Italy, was tricky. The freeway, the *Autostrade per l'Italia,* didn't allow bicycles. We were trying to head west, toward Verona, but our only route seemed to be plagued by tunnel after tunnel. Even with our lights on, it wasn't easy to see us. Many cars honked at us as we went through.

Jacky: In fact, I don't think we were supposed to go through those tunnels.

Ward: We'd gone through one and it was very loud and scary. The tunnels are full of carbon monoxide.

Jacky: They're long and dark. You have no idea if they see you.

You just hear the speed of the car coming up from behind and then "pray."

The Italians were very good drivers, who normally made way for cyclists, but they didn't expect to see us in the tunnels. We didn't want to be in them, either, so we stopped by the side of the road to try to figure out another route to Verona. Along came another bicyclist, Johnny, who only spoke Italian but clearly wanted to help us. We cobbled together some basic communication and established that if we followed him, he would show us another way.

Johnny was on his road bike, which weighed about seventeen pounds compared to our 130-pound and seventy-pound loads. We wondered how we could ever keep up with this little ant flying up the hills, but he waited for us. As we rode up and over a pass through Vicenza, he pointed out the different points of interest and filled us in on his work designing roller coasters.

After about an hour and a half, we reached a small town called Montecchio Maggiore, where Johnny suggested a café stop before he left us to continue on his way. Even at eleven o'clock in the morning, Italians drink wine, so of course there were glasses of wine being poured at our table.

We were sitting there drinking red wine and shelling pistachios when up rolled the mailman on his little scooter. His name was Thomasi. He asked, "Who are these people? What are they doing?" He could see our bikes were all loaded down, and Johnny explained the rest of our story.

"Have they eaten? Are they hungry?" asked Thomasi. We

explained that we would get food further down the road. He then left and headed off to finish his mail route.

Three or four miles down the road, we heard a little scooter pulling up behind us. To our surprise, here was Thomasi. He had diverged from his mail route to come looking for us. "Are you hungry?" he asked again.

We admitted we were, indeed, hungry, so Thomasi jumped on his cell phone, called his wife, and arranged to bring us back to his house. We rode through vineyards going this way and that way all on a little dirt path to the house where his wife had prepared a simple but savory Italian lunch. Pasta, sauce, bread, and Coca-Cola. In addition to the soda, Thomasi opened a bottle of sparkling white wine.

He then asked us to stay while he finished his mail route. Upon his return, he gave Ward two Italian cycling shirts. He took interest in us as he, himself, goes on week-long self-contained bicycle trips each year with his buddies. He was trying to encourage us to stay and put up our tent that night in his lawn. (When we got back, we sent him one of our Decorah Bicycle shop jerseys in return.)

Finally, we needed to get down the road, but Thomasi wasn't done with us yet. He jumped on his bike and guided us back to the big highway as we surely couldn't have retraced our route to his house. As he was biking with us, he pointed to a castle and said that the next time we came, he wanted to take us there.

Our day of unexpected hospitality didn't end there, either. The traffic in Verona was so bad we decided to stay in a campground in Lazise. People were packed in, so we set up in the last open spot and tried to make ourselves inconspicuous as to not invade other people's space while we cooked our dinner.

While we were sitting there, a woman from the camper next to us came over and offered us a glass of wine. A little later she brought a refill. By the end of the evening, we were over at her camper sharing homemade Kahlua. It was one of those days where we just looked at each other in astonishment, and asked, "Can you believe what happened today?"

CHAPTER NINETEEN

MAKING MONEY

Even with all the hospitality in the world, it wasn't always easy to stick with our fifty-dollars-a-day budget. Living that cheaply was nearly impossible in Europe, so we tried to figure out ways to supplement our income and still have an immersive cultural experience.

TREK TRAVEL

Tim Staton, a former employee of Ward's company, Decorah Bicycles, suggested we look into working for Trek Travel. A US-based travel company, Trek Travel runs bike tours throughout Europe. They have a warehouse in southern France that holds the bikes necessary for running tours, and they often need help fixing and maintaining the bikes.

Tim directed us to Dan Copalla who was running the tours and the contact person. Ward already knew Dan as they worked together for Trek as bicycle mechanics, traveling across the country helping with Lance Armstrong's Tour of Hope fundraiser. Dan arranged for us to work a few hours a day in return for free lodging. All we had to pay for was our food. What's more, after a morning of work, we got to ride nice, expensive light Trek road bikes all over Provence, France.

One side benefit of cleaning up the Madone bikes was that we found all sorts of things in the seat packs. People stored extra tubes or patch kits in them. They left half-eaten Power Bars and used tissues, too, but they also left money behind. We were told that any money we found was ours. Usually it amounted to a few Euros, but one cyclist left 100 Euros in their seat pack and forgot about it. We made about $150 that day.

Ward: The job of fixing the bikes didn't pay any money, but the money we found.

Jacky: However, we used it to buy things for the Trek guest house, which housed about ten people.

Ward: Yes, we shared it. One night, we bought all the food and wine for the guest house. If you find something, share it.

Two weeks there gave us time to visit part of where the Tour de France is held: Mount Ventoux. We biked up the steep inclines of Ventoux, enduring 10 or 11 percent grades most of the time. The area is known for the high winds that have shaped the bare, treeless limestone surface over time. It looked like a lunar landscape. Luckily, we had a picture-perfect day: sunny and mild, with no wind.

Ward: It was a highlight, to be able to say we rode part of the Tour.

Jacky: Ward climbed it in an hour and a half, while I took nearly two hours. Luckily, Trek Travel hooked us up with some superlight Madone bikes for the climb. We descended in under half an hour.

As happened so often on our trip, one thing literally led to another, and we were soon offered another job with Trek Travel in their Costa Rica location. We hadn't planned to go to Costa Rica at all, but they offered to pay our way.

Ward: They'd pay us each six hundred dollars to get there, plus compensation for lodging. And we could explore Costa Rica using Trek Travel's mountain bikes. We didn't make any money to put in our pockets in this deal, but we didn't spend any money either.

Jacky: We had a super experience, because the Trek warehouse was a garage on the property of a great family. We were supposed to have lodging waiting for us, but when that fell through, the family said we could camp in their yard.

For three or four days, we stayed there. Tomasita, the mother, invited us in every morning for breakfast. She made *pinto*, which is a hot egg, rice, and bean dish. She tried to feed us all day long, even when we were out working on bikes in the garage. If she saw us munching on an apple or something, she brought out a big platter of food.

Jacky: We'd have to hide around the corner so she wouldn't see us eating. Not that we weren't appreciative, but most of the time we just wanted a quick little snack. She called us the skinny ones. She thought she had to take care of us and feed us.

The work was right up our alley. Our job was to go through bikes at the end of a tour and get them ready for the next one.

The bikes needed to be as perfect as possible to protect Trek Travel from any liability and give their customers the best riding experience possible.

Jacky: With ten years' experience as a bike shop owner and a certified bicycle mechanic, Ward could fix anything. His goal was always to make the bike as good as it could be.

While in Costa Rica, our friends, Gina and Doug Mello, were at their all-inclusive resort there. So, we took advantage of the opportunity to hook up with them, along with some other friends, and stayed for a few days. It was quite a bus ride to their place, sharing seats (and smells) with chickens for five hours. But it was so much fun to catch up with people we knew and to easily converse without a language barrier.

The unexpected side trip to Costa Rica was just the sort of adventure we were courting with our flexible, unplanned itinerary. Without a strict schedule to follow, all sorts of things became possible.

TOURING TASMANIA

When we went to Australia and New Zealand, we were reasonably sure we could find work picking fruit in the orchards. Not surprisingly, we didn't go to the usual tourist spots, though. Instead, we took an eight-hour ferry ride from Melbourne to Devonport, Tasmania.

Ward: I just liked the allure of Tasmania. Maybe it was the *Bugs Bunny* show with the Tasmanian devil, which was the only time I'd heard of Tasmania. I didn't know it was an island off Australia.

We called and emailed ahead to arrange work, but it didn't come as easily as we'd hoped. Once we set up in a great little campground overlooking the water, we wanted to stay a while, so the serious job search began.

We scanned the yellow pages and asked around, but it was an unusually cold season, so most of the fruit wasn't ripe yet. Also, many travelers were "WOOFing"—it stands for Working On Organic Farms—in the area, so farms had help readily available.

> Jacky: I called many places with not much luck. I did get hold of this one apple orchard, and the guy said they wouldn't be picking for another week. He told me to call back.

The next morning, we decided to get on our bikes and ride to this apple orchard to check it out in person. It was only seven miles away, so we biked out there hoping to talk with the orchard manager. When we arrived, we were told he was out in the field. Rather than just leave our business card and turn around, we decided to bike out into the orchard to find this man.

Mountain biking through an orchard was a first, as was our "job interview" with the manager, Brent, in the field. He was so impressed that we had gone to the effort to bike to the orchard and then through the fields, that he told us to come on Monday to start work.

> Ward: We got paid eighteen dollars an hour in Tasmanian dollars, the equivalent of twelve bucks an hour in the US.

Working from eight o'clock in the morning to half past four o'clock in the afternoon for six and a half days helped replenish our funds significantly. The workday was fairly regimented, which suited us fine. We always arrived thirty minutes early; we would beat Brent. Every morning, we sat there with our bikes, waiting for him to open the shop. (Our early arrival was cushioning our travel time in case we had a flat tire. We didn't want to be late for work.)

> Jacky: He really liked that, and we were getting into the swing of having a regular schedule again. It was actually fun, getting up to make breakfast and pack lunches, and being back to the campground by half past five o'clock.

Our job was thinning apples. We worked with two other guys in the hot sun all day, getting sunburned.

> Jacky: They have a hole in their ozone layer, so the sun is very fierce. We had to wear long sleeves, and still, I was getting burned through the threads of my shirt. You could just feel it stinging. We had to put zinc oxide on our faces. We loaded up with sunscreen at every break and still we were getting burned.

> School kids weren't allowed to play outside without wearing hats.

Needless to say, people in New Zealand, Australia, and Tasmania all look a lot older than their chronological age. People there always thought we were younger than we were.

For the six and a half days we spent working in Tasmania, we made enough money for a month and a half in Asia. We learned that it paid to work where the wages were high, then spend the money where the wages were low.

We never saw a live Tasmanian devil after all, but we did hear them when we camped in Leven Canyon. They make an eerie screeching sound that spooked us, because we were camping there all by ourselves.

Other sounds in the night baffled us at first. We heard a light thumping on the ground and looked out the tent to see forty or fifty wallabies jumping around right outside the tent. Later, we heard heavier thumping, when the kangaroos joined the festivities. Thump, thump, all night long.

CLEANING UP

The key to finding work to help pay our way was to be willing to do just that...work. No job was beneath us if it offered a way to make or save a dollar. We often did more than was asked of us, for the satisfaction of seeing a job done right, if nothing else.

We had some time to spend in New Zealand, so Jacky lined up three different campgrounds that let us stay for free if we worked for them.

IN THE GUTTER

The first place said we only had to work an hour a day each to pay for the night's stay.

Ward: A New Zealand dollar at that time was worth sixty-two cents in US dollars. The campgrounds averaged thirty New Zealand dollars or eighteen US dollars a night. If two of us worked one hour each, we made eighteen dollars.

It's hard to get much work done in an hour, as our first gig demonstrated. We were at a place called Baylys Beach Holiday Park, where they asked us to fill some holes with dirt and scrub down the outside of the cabins. The gutters were so full that the rainwater ran right down the siding, so mildew was a recurring problem for them. We could see it was going to be a big job to set things straight. We wound up spending four or five hours a day cleaning before going on a bike ride or going to the beach. (They paid us for the additional hours.)

We did that for three days before we had to move on. The owners joked that maybe they should try to keep us at their place, since we were so much help getting them ready for the upcoming holiday season. In New Zealand, the biggest camping day is Boxing Day, the day just following Christmas and we were there in November.

FILLING IN

At the Kauri Coast campground, the owners were quite particular. Again, we found ourselves filling holes and just doing whatever it took to make the premises perfect in exchange for a very nice cabin stay. They were known throughout New Zealand as one of the best campgrounds. They also offered nighttime tours to see the kiwi, which we jumped on. Red flashlights let us look at the birds without frightening them with bright lights.

One of the other perks at this campground was the use of the owner's four-wheeler. He let us take it for several hours each afternoon to just poke around. The owners had us over to their house for tea and dinner, too.

SCRUBBING AWAY

Our third campground was at Bay of Islands, where we were once again relegated to cleaning cabins, scrubbing shower stalls, and cleaning out gutters. When the owners saw us tackle a job, they quickly realized we meant business. Our lists kept getting longer and longer.

We worked four or five hours at a time, including Saturdays and Sundays. The owners had offered us around two hundred dollars, but they were so happy with our work, they paid us over four hundred dollars when we left.

After working until noon, we would jump on our bicycles and loop around Kauri Coast and Bay of Islands. In the afternoons, we were also organizing ourselves to go talk at schools where we gave out pencils as part of our "Pedaling for Pencils" program, which we will cover in more detail later in this book.

Ward: We thought, "Oh, well, if we're going to be here, let's get as much out of it as we can." I am kind of a workaholic. Work is an important element of my sanity.

Even when we had some cash in hand, we didn't splurge. We were always looking at how we could use the money down the road. We were so in tune with what everything cost that we felt guilty if we spent too much.

Ward: We wanted to say, "Oh, gosh, we just got paid. Let's go get a big steak." We didn't do that, though. Instead, we said, "Oh, maybe now we can get some sauce for our pasta."

Working at the campgrounds offered us a healthy respite from moving around so much. Plus, we enjoyed helping people and getting to know them. We were feeling like part of the crew, which really felt good after it being just the two of us for so long.

Jacky: Many people try hard to get out of work. But when you're not doing it, you kind of miss it, being productive and doing something.

SUNSHINE STATE

We had a similar sort of experience closer to home, in Summerfield, Florida, when we stayed put for a couple of months. We got there right around New Years, and we knew we did not want to ride up the East Coast in the middle of winter, so we planned to work there until March.

Through one of those serendipitous connections that just seemed to happen on this trip, we had a free place to stay. We had met an American woman named Carol at a hostel in Bangkok, Thailand, who had a rental property in Florida. She offered to let us stay there if we fixed up the place, because it was a little bit run down.

Ward: The biggest problem was that she had a squirrel living in it. We had to get the squirrel out. I also did all sorts of handyman jobs for Carol, like cleaning out the septic system and putting all new piping in it. I patched a hole in the roof, things like that.

During that time, we also looked for work in the area. We went to Home Depot, Lowes, bike shops, and a number of restaurants applying for jobs.

Ward: I went to every bike shop around. There was one shop

twelve miles north of us, so I rode up there on my bike to meet the owner. He said, "Oh, sure, you can work here, but I already hired a manager." Then he said, "Ward, could you train the manager?" The new guy had never worked in a bike shop.

Jacky: They loved him because he did everything. Even when their septic system got plugged up, he went to the Roto Rooter store, rented a machine and hauled it up there in our Burley bike trailer. He cleaned out their system and hauled it back. Not many people would do that.

Ward: I was looking for a job, and if you work hard, people see that and they'll give you a job. I really liked that bike store because it was right next to a mountain biking park where all kinds of bikers came through. It was really nice to visit with people who are enjoying the sport.

We were very fortunate with the jobs we found. Our money supply was down to nothing, so we needed to make money just to buy food. We were willing to do anything.

Jacky: We met a guy who said he had some lawn work to do. He could only pay five dollars an hour per person, so we would work from eight o'clock in the morning to noon for forty dollars. We figured it was forty dollars more than we'd have otherwise. A lot of people say, "We would never do that for five bucks an hour," but when you don't have anything otherwise, five bucks is five bucks.

We were willing to stay in less-than-perfect quarters as well. Carol's house in Florida was great, because it had electricity, a refrigerator, and a bed. We were thrilled. When friends from the Midwest came to visit, though, they looked around and said, "Oh, my gosh. We have to take a picture of this to show people. We could never live here."

To us, it was more than perfect. It was our temporary home. We were very thankful for Carol's graciousness. Her hospitality was even more extended beyond the walls of her home; she shared her family.

After so long tenting and moving from hostel to hostel, Carol's house offered welcome stability and tempting proximity to a big grocery store.

> Jacky: I studied the paper for BOGO bargains, "buy one, get one free," or any bargains. I stocked up on food to be able to make casseroles and other familiar dishes again. That was really fun for me.

When people first learn about our trip, they tend to think it's something they couldn't possibly do or afford. They may think we came from a privileged position to be able to financially manage this, but that's not the case. We worked hard and lived frugally before we left on our trip and then worked our way through it.

PENNIES FROM HEAVEN

On the other hand, sometimes money seemed to fall from the sky. People were incredibly generous in supporting our trip, even total strangers. The first time it happened was in the Yukon. A gentleman came up to us and handed us a one-hundred-dollar bill. He expressed his admiration for what we were doing and the way we were doing it. He said, "I want you to have this money so you can buy food as you go along your route."

We got another hundred dollars at a campground in New Mexico, just visiting with folks in the kitchen area of the campground. The same thing happened in Florida. And New Orleans.

Ward: We were down in New Orleans visiting my cousin Russ and his wife Angela, and we presented a program at their book club. After we spoke about our travels for a while, the guy came up to us and went, "When you get to Key West, go out to dinner on us." He gave us a one-hundred-dollar bill.

Jacky: There was also a time in California when we were camping and walked into the lodge area to get some breakfast. A woman came over to us and handed us a one-hundred-dollar bill.

Sometimes the spontaneous donations were smaller, occasionally larger. We got a fair number of ten- and twenty-dollar bills on the road, in response to the sign on the back of Jacky's bike that said, "Living the dream, cycling the world." People read that and understood why we were out there on the road with our packs and gear. Because of that sign, folks came up to us and handed us money. It even happened at a stoplight in California, when a driver two lanes over waved a twenty-dollar bill out the window while stopped at a stoplight.

Jacky: I thought, "How am I going to get that?" I have to cross in front of all this traffic. I don't know when the light's going to change. So, I scoot over there, get the twenty dollars from her and scoot back. I don't think the light ever turned, but I like to think the traffic would have waited for me if it had.

A real surprise came in the mail one day. We had written to one of our friends, Hall Roberts in Decorah, a strong advocate of International Youth Hostels (IYH). We had always thought highly of their programs; Ward carried IYH brochures in the bike shop for years. In our note, we mentioned that the hostels cost more than we had envisioned. It was fall and getting a bit chilly for camping. We were just sharing our experience, not requesting funds, but he sent us a check for a thousand dollars.

The Decorah Rotary Club was very supportive. Prior to our departure, the members passed the hat at one meeting and they contributed eight hundred dollars to our adventure.

BUY A BREW

Direct cash gifts probably totaled around three thousand dollars, but we also ran the "Ward is Thirsty" campaign on our website, which raised quite a bit of money.

> Ward: Basically, if you wanted to buy me a beer, you could send money and say, "Have a beer from me when you're in China." Or, "Have a beer on me in New Zealand."

Each time, we took a picture of Ward drinking his beer and posted many of them on the website so people could see that he had enjoyed it while they were also following our progress. We probably raised another couple thousand dollars this way,

CHAPTER TWENTY

SERVING OTHERS ALONG THE WAY: PANAMA

You go on a trip like this thinking you're the strong one, that you can do it on your own. The truth is, though, you don't go around the world by yourself. Support from family, friends, our community, and Rotary members is what got us through. Knowing we were buoyed by all these different groups of people, we felt able to use our journey to assist others as well. Helping other people felt like a small token to begin to repay the people who helped us. We were pleased to do that in a tangible way in Bocas del Toro, Panama.

WATER, WATER, EVERYWHERE

We were in Costa Rica when we got an email from our pastor Bryan Robertson, from Decorah Lutheran Church, saying that our church was doing a mission trip to the Caribbean islands of Bocas del Toro, Panama. The group was going to help install water catchment systems so the locals could have clean water to drink. They were getting their drinking water from puddles and holes in the ground, which were perfect spots for breeding malaria and all kinds of different diseases. The catchment system involved gutter systems placed along the rooftops that filtered the rainwater into a five-hundred-gallon tank. A little bleach or chlorine added to the tank killed any bacteria and now they had safe drinking water. Thankfully, the daily rain showers kept the water tanks full. It was quite gratifying to learn that the school attendance rate rose from 30 to 70 percent after the water system was installed and the children enjoyed better health.

We met up with Pastor Bryan and six other people at a tiny little airport in Panama to fly to Bocas del Toro. Our boarding passes were plastic paddles with numbers on them. We crossed the tarmac and boarded a very small, very loud, very turbulent airplane.

Once we landed, it was obvious how poor these people were and the help that they needed. We boarded onto two small boats that took us from the mainland to the small island that Dave and Joellen Jeffers owned.

The Jeffers, whom were from the United States, had sold everything to come help this island community with a primary objective to provide medical and spiritual support for the Guyami Indians. This was no easy task. They bought an island and built a house for them to live in. The small island then grew with structures, as they built a house for her parents, sleeping quarters for missionaries, and a chapel to take care of the locals' spiritual needs. They also set up a medical infirmary for the people of that area. All in all, the Jeffers lived quite simply. There was no regular plumbing on the island, and no electricity. Water came from a roof catchment system and was delivered to a showerhead by a pump that used solar-charged batteries. There was one light bulb for our open-air sleeping area.

Ward: We felt like we were on *Gilligan's Island.*

Jacky: It was super gorgeous. The whole island is actually a root system. The houses are built out over the water on stilts. Flowers are everywhere. But since the island is a root system on the water, you had to stick to the paths between buildings, because it was very muddy and spongy if you got off the path.

Ward: It was a bog. There was no grass, just this root system.

Water surrounded the islands, and yet the people weren't capturing any for clean drinking water. They get about two hundred inches of rain a year, but they didn't catch it. When we asked them where they got their water from, people pointed to a hole in the ground that was filled with bugs and slime. Meanwhile, the children were covered with mosquito and vampire bat bites because their housing lacked screens. We felt very bad for the children. Knowing that we could at least help them to stop drinking dirty water and instead drink water right from the sky was very rewarding.

Our task was not a simple one, though. The five-hundred-gallon tanks had to be transported by canoe-type boats and then hauled through the jungle on a small path through the trees and creeks. We had to wear boots, because we were slogging through mud that housed leeches and snakes. Once again, we were in the jungle.

> Ward: We tied a rope through the tank, and then two men carried it on a stick across their shoulders, with the tank between them. Sometimes, the trees were so tight you couldn't get the tank between the trees. We then had to take a longer, muddier route to get through. It was well worth it, though, when you understood that these people now weren't going to be sick.

> Jacky: I felt very good and warmed when I was asked, as a dietitian, to talk to one of the women at a village about her diet, as she was diabetic. It was so rewarding for me to be able to help these locals in whatever manner I could. This happened quite a bit; once they found out I was a dietitian, people asked for advice, even if I couldn't speak their language.

The people there were so happy that we were helping them. We didn't speak their language, but we could sense their joy. We felt it was a very worthwhile mission. Our church had gone down there twice a year for several years. Most of the places within half an hour's boat ride from the island now have water catchment systems, including the schools. We believe that it truly improved their lives.

CHAPTER TWENTY-ONE

UNNERVING MOMENTS

While most interactions were heartwarming, a few were unsettling, and even frightening.

NO QUESTIONS ASKED

Trying to cross the border from Peru to Bolivia came with its own unique challenges. For starters, we heard that they required hundred-dollar bills to enter Bolivia. We didn't have any, so Ward took the bus back to the last town to get the money. Once he got back, we decided to stop at a little pub and get a beer.

The pub was basically four cement walls with a few wooden benches on one side, a table and chairs off to the other side, and a barmaid at a standup table in the back. It was full of townspeople, mostly men, so we followed our rule of thumb to befriend the locals. We walked in waving, saying "Hola" to them all. They waved and greeted us back; it seemed quite friendly.

Not long after we sat at the table, though, a younger guy

came in and sat across from us. Instantly, the locals got up and walked over to stand beside him. The seated guy had his right hand in his coat pocket. The locals aggressively tried to get this man to shake their hands. The man kept his right hand tightly in his jacket pocket and tried to push them off with his left hand.

We weren't sure what was going on, whether they didn't want him talking to the Americans, or what. At this point, the barmaid came over and shooed the locals back to their seats.

> Jacky: The locals were behind the shady guy's back. I was facing them and could see the locals waving to me with their arms, pointing to his right jacket pocket. Then they made hand gestures with their thumbs and forefingers, like a gun. I was thinking if I just sat tight, didn't panic, and didn't make a scene then maybe he wouldn't pull out his gun. Not long after, the barmaid came over to me and whispered in my ear, "You must come outside."

> In Spanish, she said, "He knows you're American. He has a gun. He's going to rob you. You need to leave." I don't understand a lot of Spanish, but I did understand that!

We had two code words we agreed to use on this trip, for safety. One was "mora," which meant be quiet, don't say anything more or you're going to get us deeper in trouble. The other was "Birkie," reserved for moments where there was no time to ask questions. "Birkie" meant DANGER, just leave the situation. Now. Ask questions later!

> Jacky: I walked back in and sat down. I calmly said, "Ward,

we have a Birkie." Instantly, he's like, "Oh, okay, well, I guess we've got to go."

We gave the guy our beers, hoping that would keep him rooted to the spot. We got up and left. He didn't follow us, which was fortunate, because we had to walk down several alleys to our hostel in the dark.

Jacky: I think if he had gotten up and gone after us, the locals would have tackled him down. We always tried to form a relationship with the locals. Then they knew we were friendly and had our backs.

One of the reasons we had so few problems was that we listened to the locals. We took their words of advice to heart and tried not to be arrogant about our ability to handle things we didn't understand. As long as we smiled and greeted them, they took care of us.

Ward: One of our pieces of advice to travelers is to choose a key word that means, "We've got to go. Don't ask me why. Go now." I didn't know that the guy in the bar had a gun. I found it peculiar that he didn't shake hands with the other men, but I didn't realize why. When Jacky said, "We have a Birkie," I knew not to ask a thing, just get out of there.

OFF-ROAD RAGE

An even more unusual encounter made staying in a Swedish city park very, very uncomfortable. The town had a strange feeling about it the moment we rode in. There weren't a lot of people around, and no restaurants or stores were open for business.

We put up our tent alongside a walking path around seven o'clock at night. We were told that it was okay to free camp in Sweden, but we didn't yet understand that we were expected to find a spot removed from the mainstream, out of sight. We were planning to tell anyone who asked us where we were from that we were from Canada, to avoid testy political confrontations, but Ward forgot and as we were putting up our tent a man stopped and asked, "Where are you from?" Ward replied, "America."

Jacky: The guy says, "I'm from Iraq." I'm like, "Way to go, Ward! The one time you messed up and said we were from America, we meet this guy from Iraq!" During the night, someone came by our tent yelling at us in some other language. It was nothing I recognized, but it wasn't Scandinavian. The man clearly appeared to be drunk.

Ward was sleeping, so I just stayed very still. The guy continued walking by, but then came back to yell some more. I was very nervous because I wasn't sure if he would come in the tent, and I wasn't dressed. When he returned a third time, he sounded really drunk and stood for some time outside our tent. He was yelling and saying the word "American" every once in a while. Nobody but the Iraqi guy knew we were from America.

My heart was racing. I thought he might be back with a weapon. I didn't sleep much that night.

Ward: The reality is, I slept through it. When I lie down to sleep, I sleep. A tornado could roll through and I would sleep through it.

Luckily, we never saw the man again.

CHAPTER TWENTY-TWO

PERU'S WONDERS

Traditional tourism wasn't our usual fare on this trip, but occasionally it was worth braving the crowds, as it was in Peru. Machu Picchu was the main calling card, plus we planned to meet our friend Jeff Freidhof there for a two-week stay. Cusco offered one of the better airports to fly into, so we had Jeff fly in there.

NITTY GRITTY CITY

When we bicycled into the mountains of Cusco, we climbed up eleven thousand feet. The descent was breathtaking, with vista views of the city nestled in the valley below the terraced mountainsides.

Cusco was a touristy city, but it was also unique in that they had preserved the past in many ways. The narrow cobblestone roads gave it a quaint feeling, and the architecture was impressive. The cathedrals, though small, were truly magnificent.

The thing that was hard to wrap our heads around was that those cathedrals were built at the bidding of the conquistadors. Evidence of the Incas' advanced architectural abilities are everywhere in Peru—Machu Picchu is a shining example—and yet their cities are dominated by Christian architecture.

The contrast was stunning. We marveled at both types of structures, knowing that the Incas were doing the work in both situations, only under conscription or slavery in the case of the cathedrals.

On the streets of Cusco, there were lots of beggars. We had been advised that we shouldn't give money to the children begging, but it was okay to help out the elderly. In Peru, it isn't unusual for families to shun their elders, who often end up on the streets trying to take care of themselves. We did see some older people begging, so we bought some potatoes and other food to give to them.

We arrived during the harvest, so there were many food festivals going on. We tried many, many different potatoes because they were celebrating the Year of the Potato. Typically, when you got a plate of food from a vendor, they'd put five of the five thousand different varieties of potato on the plate. Black, red, every color. You also got a piece of fish, or if you were especially lucky, a whole guinea pig. The potatoes really did have distinctive flavors.

When we first arrived, we saw a lady filling a four-foot tall sack of potatoes that was basically the same height and shape as she was. We took a picture because it was so striking.

Jacky: The men seemed like they were taller and thin, but the women were short with a stocky stature.

Ward: Jacky's five feet, three inches, and she was tall relative to the Peruvian women.

Our hostel in Cusco was an old colonial building with great character. When we arrived, the desk clerk immediately offered us *mate de coca*. The remedy is supposed to help you adjust to the altitude as we were at eleven thousand feet, but it only made Ward sick. The hostel was fun to be at; it had people of many different nationalities there, so we got to hear their stories.

Jeff was the first biker to join us on the trip, so we were eager to make it a good experience for him. We arrived in Cusco a few days before Jeff to prepare for his visit. We biked from Cusco to Machu Picchu to scope out the towns, etc. We wanted to make the most of his time with us, so we familiarized ourselves with the area, arranged a visit to a school and set up Pedaling for Pencils stops. This is as calculated as we got in three years, only because we knew someone would be joining us. As we were scoping out the route, we came across two local mountain bikers. They told us to follow them and they took us on a World Class mountain bike trail. It was interesting to see two fully loaded bikes tackle this challenging downhill course, but we did it. Days later, after Jeff arrived, we rode the same route to Urubamba. When we came to the location of this mountain bike trail, Jacky told them she would be their Sherpa and she carried all three of their bags to town.

Jacky: What I don't do for those guys! What's the going Sherpa rate anyways!

Ward: It was considered one of the South American downhill routes. It was tough. I do a lot of mountain biking, but this was a challenging route, and fun.

As we rode over gravel roads throughout the farmlands, we also hit some roadblocks caused by donkeys carrying corn stalks. You could barely see the actual animals, because they were so buried. Our only option was to patiently bike behind them as they moved massive amounts of fodder down the road. We also had school kids that just got out of school come running up to us, slapping our hands, giggling and saying, "Hello."

TOP OF THE WORLD

Some people take a four-day hike over the Inca trails to get to Machu Picchu. We would have done the same, but Jeff had a limited time with us, so we wanted to show him as much of Peru as we could in the ten days of biking that his trip allowed. The rest of the tourists have to arrive/depart by bus and many stay in Aquas Calientes at the base of Machu Picchu for sixty dollars or more a night, and that wasn't in our budget, so we stayed in a town close by, Urubamba, for fifteen dollars a night.

Machu Picchu was spectacular. The mortarless stonework is so precise that you couldn't put a knife in the cracks between stones even now. Along the edge of the sheer mountainside, the Incas had built little stairways. We were very interested to see how these people had developed this whole city.

The backdrop took our breath away as well. The heights, the openness, and the exposure were breathtaking in other ways, too. We went to a less-developed section, Huayna Picchu, where only four hundred visitors are allowed each day. It is the mountain that you see behind Machu Pichu. There were no buildings here; we were told it was the place where young women were once taken by tribal priests.

When we started the climb up Huayna Picchu, we were walking up steps with a lot of brush and foliage on each side, so we didn't actually see how high we were going so it didn't seem that bad. It was very humid, so the steps were slippery but it was okay.

It was when we got to a little open area where we took a break. As Jeff looked down at Machu Picchu, he quickly realized how high he was and couldn't go any further.

Jacky: While Jeff waited on the ledge, Ward and I continued up. I am afraid of heights as well, but as long as I didn't have to look down, I was okay. Soon, the steps ended. We had to crawl through a cave to get to the top. It was pretty neat to be able to look down over Machu Picchu, but now we had to go down again.

You didn't go down the same way you came up. You went down on the side, where it was totally exposed. It was just a steep staircase with no railings and going straight down. Ward was walking normally down the steps, but I was nervously scooting, crab-style, all the way down.

Other Americans on the descent felt my concern as they stated, "This would never fly in the United States. We'd have nets. And fences. We'd have everything all over the place."

The steps were very irregular, which only added to the challenge. They were maybe ten inches wide and seven inches deep, so you had to step carefully. It was also damp, which made everything slippery.

ISLAND LIVING

While Jeff was scouting out different things to see in Peru, we knew we wanted to visit Lake Titicaca. We were heading toward Bolivia, and the lake was on the way. It's the highest navigable lake in the world at 12,500 feet and known for its floating islands. The islands developed when the Incas took reeds from the edge of the lake and piled them on top of each other. They floated. They put together such large masses of reeds that they created islands.

The islands were handy, because the Incas could float into the middle of the lake when the conquistadors came. The conquistadors had no boats, so the Incas were pretty safe out there. They also fished from the islands.

Today, the islands are maintained as a tourist attraction. You can take a boat out to the islands, eat frog head soup, and actually sleep. You're out pretty far, the water depth is over sixty feet. The boats that were used to take you to the islands were made of reeds. The island dwellers constantly collect more reeds as the islands are continually decaying.

> Ward: It was cool, because we were just on a bunch of floating reeds. You'd see little houses out there—people live there—and there are restaurants. There might have been fifteen to twenty islands you could go around and look at.

There was even a government of sorts out there. Each island had a mayor, and a teller. The teller used a loudspeaker to communicate with all the other islands. It was quite rustic, but they did have solar panels to generate electricity so you could have light at night. They also had a satellite dish to watch television.

> Ward: You don't want to have a candle, because you'd burn your house down with all those reeds.

One fascinating, if uncomfortable, facet of staying here was using the bathroom. You had to row out to a place known as Poop Island, made just for this purpose. Our friend, Stacey McClain, stayed on one of the islands with her friend. During the night, they had to do their deed on Poop Island. One of the local ladies rowed them over. There was a dog on Poop Island protecting it. They said it was so strange to go to this barren island and try to do their business while the lady and the dog watched and waited.

SPORTING FELLOWS

Lake Titicaca at 12,500 feet does not provide an ideal running climate, but Ward was training for a marathon. He wanted to enter a marathon in New Zealand with a goal of running the

Boston Marathon when we returned to the United States. The training started by climbing up a hill to get a better perspective of Puno. At the top was an eagle, and many visitors climbed to see it.

We were warned that many bandits waited along the route for the out-of-breath and tired visitors and then robbed them. Jeff was hopeful that he would be accosted. (Jeff is a state high school champion wrestler and a college All-American in wrestling. An attack would allow him to do takedowns on the stairs.) The suspicious guys hanging out at the many landings saw Ward and Jeff basically running up the stairs. They just looked and thought they should wait for some easier targets.

Not having had enough fitness training from climbing up to the eagle, the next day, Ward and Jeff went for a fifteen-kilometer run that proved to be more difficult than the previous days' training.

> Ward: At 12,500 feet, you don't go running. You're just looking for every bit of oxygen you can get, but here Jeff and I are running. We have a little video clip of me saying, "This really hurts," because there was zero oxygen.

Undeterred, Jeff was still interested in pursuing as many sports-related events as we could while in Peru. It was lucky that Jacky learned about a soccer tournament to be held on a basketball court in town. It was sponsored by the Peruvian Navy. There's one ship on Lake Titicaca, the Yavari, which is a British ship, and it's from the Peruvian Navy. They brought it over—in pieces carried by pack mules—from 1860-1862. It's so old they have to manufacture replacement parts for it.

The Peruvian Navy guys, seeing that we were interested in what was going on with the tournament and the other activities, waved us over to join them for a beer. We learned that different cultures have different drinking rituals. In Peru, they buy a case of large beer bottles and open them one at a time. Each bottle is accompanied by one glass. They pour two or three ounces in the glass, drink it down fast, then hand the glass and bottle to the next person.

> Ward: They wanted to get us into that circle to help drink the case of beer.

> Jeff and I decided to get our own glass and join the circle, just to be culturally with them. They noticed I had on a Dewalt Tools baseball cap, and they thought that was pretty cool. One gentleman said, "I'll trade my Navy baseball cap for your cap." I thought, "Oh, that would be pretty cool to have a Peruvian Navy cap." We exchanged caps, and then pretty soon, they switched caps with Jeff and Jacky, too. I think we're the only ones in Iowa with Peruvian Navy baseball caps.

Because of our continuous cultural experiences, we were lucky enough to be given a tour of the very old ship the next day. Ward found it extremely fascinating because of its uniqueness and age of the mechanical elements.

MAKES YOU WONDER

One other wonder we saw in Peru was the Nazca lines. These geoglyphs are huge drawings made in the sand of the Nazca desert. We actually took an airplane ride to see them better.

Extremely large animal, geometric, and botanical shapes were formed from lines drawn in the sand. We were fascinated to think about how they had been made. The lines are so straight and precise that it's amazing. How could that have occurred so many years ago when the technology we have today could barely do it?

GOING TO THE DOGS

One downside of traveling in Peru, though, was the dogs. There were stray dogs everywhere, some with fur missing. You don't want to get bitten by these dogs, because you don't know what kinds of diseases they might have. We carried sticks in our front racks, so that we could easily take them out when the dogs came around and whip them in the air and yell to scare off the dogs.

We were always a little nervous in Peru. We had heard that we should stay together, because bandits might stop us along the road to rob us. The economy and the culture there were rough around the edges. We just changed the way we did things. We didn't camp in Peru at all. We had heard stories about campers being victimized. Happily, it never happened to us.

CHAPTER TWENTY-THREE

THE WINDS OF PATAGONIA

Does getting blown off your bicycle make you afraid? How about blowing off a mountain? Welcome to Patagonia.

Our philosophy of setting out, seeing what was in our path, and dealing with it as it came served us well most of our trip. Some moments were more harrowing than others, though. The winds in Patagonia stand out as one of those moments.

SOUTHERN HOSPITALITY

We were in Southern Patagonia, traveling on rough, loose gravel. It was all gravel. Riding along, we saw maybe four or five cars a day. We heard that between towns, there were *estancias*—small places where ranchers live—where they would let you stay in a shed or a barn. This is how people traveled the miles between towns years ago, when they went by horse. The custom of accommodating travelers remains today.

One day, the winds in Southern Chile were so relentless that we declared defeat and found an *estancia* hoping to get some reprieve from the wind. The gentleman we mentioned in our prologue, Aquarius, answered our knock on his door and kindly let us pitch our tent on the east side of the barn out of the wind. A little later, he came out to us, asking us something. His Spanish was a different dialect than anything we were used to, so we didn't fully understand him, but he seemed to be inviting us to cook our dinner in the farmhouse kitchen.

That sounded good, so we gathered up our pots and pans and some rice and went into the house. On the table, Aquarius had spread a feast: a plate of meat, a plate of potatoes, and some bread. He had asked us to come in and share his food!

> Ward: Jacky looks at me as if to say, "Stupid Ward, why did you bring all this stuff in? He invited us to dinner!"

Aquarius lived there with another man. They prepared everything on a wood-fired stove, including the fresh bread we were enjoying. The men were ranchers who took care of the fences and the cattle. They didn't have a vehicle and about once a month caught a ride into town for supplies. Otherwise, they lived out on the land.

They didn't have any electric lights, only oil lamps. There were no books, no radio. It was just a very, very simple life, but he was the most hospitable host.

> Ward: And here's the wood-chopping story for this stop. I saw he had a big pile of wood out back, so I asked him if I could split some. I went back and chopped wood for an hour to show my gratitude for the evening dinner.

The next morning, Aquarius came to our tent saying, "Come inside. I have coffee for you." That was probably the best cup of coffee we ever had. We were out of the wind, huddled in the warm kitchen eating fresh oven-baked bread and drinking coffee. It doesn't get any better than that.

BLOWN AWAY

As we mentioned in the opening paragraphs, we knew something about the Patagonian winds, and friends had told us about their harrowing experiences, but we didn't truly realize how rough this section of our trip would be. These were serious winds: straight headwind all the way through Argentina and Chile, averaging 15-20 mph and hitting gusts of 60 mph when you rode through open valley areas.

The gravel roads going up the Chilean side were slow going. People had told us it took them four hours to go sixty miles in a car. At that rate, it would take us four days. As we headed out, it became clear that the two of us had different ideas about this leg of our journey.

> Jacky: Ward took on the whole attitude of, "Hey, this is a challenge. This is great. This is survival." I was more like, "What are we doing? Let's ask some questions, get some answers. There are no towns, no food."

This was probably the most challenging time for me because of the wind. I got blown over on my bike in the Andes. The side winds blew me right off the road into the ditch. When semis went by, it was really scary because of how the wind swirled. One time, I almost got pulled into the back wheel of a semi. I was afraid for my life. It was mentally and physically demoralizing.

We didn't see a lot of other bikers out there, although we did see one couple traveling in the opposite direction with clothes hanging off the back of their bikes. They had made a sail. They were just flying! We were averaging about 6 mph and they were averaging over 30 mph.

Even hiking in Torres del Paine National Park in Patagonia was a trial. Many people go there to do multiple day hikes through the park. It's rated as the fifth most beautiful place in the world by National Geographic.

> When we arrived, we should have used our cues and realized that the other campers had tents with longer flaps that were held down with ten-pound rocks. Most had at least fifteen ten-pound rocks holding down their tent. You think we would have learned from Slovenia that the usage of rocks to hold down tents and tile roofs would indicate the potential for high winds.

We didn't have backpacks, and our panniers were not suitable to carry our sleeping and cooking gear for a multiple-day trip. So, we decided to do a one-day hike to Mirador Base. The day we hiked started out sunny and beautiful, a picture-perfect day. The route was loose pea gravel along a glacial stream that wound up the side of the mountain. It started out easy but then became very nerve-wracking as it led us up to a narrow ledge called *paso de viento* (passage of the wind). The ledge itself was only about three feet wide. There was dangerous exposure on the right side of five hundred feet straight down and on the left it went up seven hundred feet. This geological shape created a wind vortex that more than doubled any wind speed. Hikers had to pass one at a time for safety reasons.

Jacky: As we were hiking around this narrow pass, it got super windy. I was bent down to lower my center of gravity, getting close to the ground but not quite on my knees. After I nervously made it around the ridge, I said to Ward, "You have to stick by me when we go around the ridge on the way down." This wind exposure was too spooky.

The rest of the climb to the top was beautiful, still somewhat windy but manageable. We passed many campsites and *refugios* along the way and we were informed of an incoming storm. Once we reached the vista on the trekking route, Mirador Base, we viewed the Torres del Paines towers of mountain peaks. They were beautiful! But then the winds picked up significantly and the sky turned gray. We decided not to go any further and to turn back. We stopped at a little refuge kiosk that was full of backpackers getting some reprieve. After a short stop, it was time to face the forces again. The weather can change very quickly in these mountain ranges giving winds of 110 mph and known to take hikers with backpacks airborne.

Jacky: It was challenging just to hike down the regular path. All I could think of was, "The ridge. How am I going to go around the ridge?" We passed two girls that were struggling with the descent with huge backpacks. They said, "We want to take the bus!" If only that was an option. As we approached the ridge, I made sure Ward was right behind me, like he promised. The wind was wicked, gusting up to 100 mph. I had total fear in my eyes, in my bones. My arms and legs were shaking. As we neared that narrow ledge, I was pretty much forced to almost crawl. This ferocious merciless wind picked me up and I could feel myself getting blown off the mountain. Ward jumped on top of me and we grabbed onto a rock. We laid there and I held onto that rock so tightly like it was my new home. I didn't think I was ever going to get up again. I was petrified! I prayed so hard and asked my guardian angels to help me make the crossing.

Then the wind let up a little bit and Ward yelled, "Run!" We quickly got up and scooted around the ridge to some relief! Thankful to be alive. The rest of the descent was much less fearful but still very windy.

I was worried for all the other people that we had met hiking the mountain that were still up there. Are they going to be okay?

Other hikers we talked to were frightened in that section as well. A few days later, in fact, we met a couple that had been there the same time we were. They said a man did get blown off that ridge that day. It took the rescue crew three days to get him out of the crevice. He had a broken pelvis.

The winds of Patagonia challenged us for a long time. Not just physically but mentally as well.

Ward: The winds in the Patagonia area were so strong they beat me. I had a goal at the start of the trip to ride the whole trip without shifting into my smallest gear, the granny gear. This road was so steep and gravelly, I couldn't maintain traction. The wind just buffeted me around. I shifted into my granny gear and I still could not get traction and balance my bike. I ended up walking my bike up to the top of the pass. I started riding back down the other side but the wind had not subsided. I was getting whipped around the narrow road that had a three hundred foot drop off. I decided that day, March 1, 2008, was not my day to die. I walked down the other side, my pride was hurt and it made me feel like a loser. Male ego, you know.

Jacky: For me, I didn't have any problem walking my bike up or down a hill. Screw ego; it's all about survival!

Another very windy day. Another day of biking only 5-7 mph. The road today was busier with more traffic than other days. This was always scary for Jacky as the gusts of winds made it hard for her to control her bike and she couldn't predict where she would end up on the road. We stopped and ate some bread in the ditch. (When we weren't in the mountainous regions of Patagonia, the area was relatively flat and treeless. We had to seek out windless areas. Many instances, a manmade structure in a roadside ditch gave us some blockage from the wind and created a low point for us to take refuge. In this case, it was a manmade berm.) Once we were back on the road, we came to a gravel detour. As we remained at the mercy of the relentless winds, we looked up and there was a dump truck parked on the side of the road with a man standing next to it. He must have seen how we were struggling when he passed us on the road and pulled over to see if we needed a ride. Did we ever! We put our bikes in the back of this huge dump truck and took the three-hour-long lift to Porte Natalia, which would have taken us two to three days to bike. The driver's name was José. He didn't say much, just gave us the help we needed.

Jacky: I was claiming defeat. The winds had won! There was no escape! There was no end to the winds! It wouldn't have taken much more to bring me to tears.

Ward took this dump truck ride more for me than for himself, because I was having such a hard time. It takes a mental toll on you when you have that wind blowing in your ears all day long.

Ward: Your arms were tired because you had to constantly fight the wind. You were tired.

Jacky: It was tricky. When you were up in the mountains and got to a little opening, all of a sudden, the wind came flying through and whipped you all around. You constantly had to hold your handlebars really tight because you never knew when these swirling winds were going to throw you into the ditch or into the lane of traffic. The wind had no sympathy.

THE SPIRIT OF "GOAT MAN" PAUL

While we couldn't trust everyone we met, we seemed to have some spirit guides looking out for us—one of whom came to us as we faced those Patagonian winds. We knew him as "Goat Man" Paul. Paul Walker was a goat farmer and excellent biker and cross-country skier from Wisconsin. We saw each other at bike and ski events throughout the years. We weren't close friends, but we kept up with him through other friends. We had heard the sad news that he had extensive cancer and had been hospitalized.

Jacky: One day in Patagonia, I wasn't doing so well. Oh, man, I wanted to quit. We had just climbed a glacier the day before and I was very sore. The whole terrain this day was rolling hills and it was very windy. We had about twenty-six miles of biking left ahead of us, though, so I was trying to muster the strength to continue.

Strangely, Goat Man Paul came to mind. I thought, "He's sitting in the hospital and he'd do anything to be on his bike down here in Argentina." All of a sudden, my pace picked up. I caught up to Ward and passed him. Ward's like, "What got into you?" I said, "I'm riding for Goat Man Paul today!"

The next day, I got the email from my friend telling us that Paul had died that prior afternoon, the day he helped me. Was it just a coincidence? Whatever it was, it was just so strange to have him come to mind at that very moment. We know that the positive thoughts and prayers sent to us from our families and friends added to the same spirit we got from Goat Man Paul. You don't go around the world by yourself.

CHAPTER TWENTY-FOUR

A TYPICAL DAY ON THE ROAD...WHEN THERE WAS ONE

Whenever we wrote blogs or newsletters, they were always full of stories. On a typical day on the road, however, things could be downright boring. We were always a little nervous when people joined us on the road, because we didn't know what their expectation was. Did they think these stories happened all the time? In reality, we could go a couple of weeks with no good stories to tell at all. It could be grueling.

I CAN SEE FOR MILES

Chaco Province, Argentina, is a prime example of how days sometimes seemed to go on forever. The Chaco is an extremely flat portion of Argentina near the Paraguay border. Not only is the region very flat, but it's extremely hot and arid. The vegetation of shrubs and short statured trees (fifteen feet tall) added to the boredom. Imagine this monotonous landscape day after day: straight, unvarying roads that go on for twenty miles or so between towns. For miles on end, we saw nothing interesting. There were no farmsteads and the denser vegetation blocked any peripheral view and created a tunnel-like roadway. There was nothing to ease the tedium.

We got so bored in the Chaco that we started inventing exercises to do on our bicycles. At each kilometer marker, we came up with a new activity to try. We did push-ups off the handlebars and tried to pedal with just one foot, among other exercises. We were desperate for entertainment. Unfortunately, our kilometer marker workouts only slowed our pace and made the days last even longer.

> Ward: We were trying to speed it up, but in fact we were slowing it down. It really got very boring. You could see for miles straight down the road with no view to the side. The road was just straight and flat with very little traffic. It was worse than North Dakota.

> Jacky: Sometimes, we would see an electric pole or water tower (anything) off in the distance and bet each other on how many kilometers away it was. We would do anything to take our minds off of the monotony and to pass the time.

DAILY GRIND

A typical day started with boiling water for coffee, oatmeal, or maybe ramen noodles. If we knew the day would take us where there were no restaurants or stores, we bought some bread to take with us and cooked more noodles or rice to have at lunchtime. Meals were basic.

We always tell people that we planned where to start each day, but not where we would finish. We looked at the map and said, "Maybe we can reach that town." We didn't know what the roads were going to be like or what obstacles might come our way. If we thought it was going to be a long day, we tried to get an early start so that we could make it to our destination two hours before sunset.

> Ward: It was always imperative to get there two hours before dark because we were arriving into areas we had never been to before. From a safety perspective, those two hours were critical. I'm glad we always stayed to that rule with only a rare exception.
>
> Also, it's not fun to use your little headlamp to cook, set your tent up, and organize yourself in the dark. It's always best to do that during the daylight.

We usually managed to make it to the next stop before nightfall. A few times, we missed our mark. In Slovenia, we got delayed because of the cricket match. We ended up passing the campground we wanted to camp in without realizing it. We went six or seven miles beyond where we intended to stop, so we had to turn around and go back. That added another hour and twenty minutes (twelve to fourteen miles) to our ride that day.

In the Southern United States, we struggled with longer distances and the waning fall and winter sunlight. The days were simply shorter, so we did end up riding at sunset and cooking in the dark.

In Argentina, on the other hand, everyone is active a lot later in the day. Nothing closes down very early, so we were always able to get to a store and buy meat for barbecuing. If time was short before sunset, we worked in tag-team fashion: one person got a shower while the other one guarded the camp and got the water boiling. Or if someone went to the store, the other set up the air mattresses, etc.

We didn't always agree on what chore should fall into which hands. Sometimes nobody wanted to go to the store, but it was just one of our daily tasks. We couldn't carry a week's worth of groceries with us.

Checking out hotels and hotel prices was another chore we took turns handling. Neither of us wanted to do it all the time. It was always a struggle to convey what you were asking when the language was different. Plus, we were tired from biking that day, so the whole routine of checking out rooms at different hotels and negotiating a price was often just more than we felt like dealing with.

> Jacky: When it came time to check for hotels, it'd be like, "Well, I did it yesterday. It's your turn." It was much worse than having to take your turn to go to the store.

Hotel choices were often hard to make, especially in Asia, because some of the places were not very nice. We looked for things like internet, showers, fans, or air conditioners, but often it came down to just how clean the room was.

> Jacky: They were very dirty. Sometimes, bugs were smashed on the walls. It was not uncommon for us to sleep in our own sleeping bags.

> Ward: Our tent, even though we were sleeping on the ground, was cleaner than some hotel rooms.

Often, it was a matter of choosing the lesser of two evils.

Jacky: When we were in Anta, Peru, Ward went and checked on two hotels. He came back and said, "They're both bad, but one is the best of the bad." It had a communal toilet. The bottom and the inside walls were brown. The caveat was that the toilet was also the shower. So, you stood in the brown colored tile while you tried to wash your body.

Ward: And this was the better choice.

Jacky: Needless to say, we didn't shower that day and we used the wilderness for our other needs.

After finding a place to stay, doing laundry was often our next chore, so we'd try to find a river or a sink to wash our clothes in. Because we didn't have a clothesline, we hung our clothes in the trees when camping or around the hotel room to dry. If they weren't dry by the morning, we hung them from our bikes to dry some more.

Jacky: Sometimes, I rode with socks and underwear hanging from my handlebars. (I removed them when we entered a town or village.)

RAIN, RAIN, GO AWAY

When it rained, we stayed put as much as possible. This was one of our rules, to avoid riding in the rain. If we were already staying in a hostel or a hotel room, we would just stay an extra day and spend it journaling or reading. There were times when it rained while we were camping. We would stay put and try to take refuge under shelters, pavilions, or any coverage available. If we would have headed out on our bikes, that would have guaranteed that everything would get wet. Our bags were waterproof, but it always seemed that everything got damp.

We used Weather Underground to check the forecast and planned accordingly. If it looked like a stretch of nice weather was coming up, we pushed ourselves to cover more miles on those days, knowing we'd get a break when it rained again.

One showery day in the Czech Republic, though, we broke all our rules. It was raining that day, but we went out in full rain gear, even Neoprene gloves. We rode for two or three hours in thirty- to forty-degree rainy weather before our fingers were completely frozen. We made it to a small town with a café. Coffee beckoned. Not only did the hot coffee warm us inside, the warm cup also defrosted our fingers. We wanted to find out if the locals thought the rain would let up. Unfortunately, the people at the café informed us it was going to be a long rain.

We gave up and hired a young man to take us to a hostel in the next town, Brno. It turned out to be more expensive than we could reasonably pay, but it rained for three days straight, so we stayed there.

Ward: I got really depressed because we were spending money and we couldn't go see anything. We watched the news and it had been one of the worst rainstorms they had had in a long time. I tried taking the city bus, but the windows were all fogged over, so you couldn't even see the city.

Jacky: There was one good thing that came out of it. Ward went to a Rotary meeting and then we got invited to a Rotarian's house for dinner and an overnight stay and learned a lot about the Czech Republic.

LOST TREASURES FROM THE DITCH

We had to be seriously thrifty to make a trip this extensive possible. We've talked about how we stuck to a tight budget, worked along the way, and camped anyplace that was cheap, or better yet, free. Still, we took our frugal habits to a higher level by taking advantage of Ward's inability to pass by any useful item, even if it was lying in a ditch.

Ward: I am a ditch diver. It's just kind of an overriding state-ment. I do it in my vehicle. I especially do it on the bicycle because you can see so much when you are going 10 mph. I stop for coins on the side of the road or even in the middle of an intersection. I can't help myself. Growing up poor, what-ever came out of the ditch was probably as good as what I had, or maybe better.

Fishing gear, for instance, is expensive. When Ward wanted to fish in South America, he bought a telescopic fishing pole but still needed a fishing reel. He tried three or four different fishing stores, looking for something used. No luck.

> Ward: I didn't want to spend sixty bucks on a fishing reel that early in the trip. If you spend sixty dollars then, you may be short later on. As we left the town, it wasn't but ten miles down the road that I saw a brand new fishing reel lying along the side of the road. Somehow, it had fallen off somebody's car or God threw it down from the heavens. I tell people that God provided for me with the fishing reel, but the thing was he didn't teach me how to fish.

A fishing reel was a nice extra, but often we were scavenging for the basics. In Montessori, Spain, for instance, someone stole Ward's helmet, a piece of gear he couldn't do without. As we were traveling south from there, we came across a construction helmet in the ditch. Ward fashioned a strap to hold the bright blue hard hat to his head and used that until we could purchase a real one.

> Jacky: Wow, was he styling. I said, "I married that guy."

> Ward: I looked like a nerd.

Other times, we picked up items that didn't have a clear purpose at the time. They almost always proved useful in the end, though. In Portugal, for example, we kept seeing seed sacks from wheat. Heavy, woven nylon seed sacks were just strewn in the ditches. Ward got an idea and started grabbing bags from the side of the road.

Jacky: I asked, "Why are you picking up all those sacks?"

Ward: I was picking all this up so I had enough to make a couple bigger bags that we could sew together and that would allow us to put our panniers in for flying back for a visit to the United States. That way, we didn't have to check as many panniers at the airport.

Jacky: When we flew into Minneapolis, I was at the baggage claim, waiting for our bag at the carousel. I saw our homemade wheat sack bag coming around on the conveyor belt and was getting ready to grab it when a guy in front of me said, "Now, that's a bag you wouldn't want to claim!" But I did!

Some things were easier to carry on the bike than others. Five-gallon pails, for instance, are a bit unwieldy, but when the opportunity arose on the way to the Arctic Circle in Alaska, Ward gamely tied his latest find to his bicycle with bungee cords. (The pails had blown out of the oil field service trucks.) Our friends that joined us for that section of the trip wondered what he would possibly do with a huge bucket.

Ward: As we got closer to the end of the day, I went over to a snowbank and filled the pail with snow and ice. It was perfect for icing down a twelve-pack of beer for all of us at the end of a long ride.

It wasn't long before our friends that were with us for this Arctic leg of the trip were picking up pails to increase the cooler capacity. We were traveling with a motor home, which had a refrigerator, but that was dedicated to food. There were eight of us, so we needed a few buckets to keep the beer chilled.

All sorts of treasures made their way onto our bikes. It might be a piece of plastic that could serve as an additional drop cloth for the tent or for us to sit on instead of the wet grass or dirt at the campsite. It could be a piece of rope that could make a temporary clothesline or a strap for tying things to the bikes. Who knows, it might really be helpful in winching a runaway boat back onto a trailer.

Ward: One of the best finds was a brand-new Therm-a-Rest air mattress. It had blown out of the back of somebody's pickup, we suspect. I carried it for several days, while Jacky wondered what use I had for a second mattress. Well, we ran into two young men in California traveling light, with no sleeping mats. I gave them the extra Therm-a-Rest so they could have a little softer sleep.

I never really regretted picking up anything, but Jacky had her doubts. She questioned me a lot.

In Texas, I averaged over a dollar a day in found change, mostly in the intersections. I wondered, do they just throw money at the intersections? Is it an offering to the highway gods or something?

Jacky: He would also stop on a dime for a penny! When we would bike through an intersection, all of a sudden, Ward would stop in the middle of traffic, bend over, and pick up change he saw in the street. There were many times he almost got hit by cars. At one point, his bike looked like it belonged to a hoarder. I get it if the things have value, but at times I had to stretch my imagination as to what use it had.

Most things did have value, like wrenches, bungee cords, and other things previously mentioned. If we didn't have a use for an item ourselves, we could often leave them at campgrounds for others to claim. We did have some heated discussions, though, over what we might leave behind.

Ward: Jacky appreciated it when I found a nice windproof jacket in Italy, or a pair of warm fleece pants for her that she so appreciated when we were camping in the chilly December temperatures in Spain and Portugal. One time, though, I found a dry fit shirt where someone had gotten sick on it and also some underwear. I just hand washed them and then I could wear them, but Jacky wasn't impressed.

We found Spain, as a country, had far more bras and underwear and random items of clothing along the side of the road. What causes this to be part of the Spanish culture? We are still looking for an answer.

Ward also happened to score a piano chair in the ditch. At that time, Jacky was learning how to play the harmonica. Russ and Angela Carll, Ward's cousins, rented two Gites for family and friends to come and stay at in France. The Gites would take turns hosting that night's variety show. Jacky would sit outside on her piano chair late at night practicing for the next night's show. (Ask her about the key of "four"). Another time, Ward decided he was going to replenish his beer fund by picking up cans in the ditch. It must have been the five-cent can redemption that you get in Iowa that struck his interest as Sweden has a similar can law, so we thought. He happened to pick a rainy morning to try this.

Jacky: He would stop every time he saw a can, lay down his bike, retrieve the can from the ditch and then place it in a bag he had hanging from the back of his bike. It became quite a site as the bag was filling up. Needless to say, it became very annoying!

I get his frugalness and pleasure in making some money this way, but did he really have to pick a rainy day to do it? Every time he stopped, I had to stop and wait in the rain. It took us all morning to only go thirty kilometers. Then, when we finally reached a store that would redeem the cans, he only made 30 cents! Sweden doesn't redeem all cans, just certain ones. This cured Ward from picking up cans. He didn't even have enough to buy himself a beer.

All in all, the ditches were good to us.

CHAPTER TWENTY-FIVE

NICO

This chapter about Argentinian culture tries to explain the blunders that a gringo can make while preparing an evening meal. As you travel through Argentina, you will notice in all of the parks, rest areas, truck stops, everywhere that they have barbeque grills. The *asado*, the Argentinean term for barbecue, is recognized as a very cultural aspect of their lives. The Argentineans love their barbecued meat!

The barbecue grill and its design are much different than our American-style grills. The Argentinean *asado* grill is a three-sided cement structure (approximately two and a half feet by four feet). Cooking is done by building a fire with wood kindling in one corner, and when the coals are proper, they are pulled underneath an elevated grill to cook the meat and vegetables with no flames below.

> Ward: Well, as a not-so-smart gringo, I built a fire and tried to cook the meat over an open flame. I didn't wait for the coals. I didn't have a stick.

This young boy, thirteen years old, came over with his younger sister and cousin to see who these foreigners were and what they were up to. His name was Nico. He saw my grilling technique and kept asking me, "Do you need a stick? Do you need a stick?" I said, "No, no, I don't need a stick." (Why would I need a stick?) I could just hear him thinking, "Stupid gringo, you need a stick. You're doing it all wrong."

He left me to it, but soon returned with his grandmother. The grandmother said, "Nico says you don't need a stick. How would you like to come over to our camp? Nico is preparing dinner. You just bring your meat along and be our guests."

Jacky: We had biked one hundred miles that day. It was hot, almost one hundred degrees. I was exhausted and I had a bad headache. All I wanted to do was to eat supper and to go to bed but, our purpose for the trip was to learn the cultures. So, I mustered up whatever energy I had left and we packed up our food and went over to their camp.

Nico, it turned out, was hosting a dinner party for his grandparents, his sister, and his cousin. Nico prepared all the food—the right way, by pulling coals over. We enjoyed the varieties of meats, sausages, and vegetables he cooked, while listening to the grandparents talk about their interests and hobbies.

The grandfather, Daniel, owned a radio company. What he and Nico did in their time off, for fun, was ride motorcycles in the desert. Grandma offered that she liked to go down by the river and look for arrowheads and Indian artifacts. Around her neck, she had an arrowhead necklace that she said was twenty-five hundred years old. She went into her camper and brought out a different arrowhead, which was thirty-five hundred years old.

It was a perfect evening with a little wine and beer, sharing experiences and telling stories. At the end of the night, we said goodnight and returned to our tent.

In the morning, as we were packing up, Nico and his sister and cousin hung around our campsite. Once we were packed up, the grandparents came over to say their farewells. Everyone gathered around, excited to see the gringos take off on their bikes. It was very sweet, but we never expected the parting gift they gave us. At the last moment, Grandma took the twenty-five-hundred-year-old arrowhead necklace from her neck and placed it around Jacky's neck.

Ward: The grandfather said, "She's never sold one or even given one away before."

Jacky: I gave her a hug and tried not to cry.

The necklace remains a warm symbol of the hospitality of this thirteen-year-old boy and his family, an evening of enjoying Argentinian culture, food, and conversation. It was a beautiful moment.

CHAPTER TWENTY-SIX

A VERY SPECIAL ARGENTINIAN BIRTHDAY

Holidays and celebrations on the road were always very different from our usual traditions. We arrived in the town of Catriel, Argentina, on the Saturday before Easter. We stopped at a fruit store to buy some fruit and to pick up some snacks for the day. Here we met a gentleman, the owner of the store, who was curious about who we were, where we were going, and so forth. He said, "We don't get cycling tourists around here." Ward explained that we were trying to experience the different cultures of the world by our bikes.

We were planning on spending the weekend there and taking a day off to celebrate Easter Sunday. That we did, spending a beautiful and quiet day in our campground. Monday, we packed up and stopped in town to pick up a few last supplies. The manager from the fruit store, that we were at the day before, saw us and came out to the corner waving us over. "What are you doing at one o'clock?" he asked. We said we were leaving town. He said, "No, you come back here at one o'clock. I close up my fruit market. You're coming to my niece's birthday party."

Jacky: Even though we were on a bit of a schedule, as stated earlier we reminded ourselves of our trip's purpose.

This was unexpected but very thoughtful of him, for he knew we wanted to experience true Argentinian culture, not just the usual things tourists saw.

We followed his rickety car down a rough, rocky road to the place his sister lived. Here, the niece was celebrating her seventeenth birthday, and we were invited as special guests. That afternoon, Grandpa and Grandma and all the aunts and uncles were there. Meat roasted on open grates over a charcoal fire.

Jacky: They were really poor. It was a mud-style house with a cement floor, no plumbing and really no kitchen. Only a few people there got cups and plates. They were treating Ward and I like celebrities; we got wine glasses, plates, and a chair.

The menu included chorizo, chicken, and beef cooked on the coals that were spread out on the ground. Entertainment was provided by another uncle who had cassette tapes of music from the band he played in. Grandma and Grandpa danced the tango in the backyard. The birthday girl had some friends over. It was unbelievable that two gringos got invited to an Argentinian birthday party.

Although the family was not wealthy, we could see that everyone was so happy. We looked at this place with no running water and a cement floor, and yet everybody was dancing and smiling. It made us wonder, "Why do we want so much?" It was one of those magical moments.

We were having a great time, but we knew we needed to get

going by four or five in the afternoon or who knows when we would end up leaving. They wanted us to spend the night and kept telling us we shouldn't bike because it was going to rain. We knew if we stayed we wouldn't leave until the following afternoon, because of their great hospitality, and we had quite a distance to cover. However, before we left, though, Ward wanted to fix up the father's bike. A small gesture for such a wonderful and cultural experience.

Jacky: It was one of those eye-openers, where you realize how much fussing one does when guests are coming over, but you see that's not really what's important. I swore that when I came back to the US, I wasn't going to worry about those things. But I've turned back into the "it has to be clean" person after all.

Ward: I've got to get her back to Argentina and get that out of her.

CHAPTER TWENTY-SEVEN

SPECIAL NEW FRIENDS MADE ALONG THE WAY NUMBER THREE: WILSON

Making new friends was a wonderful part of our journey, but sometimes old friends were just the thing we needed. One such longtime friend was Wilson Daltou, a Rotarian Ward knew long before the trip. He lived in Brazil, so we knew we had to stop and see him. On our first map of South America, which we tore out of the center of the airline catalog on the plane, we wrote "Wilson" in the center of Brazil. Whatever else we might do in the southern hemisphere, we knew we were going to connect with Wilson. That set the stage for our route in Brazil.

Wilson lives in Tangarra de Serra, Mato Grosso, in the north-west section of Brazil. As we made our way north to see him, we sent emails to let him know we were getting closer, to check addresses, and confirm arrival dates. We checked our email more and more often as we got closer, in case plans had changed. However, getting there was not so easy. The distance between cities and villages was great (eighty to 120 kilometers on average). The road was deep powdery dirt and deep loose sand. The temperatures were reaching 109 degrees during the day and the sun was very, very intense. The red dust of the road was sticking to our sweaty, sunscreened bodies. The poorly maintained paved roads were narrow, had lots of potholes, and were busy with grain semis.

> Jacky: Due to the red dust, it was hard to read the road. Some spots were firm and packed, so I felt confident in picking up my speed only to be surprised by stretches with dust six inches deep, which would take me to the ground. One day, I had fallen several times in the deep powdered roadway. When we finally reached our destination, we sat outside a restaurant and had a cold beer. People were coming up to me and pointing at my arms and legs and telling me how sunburnt they were. No, they were filthy with the red dust.

On the final day, as we were riding into Tangara da Serra, we stopped at an internet café about thirty miles out of town for one last email. As we turned to go into the café, a car cut us off.

> Ward: Jacky goes, "Gosh, the Brazilians are so rude in their driving. They just cut me off!"

We looked up, and on the back of the car was a sign, saying, "Welcome, Ward and Jacky." Wilson, and his friend, had come out on the route to find us. He was so excited, but we still had more miles to ride. Wilson wanted to know how long it was until we got to his town. We said two, maybe two and a half hours.

"There's a hill in the way," said Wilson. "A big hill."

He wasn't kidding. We were going to be climbing a mountain and it was over one hundred degrees out. We navigated switchbacks with the sweat dripping off our elbows and brows. Luckily, when we got to the top, we saw an oasis: a Coca-Cola stand in the shade.

After that brief rest, we headed out again. Fortunately, the road started to flatten out; the hills were done. The next thing we knew, a car pulled up next to us carrying a television crew. They were videotaping us. Wilson had sent the town TV station out to record and interview us! It was tough, because they didn't speak English, only Portuguese. We tried to communicate, smiling and pedaling, for three or four miles. It was insane.

By now, we were well behind our planned schedule. But when we arrived at the entrance to Wilson's town, his entire Rotary Club was standing at the entry with a twelve-foot-long banner that said "Welcome, Ward and Jacky, to Tangara da Serra. Rotary Club welcomes you." They stood there in the baking sun for one and a half hours waiting for us!

> Ward: All I can say is WOW! I felt like a president or king, not a cyclist. Wilson rolled out the red carpet.

The newspaper was there, and the television crew. Everyone wanted to interview us, and while we were so charmed, we were also so exhausted. We were totally drenched in sweat; it was just dripping off our hair. They talked to us for half an hour in the hot sun.

We planned to stay five days with Wilson and his wife, Mariza, but it ended up being twelve. Wilson is an energetic guy. He's a lawyer, plus he owns a school where they teach adult Brazilians to read and write. He's also one of the founders of the town, which was founded in 1976. He was instrumental in education and helping the town grow.

On our first night in town, Wilson had a little barbecue at his house with family and friends. The next night, he rented a cabin in the middle of a river. The cabin was on stilts, right below a waterfall. It was astounding. We spent the night with Wilson, his friend Gioconda, and their wives. We slept in the middle of the river, with water flowing underneath the cabin. It was unbelievable. There was a long catwalk leading out from the beach to the cabin. To top it off, Wilson had arranged a special buffet for us, with a ten- to fifteen-pound Dorado fish they had caught as the main dish.

Jacky: It was funny, because it was this big buffet and I was like, "Where are the rest of the people?" But Wilson had ordered it, just for the six of us. The next night Wilson took us to an island that Gioconda owned, to spend the night. Again, it was the same three couples, but this time some of their kids joined us too. They have three very nice buildings on this island. We had running water, electricity, and satellite TV. The highlight here, for Ward especially, was the fishing.

Ward: Giocanda would feed the fish corn, which enables more fish to be caught. (I believe this is illegal.) Gioconda and I were standing in the Sepatu River, which had a pretty strong current. I was holding the flashlight while Gioconda was throwing out a net. We were catching so many fish, and we didn't have any place to put them. We ended up putting them in our pockets.

Jacky: When they came back to the house empty-handed, we said, "Oh, you didn't catch anything!" Then they started pulling fish out of their pant and coat pockets. The fish were live, flopping around on the table. Unbelievable!

Wilson made sure we understood his town, what his Rotary Club was doing, and all about the Brazilian culture. We toured a forest preserve where a Swedish company was raising teakwood. We visited schools. We rode with Wilson to different towns while he worked and we immersed ourselves in the culture.

One of the things the guys bonded over was beer. Cold beer. Wilson taught us how to look for the coldest coolers in the convenience stores. We learned to look for the beer cooler's temperature, often minus seven or minus eight Celsius, which is below freezing, though the beer didn't freeze. Wilson wanted to make sure we got the coldest beer. Do remember that it was over one hundred degrees Fahrenheit at that time.

OPEN DOORS

Being on bicycles opened a lot of doors for us. People heard about how we were traveling, and it made them want to take care of us. They admired us for riding our bikes that far in the heat, and they could see that we were putting a lot of work toward our goals.

Ward: I don't think people who get on and off the bus get the same kind of experience that we did. When we talked with backpackers or hitchhikers, we found they hadn't received the same kinds of invitations that we had.

Jacky: Plus, they could see we were trying to learn their cultures, so they were more likely to open up to us.

One of the main differences was that we rarely ended up where the regular tourists went. As mentioned, many people use guides like *Lonely Planet*, which is wonderful, but they were all following the same route. *Lonely Planet* puts you where the bus stops. The bus never stopped where we stopped.

Jacky: No one is ever going to experience exactly what we did. There's no way you can duplicate that. You just have to set your own goals and enjoy what you're going to enjoy. Where you end up, you end up.

Another factor was that it was just the two of us traveling together. We weren't part of a group, so when we came to town, we weren't obviously pegged as, "Here comes a tourist group." We were approachable as individuals, so other people felt comfortable treating us like friends.

Since the trip, we have gone on group excursions, and we have a different experience. We noticed we don't automatically get the same hospitality. Part of it is that people don't feel comfortable coming up and approaching you in a group. Also, when you stop to eat or have a drink with your group, you tend to talk with each other. On our trip, it was just us and we talked to each other all day. So we were eager to speak with other people when we would stop. It wasn't usually hard to find someone to talk to. The bike opened up many opportunities for us. When we would stop at a bench to have lunch, typically people would come over and ask us what we were doing, where we were going, and where we were from. The number of people we have traveling with us and the mode of travel changes the dynamics of the way people interact with us. To this day, every so often we just do a bike trip with the two of us.

CHAPTER TWENTY-EIGHT

SERVING OTHERS ALONG THE WAY: ORPHANAGES

We received so much from others on our trip. When we could, we tried to give back. One of our missions was to help some of the world's orphanages, whether through donations or by helping with things like building projects.

BOYS WILL BE BOYS

We had a connection to an orphanage in Lurin, Peru, through the La Crosse Catholic diocese in Wisconsin. Jacky's first cousin, Joe, is now a monsignor priest in that diocese, who had visited this orphanage many times.

The place is called Casa Hogar and it is run on the same model as Boys Town in the United States. At Casa Hogar, the children live in small family units of about eight kids and two support parents. There's a common eating area. When we were there, the support parents were all Peruvian, but the office workers, other staff, and volunteers were from the United States.

When we arrived, they were preparing for an upcoming visit by the Archbishop of La Crosse, so they wanted to give Casa Hogar a nice facelift. We were put to work on the paint crew. As a gift, we purchased all the paint they needed and stayed on to help for about seven days. They discouraged us from buying the paint, saying we didn't have to do it, but it was something we felt good about doing.

We were sort of put on a pedestal while we were there, because we knew the priest, Jacky's cousin, Father Joe. The kids loved to have Father Joe visit because he played the guitar and engaged and entertained them. Because of our special connection, we think, we stayed in very nice guest quarters in the rectory rather than in a dorm room as we had anticipated.

Father Joe is now the director there and, as mentioned, a monsignor.

Our personal relationship was valuable, though, in helping us reach the children. At a certain hour each day, the kids could go out and play, so we joined in on all their games. They gravitated toward Ward, because he was so tall, and a male. We wanted to do something special with the kids, and we were relatively close to the ocean, so we thought of taking some of the boys fishing. Father Sebastian, the director at that time, didn't take us up on it. Then we suggested taking them to a soccer match, but the director thought it might be too dangerous with too many fights in the stands.

In the end, though, he called in some favors from a few community members and we got tickets to go to a Lima pro team soccer match. Around ten of the boys joined us. We wanted to contribute so we bought them a meal in the stadium. To see the smiles on their faces from something as simple as attending a soccer match was amazing, even if things did get a little tense.

Jacky: Two rival teams were playing each other. As we were entering the stadium, there were riot police all around; kids were throwing rocks at the police and the police were chasing them and hitting them with billy clubs. This whole group passed right in front of us. We had to push all of the boys up against the fence to shield them while this all went on.

Ward: A riot ensuing right in front of our eyes. It was kind of scary, because we knew we had to protect these young boys.

Even as we got into the match, there were fights in the stands. But it was a real treat on the way home to see the smiles again light up the boys' faces.

There are over fifty children in the Casa Hogar orphanage, but it's not an institutional environment. The children thrive in family units, and they are required to go to school and study. Mass is part of every day's schedule. This was by far the most successful orphanage we saw.

Casa Hogar had many challenges. They had the same wild dog problem we saw all over Peru; here, the danger was feral dogs coming onto the orphanage property and biting the children. Father Sebastian, the director, had a no-nonsense solution, though: he climbed to the top of the chapel with a high-powered rifle and shot them.

Ward: I was sitting up there with him one day and he's shooting dogs. He looks over and there are two dogs, going at it. They're trying to make more dogs. I said, "Well, shoot them before one impregnates the other! You don't want more dogs." He's like, "You can't shoot them when they're doing that!" Here I was encouraging him to shoot them. It was surreal.

LEGACY OF LOSS

We also spent time at an orphanage in Phonsavan, Laos, which was quite a contrast to Casa Hogar, largely due to the political history of the area. We were drawn to the area by a fascination with the Plain of Jars near Phonsavan, an archeological mystery featuring hundreds of open-mouthed stone jars, possibly serving as an Iron Age burial site. Exploring the site led to other discoveries.

> Jacky: One day, Ward went out roaming around and when he came back, he said, "Jacky, you have to see this." Everywhere he went, he was seeing the damage from the United States' actions against Laos in the wake of the Vietnam War.

A cluster bomb has many, many small "bombies" that are ejected and designed to cause massive injury to people and damage vehicles.

From 1964–1973, the US dropped more than two million tons of ordnance (over 270 million cluster bombs) on Laos during 580,000 bombing missions—equal to a planeload of bombs every eight minutes, twenty-four hours a day, for nine years—making Laos the most heavily bombed country per capita in history. Up to a third of the bombs dropped did not explode. Over twenty thousand people have been killed or injured by these unexploded bombs since the bombing has ceased. Close to 60 percent of the accidents result in death, and 40 percent of the victims are children (per Legacies of War).

During the Vietnam War, when the United States agreed to stop bombing North Vietnam, they turned their attention to Laos. This was a secret war, not even known to the US Congress. The planes sent to bomb Laos deployed cluster bombs that not only decimated the country at the time but left behind countless undetonated "bombies" that are now buried in the soil. Literal fallout from this attack is still there to this day, which creates the need for an orphanage. Additionally, the unexploded bombs prohibit them from farming their fields, causing economic hardship.

> Ward: Millions and millions of bombs landed and about 30 percent of them never blew up. Millions of these bombies still lie in the ground. Because of the metal cleats on the bottom of our cycling shoes, we didn't even go off the road to urinate or anything. The bombies can be underneath the side of the road and you can set them off.

The children at the orphanage were there because their parents had set off a bomb while they were planting or harvesting crops in their fields. These bombs and their remnants were part of everyday life in Laos. We noticed bomb shells in front of many homes, some of them used for flowerpots. People went out and retrieved the shells because the metal was valuable. They could sell it.

While it was rewarding to greet the orphanage kids who gathered together to meet us, it was also a disturbing moment. We couldn't help but realize it was our government that caused their parents to die. Nobody there had any animosity toward us individually, but on an international level, they do not trust the United States any longer.

Even in the schoolyards, kids still get hurt by the bombies. As they play, they stir up the soil and bombies surface.

> Ward: I'm so glad we went there and learned about that. It was so sad to see the kids as victims of our prior military actions.

> Jacky: The war was over so long ago and still we are seeing the aftermath. And to think, Laos wasn't even in the war. They were a neutral country. It is so upsetting.

There is an active clean-up program there, called MAG, which uses metal scanners to find metal in the fields. When a bombie is unearthed, it is isolated and detonated safely. As we rode through, we spotted little flag markers in the fields, connected with ribbons cordoning off the bomb sites. Some of these undetonated bombies were within five feet of the edge of the road.

> Jacky: Actually seeing the bombs marked on the side of the road made it so real! This wasn't just something we read in a history book. We saw it. We felt it. It was so surreal.

Amazingly, we never felt judged as Americans anywhere in Asia. In a lot of places, we felt like the people would have been well within their rights to chase us out of their country after all of the devastation our country had inflicted. Yet, there was no hostility. It was amazing how forgiving people were.

FAMILY FRIENDS

In Vietnam, our way was paved by family connections. A cousin of Jacky's had married a woman from Vietnam, Hun Hirsch, that helped start a technical school in Hue that drew students from the local orphanage. When we arrived, we were treated as very special guests because of this family link.

After arranging a visit to the school, some of the staff came to our hostel, on motor bikes, to pick us up. Once we arrived at the school, we were greeted with a big bouquet of roses. Soon after, we were invited in for tea. Then they said they wanted to take us out for dinner. They wanted to order for us so we let them. It turned out to be a bit awkward because they ordered huge meals for us while the rest of the group just had soup. They were quite eager that we enjoy our food, asking, "Is it good? Do you like it?" It was very good, but we felt uncomfortable keeping it all to ourselves. We tried to share it, but nobody would let us.

By the next day, we figured we would be able to do our part and pay for the meals and entry fees while we toured the city with some of the boys from the orphanage, but because Jacky was a relative, they wouldn't even let us pay our own way. We tried, unsuccessfully, to spring for lunch. Again, no go. We were able to buy everyone a Coca-Cola, but that was it. These were boys who had been through the orphanage and the technical school.

The orphanage itself served two hundred kids on a shoestring, with a staff of seven to handle everything; cooking, laundry, maintenance, management, taking care of the children, etc. We saw all the kids chipping in. Older kids were feeding and caring for the younger ones. There was love and a family feeling. We always tried to give money to places like this that so obviously need it. We tried to give the orphanage two hundred dollars. They took it, but then they turned around and bought pencils for us!

> Ward: We thought they would buy food or supplies, but they went and bought pencils for us to give to the children through our Pedaling for Pencils program!

We were overwhelmed by their welcoming and hospitality. After everything else, the children did a music program just for us.

The biggest heartbreak of this orphanage visit was undoubtedly the day we saw a tiny newborn baby who was left at the gate. She was less than a week old.

> Jacky: I was ready to pack her up and take her with me. I'm

so glad they left the baby at that place, but it broke my heart to see this tiny little baby left at the gate.

We never learned of any program to adopt the children out of the orphanage. The intention seemed to always be to make sure these kids got a good education. School was a very important part of the program. All of the children's other needs were taken care of so they could concentrate on school.

When we came back to the United States, we learned that the orphanage had spent the contents of their savings account on us while we were there. We didn't want that; we wanted to help.

We hope that talking about our experience there with so many people since our return will help the orphanage more in the long run. One of the things we want to do now is to give to more orphanages and charities like this.

SO MUCH NEED

Probably the toughest orphanage to visit was in Rwanda, where there is so much need it's hard to know where to even begin. This site was the poorest place we had seen, with a number of scattered buildings in poor condition. It was very dark, without much lighting and had a peculiar smell of close bodies. We brought food: a couple hundred pounds of rice, which they needed, but we didn't feel like we were making a dent in the problems there. Still, food was the main need. With 70 percent unemployment in Rwanda, things were tough. If you lived in Rwanda, you might eat one day and not the next. So, we were able to help the thirty or so children who lived there a little bit, but it was hard to feel good because the whole country was in such a dismal state.

One thing we've learned from our travels is that we are wealthy here in the United States. Even our poor people are wealthy compared to some other places.

CHAPTER TWENTY-NINE

ASIA

We had biked in some heavy traffic during our trip, but nothing compared to the chaos that we faced in Asia. Entering Bangkok was an education in a whole new way of navigating. There are no rules. The key is to never stop moving. This seemingly reckless method of crossing intersections worked surprisingly well, but it took some getting used to.

GOING WITH THE FLOW

Jacky: We were biking out of the Bangkok airport and there was traffic coming at us from every direction. It wasn't just cars. There were carts carrying anything and everything, some motorized, some pushed by people and some pulled by animals. I kept yelling to Ward to signal where he was going. I wanted him to stop. He said to me with a tone of disgust, "You don't get it; you have to keep moving."

Ward: I made her pull over at a McDonald's and I just had to get it through to her that we needed to keep going; otherwise, we were going to get hit. I had never been in traffic like this before, either, but I just kind of understood. Nobody was going to stop and wait for bicycles. It's just a different rhythm of life. Once we got through that, it was better.

Jacky: Somehow, everybody works it out and everybody moves around you, but you can't be unpredictable and stop to let people go by. That's when you're going to get hit. It was a huge learning curve for me.

I always thought it might be good to have a mirror on my bike, but after that, I never wanted a mirror. I didn't want to see what bus, cart, motor scooter, or animal was coming up behind me because I know I'd get nervous and want to stop and get out of the way. It was better not to know. It was enough just to handle all the traffic that was coming at us. Now I had to get used to vehicles rubbing my panniers.

Traffic was the worst in Thailand and Cambodia. One helpful thing we learned to do was to use buses and trucks as blockers on turns. If we saw that a vehicle was going to make a turn across traffic, we scooted in on the inside of them so they would effectively block the cross-traffic for us. We noticed that scooters, bicycles, and even pedestrians jumped in behind big trucks or buses to cross the main thoroughfare. Otherwise, it was a crapshoot.

One spooky thing we saw on Asia's roadways was the outline of scooters painted in the street to mark where an accident had occurred. It looked like the chalk outlines of bodies on murder mystery television, except these were scooter outlines. There were lots of them. We went along, saying, "Oh, another scooter got hit. Oh, another scooter."

One day we were biking in Laos to visit a cave where the Laotian people took refuge during the Vietnam War. As we were biking along, enjoying the beautiful scenery, we suddenly heard a crash and skidding tires behind us. As we turned around, we saw that two scooters had collided coming from opposite directions. One young driver was on the ground unconscious. The passenger of one of the scooters was standing there with blood streaming down his arms. The other driver was walking around trying to make sure everyone knew that it was not his fault.

> Jacky: I started yelling, "Call an ambulance, call an ambulance!" Well, number one, they don't have ambulances, and number two, they don't speak English!

> Ward: I said, "Jacky, do you realize where we are at? There's not a medical facility for forty miles."

We immediately took the water from our water bottles and started to help clean up the bleeding man. Through gestures, he did inquire if the water was purified and we assured him it was, as their unfiltered water could have caused infection.

As stated, an ambulance didn't show up but a pickup truck did. They grabbed the unconscious man by his arms and legs and swung him into the bed of the truck...no blankets...nothing, and away they went. We hoped this man didn't have any neck injuries because he wasn't handled very carefully.

> Jacky: It was an eye-opener for us. I thought, "Hmm...I really don't want to get hurt in this country!"

> Ward: We didn't stick around to see if they spray painted the outline of the scooters on the road.

Another fact that we learned, when it comes to helping injured people, is that in China they do not have the Good Samaritan law. So, if you come across an accident or someone that needs help and you help them, then you can end up being responsible for their medical bills. And, if they die, you can be responsible for their death. So, when there is an accident, people stand around, but no one is willing or dares help them. Quite sad.

In Asia, speed wasn't always the problem. In much of China, the traffic moved quite slowly. Roads were wider and people were used to seeing bicycles. We didn't feel pressured to move over or anything like that. On the other hand, the truck drivers in China seemed not to look before pulling out in front of us. We were astonished. We kept looking at each other for confirmation each time it happened. We'd say, "Did you see that? He didn't even look!" Sometimes, the trucks would pass us and then immediately turn right in front of us. We'd have to try to avoid running into their back side as they turned the corner.

Signaling rules were different everywhere as well. In Vietnam, people used their car and truck horns to notify us that they were approaching. They honked repeatedly on average, four or five times, before passing. The last blast came when they were right next to us.

Jacky: It's this high-pitched, shrill horn. I should have been wearing ear plugs, because I think the high tone damaged my hearing, so Ward tells me.

CALL OF NATURE

So many stories from our trip are filled with beautiful scenery and high adventure, but a lot of the time, we were taking care of the essentials of life: sleeping, eating, and using the bathroom. That last wasn't always pleasant. Our toilet experiences in Asia made any Porta Potty nightmares from the United States pale in comparison.

For starters, a lot of places didn't have toilet paper, so we always carried some with us. The facilities themselves ran the gamut. A place to sit was not a given. Women's rooms could be particularly unpredictable, requiring various contortions unfamiliar to most Westerners. The standard American toilet was a rarity.

When we stayed in cities, most hostels had standard European-style bathrooms where you stood and squatted, which were decent and clean. When we ventured out to more remote places like Mongolia, however, we primarily used outhouses.

> Ward: In one, you moved a board over to squat over a hole. There was no place to sit down or anything like a standard outhouse here.

> Jacky: In China, I went into a bathroom at a gas station. There weren't any stalls. There weren't any toilets. It was just a long trough that you would stand or squat over and do your business. No privacy at all. Then, every once in a while, a flush of water would run down the trough. The visual and the smell were repulsive. There was no lollygagging. You got out as quick as you could.

GOT A LIGHT?

Making connections without a common language was a challenge, but we had a few tricks up our sleeves. Neither of us smoke, but we learned to carry cigarettes in Asia. A lot of Asian people smoke and we found that if we offered them a cigarette, we could easily "strike up" a friendship. After we handed out a few cigarettes, people were much faster to help us out with whatever we needed.

> Jacky: Even just standing around, if you pulled out a pack of cigarettes, everyone took one. You always want the locals to be on your side.

We used this technique to ease uncomfortable situations, like when we stopped to eat and people gathered around to watch us. If we took out a pack and said, "Take one," they said, "Thank you," and the tension lessened a little.

Another small gift that could make a difference was a pair of sunglasses. Most people in Asia didn't have sunglasses and were fascinated by ours. We picked up a few inexpensive pairs to give out to people we met. For maybe fifty cents or a dollar, we could give them something pretty cool to break the ice or maybe negotiate an extra service.

UNSETTLED

In January of 2009, we were scheduled to land in Bangkok. While we were still in Australia, we saw on the news that the Bangkok airport was under siege due to anti-government protesters. We kept hearing about the Red Shirts versus the Yellow Shirts and worried about getting caught in the crossfire. For a while, flights from Australia to Bangkok had stopped altogether, so we had to be ready to change plans. The Australian visa, which was for three months, was not a problem, but changing the flights could have been.

These situations taught us about the uncertainties of the world. We never knew what we might have to deal with. Knowing the airport had been taken over by protesters when we were scheduled to fly in there was pretty unsettling. We had to be ready for anything.

Beyond the political struggles, Asia has natural disasters that can also affect your travels: earthquakes, typhoons, tsunamis.

The Bangkok situation got resolved before we got there, so we didn't have to alter our itinerary, but it made us wonder how people do manage it when a visa runs out. We never needed to overstay our visas, but we thought about it. It would have entailed a trip to the consulate, some explanations, and maybe some documentation of our plane tickets so they could verify our plans. It certainly would have been a challenge in non-English-speaking countries.

Planning around known visa specifications presented logistical challenges, too. We had a one-year, multiple-entry visa sixty days at a time to China. Our first sixty days had almost expired so we needed to leave China. We decided to go to Mongolia for two weeks. We could then return to China and have another sixty-day stretch on our visa. Therefore, we headed to Mongolia and then returned to China before continuing onto South Korea. Any deviation from our timeline was extremely complex.

International relations had big repercussions for us on the ground. When we were ready to take a boat to South Korea, for instance, we learned that North Korea was testing their missiles. The thing was, they were pointing them right at South Korea.

Ward: As we were going along, we'd hear on the news that, "Oh, now they're shooting at the country we're going to."

We went anyway—the South Koreans told us, "Oh, they're always testing the missiles." They were completely unfazed.

SHOW US THE MONEY

Getting money when we needed it also required extensive planning, plus the flexibility to hatch a new plan when the original one didn't pan out. This was especially true regarding ATMs. We looked ahead to see what cities had ATMs so we could take out the minimum amount of cash we needed to make it to the next ATM. These machines were surprisingly scarce. In Laos, there were only three cities that had ATMs, which meant we needed to take out enough cash to get us to the next one, but not so much that we had to worry about losing it or being robbed.

Here's a story on how this can go all awry. When we were in Luang Prabang, Laos, a tourist area familiar to many Westerners, we didn't expect banking to be a problem. We knew there were ATMs there that everybody used. When we went to the ATMs, though, we couldn't get any money. It turned out the telephone connection had gone down between Laos and Vietnam for several days, taking out the automatic teller system along with it. A quick inventory showed that we had sixteen dollars on hand. Our hotel room was eight dollars per night. If the ATM didn't start working soon, we were in bad shape. We downgraded to a four-dollar room and ate on a dollar a day, which meant a lot of rice! We were prepared to leave our passports as collateral just to eat and sleep.

As we made our way around the town, attempting to look at

all the tourist attractions but unable to due to their entrance fees, we tried to figure out how we might ask someone who had a credit card to buy us lunch if we promised to send them money later when the ATM started to work. The tourists were also in a quandary, but at least they had credit cards that they could use at the hotels and restaurants. Our credit cards had expired while we were in Chile in February of 2008.

> Ward: Even though we knew we had money in our ATM account, we couldn't access it. But I felt assured, because of the kindness of the Laotian people, that our temporary cash problem could be worked out. I think our passport could have been used as collateral until our cash problem was worked out.

We even tried to have money wired to us from our friends in the United States. Luckily, on day three, Ward woke up early and headed to the ATM machine like he did the mornings before. This time, the ATMs were working! Ward took out seventy dollars. This wasn't enough to get us to the border, so Jacky sent him back to get more money before the ATM ran dry from all the tourists flocking there. He went back and took out another seventy dollars and we now felt comfortable that we had enough money to get us to the next ATM. Whew!

HOT AND BOTHERED

Rides between towns in Laos were brutal because the weather was extremely hot and humid. Sometimes, we had to pedal a hundred miles to reach the next town. The sun was so strong that our skin was getting leathery even though we wore hats that protected our faces and necks.

Laos is mountainous, so one hundred miles meant a lot of

uphill pedaling before we reached the next place to stay. We tried to get on the road by five o'clock in the morning, so that by one o'clock in the afternoon we might be done for the day and able to rest in some shade or air conditioning.

We never got heat sickness, even though the temperatures hovered around 105 degrees, but the climate was very dehydrating. Because it was so humid, sweat just dripped off our arms and down the handlebars of our bikes. Staying hydrated was crucial.

"DID YOU SEE THAT?"

No two countries in Asia were exactly alike, but the clear division between Thailand and Cambodia was stunning.

Immediately after crossing the border, everything changed. Suddenly, we saw more people and even more chaos.

> Ward: In Thailand, the commercial charter buses were very vibrant and colorful and they reminded me of Disney World. In Cambodia, the buses were more run down. We saw one bus that was parked in the middle of the road, with its broken motor removed waiting to be fixed. Cambodia used more scooters and small tractors, which very often were in a state of disrepair.

On the bikes, we witnessed strange things every day. We were constantly saying to each other, "Did you just see that?" One motor scooter had about twenty-five live ducks hanging off it. We also passed a woman riding on the back of a scooter holding her sick baby in one arm and a stick with an IV bottle dangling off it in the other. A very talented scooter driver had a live, caged 150-pound hog on the back.

When we rode past buses (Toyota Hiace), we often saw more people sitting on top of it than inside. We also marveled at the many long agricultural carts that were pulled by small tractors. These carts were so packed with furniture and feed that we could barely see the person driving. He was nearly buried under his own load.

There was no end to the variety of things people hauled on bikes and scooters. One day, we saw a man driving a scooter with a block of ice on the floor between his legs, and a dead chicken on top. His buddy was hanging on behind him carrying a fan.

> Jacky: It's super hot, so a lot of times we saw people transporting ice on their bicycles. I wondered how much of the big blocks were left once they got to their destinations.

HOT AND COLD

We understood their desperation; we were always looking for coolers holding cold drinks. In Cambodia, they have very little electricity available for coolers, so they put huge blocks of ice in chest-type coolers to provide refrigeration for the day. We hated it when we followed the ice truck into town, because that meant the sodas in the coolers there hadn't had time to cool yet. We kept going, "Jeez, we're too close to the ice truck!"

Like ice, electricity was a precious commodity in Cambodia. Often, if we saw a lamp, it had only one bulb in it. Lighting was always dim because people tried to conserve. Many things ran on twelve-volt car batteries. Once the batteries started to weaken, people stuck them out on the edge of the road for a truck to pick up and exchange for fresh batteries.

Ward: In the rural parts of Cambodia, they'll have a charging station—a one-cylinder engine running a generator. They put forty or fifty batteries in series to trickle charge them. Then in the morning, a guy with a cart or truck picks up the charged batteries and delivers them.

In the cities, people were connected to the grid, but in the rural areas, we didn't see any grid at all. We noticed that houses in Cambodia were elevated on stilts, probably because of the rains but also to provide shade. People spent a good portion of their day underneath their houses, cooling off.

It was so hot, many of the children didn't wear clothes, even up to the age of seven or eight. When they saw us, they came running as fast as they could, totally naked, yelling, "Hello! Hello!" Very friendly and curious.

HAUNTING HISTORY

Most of Cambodia was joyful and full of life, but we did spend some somber moments in Phnom Penh, visiting the "killing fields." These were the places where an estimated one and a half million to three million people were killed and buried by the Khmer Rouge regime between 1975 and 1979. During our trip, we had seen the genocide locations of Auschwitz and Rwanda. This was no less unsettling.

In Phnom Penh, we also witnessed the long-term effects of Prime Minister Pol Pot's efforts to eliminate the thinking class.

Ward: If you wore glasses, you were killed. If you could read or write, you were killed. He wanted to take Cambodia back to an agrarian society. I think those actions have really affected

Cambodia long term. Three million of the smartest people in the country were killed.

On the other hand, modern Phnom Penh is full of first-world amenities. Not only do they cater to Westerners with nice hotels, we managed to find excellent Cambodian accommodations, too. All we had to do was find the Marriott or Hyatt that served Westerners, and just go around the corner. There we often found a beautiful Cambodian hotel for a much lower price.

For fifteen dollars a night, we booked a room with air conditioning, marble floors, a beautiful shower, refrigerator, writing desk, and colored TV with breakfast included. We could have gone down the street to a spot where all the backpackers go; a dorm room cost eight dollars a person per night. That would have cost us sixteen dollars sleeping in a big room with others versus our very nice private hotel room. Learning the culture let us see how to get better value for less money.

BEHIND CURTAIN NUMBER TWO...

The hubbub of Asia was never more apparent than in the markets in Thailand. Some guests at the International Hostel in Bangkok recommended we take the metro train to the market, so we did. You could get anything you wanted there. Navigating the tables, shops, and booths was like winding your way through a maze. There didn't seem to be any particular rhyme or reason to how it was set up.

At one point, we saw a curtain that made us curious. We dared to look behind the curtain, where we found a cockfighting ring. We could see the cages with the roosters inside. Then, just beyond the ring, we spied another curtain. Of course, we were too tempted not to peek, so back we went.

Behind this curtain, all we saw were fishbowls, or fish jars, really. Men were sitting there, looking at the gallon jars. Each jar held two fish, and the men were betting to see which fish would kill his roommate. Money was getting thrown down and everyone was intently focused on these fighting fish. It was very strange to see all these grown men betting on two little fish.

> Jacky: I don't know how you could tell the fish apart. They both looked the same.

We felt a little uneasy in there, being the only Westerners. The men were kind of staring at us. We sensed that taking pictures was forbidden, so we didn't. We definitely got the idea that we should just leave. We stayed only a minute and then made our way back out through the cockfighting ring. Looking at it, you could just picture twenty-five people perched at the edge of this ten-foot diameter ring, watching a cockfight.

HAPPY ENDINGS?

One thing we did want to try in Thailand was a Thai massage. Massages were very inexpensive and quite aggressive. Ten dollars bought two hours of deep massage, which was welcome after a day of riding.

AnnaMarie and Frank, friends from Thunder Bay, Canada, joined us for three weeks. AnnaMarie was familiar with the Thai massages and was the one to suggest it. She likes a deep massage, so she picked a masseuse that was bigger and appeared strong. Frank and Ward were also game. The masseuses gave the massages in your hotel room.

Jacky: AnnaMarie had her own room, and Frank, Ward, and I shared another room. I knew the Thai massages were very aggressive, so I bowed out from getting one and left the boys alone in our room to enjoy their massages.

Ward: Frank and I joked that our shared room couldn't offer enough privacy if Frank wanted a "happy ending." So we agreed that he would give me a heads up if he wanted me to leave the room. Apparently, he didn't want me to leave the room even though his masseuse was playing with his nipples. After the massage, we joked about his Thai massage fantasy.

For AnnaMarie, you can't say that she had such a nice experience. After one hour of her massage, the masseuse said she was done. AnnaMarie indicated that she had paid for two hours. The woman put AnnaMarie on her stomach, pushed her head into the pillow and stood with one foot on the back of her neck. She then put the other foot on her back and grabbed her ankles and arms and pulled her body up backwards. AnnaMarie was forced to surrender and had to call "uncle."

Another time, the four of us went together for general massages in Cambodia. When we arrived, they washed our feet and led us to an open room with four cots in it. We were asked to take off our clothes down to our underwear. Apparently, Frank didn't hear that last bit of instruction. Even though we were in an open area, Frank just took it all off. His masseuse started screaming, but Frank couldn't see anything, especially in the dim light—he's blind at night with even poor vision during the day—so he didn't know what was going on. Why was this young girl screaming? Why are my friends laughing? It was quite comical. Another masseuse came in to relieve this shocked young girl from her duty. Frank is a good sport and always lends some comic relief.

GOING SOMEWHERE?

Moving from country to country generally went smoothly because we planned everything based on visa requirements. On the other hand, when those requirements changed, confusion could suddenly set in, as it did in Mongolia.

We took the train from Beijing, China, to Mongolia due to our Chinese visa getting close to reaching its sixty-day limit. (As stated earlier, if we left China and then returned, we would get sixty more days on our visa.) We had done our research and there was absolutely no need for us as Americans to have a visa to visit Mongolia. Or was there? Everyone on the train seemed to be getting lots of paperwork ready, including visas. We said "No, we don't need a visa. We checked." But the others were saying, "You do need a visa."

This made us a little nervous when the time came. It turned out we were right; due to an eighty-million-dollar foreign aid deal between the United States and Mongolia, Americans were exempt from the visa requirement.

Taking the train from China to Mongolia was interesting, because the track gauge literally changed at the Chinese Mongolian border. The width of the tracks in each country is different so the countries could maintain border control. To make the switch, they raise the cars up on hydraulic jacks and then roll out the Chinese rail car trucks, and replace them with Mongolian rail car trucks.

Ward: They switched the undercarriage of the train. Everyone got off, but I wanted to stay on and watch the whole process. It was super cool, because the four hydraulic jacks come under each corner of each car and they raise it up six or seven feet. Out goes the old undercarriage and in comes the new one. When we crossed the Gobi Desert, we learned the true meaning of the term "sandstorm." The train was not very tightly sealed, so when the sand started blowing around, it blew right through the train. By the time we got out, everything was covered in dust.

Our original plan was to bike a loop in Mongolia and then return to China, but when we biked from the train to the hostel in Ulaanbaatar, it was horrible. The traffic was intense and the drivers were not used to having bikes on the road. We almost got hit many times. It wasn't long before we decided to give up on biking there. If we had decided to bike, we learned that we would have been cycling primarily on dirt paths as Mongolia only has twenty-eight miles of paved roads.

Luckily, an alternative presented itself to us almost immediately. The hostel manager told us he had a few people signed up for a Jeep tour and they had a couple of spots left. Would we like to go? It was a four-day trip into the middle of Mongolia, exploring by Jeep and sleeping in yurts, the Mongolian version of a portable round tent covered with skins. The Jeeps were rugged old Russian-vehicles, perfect for the miles and miles of dirt that cover most of Mongolia.

Riding in the Jeep felt like riding a dune buggy through the desert. We buzzed through wide open plains and highlands and streambeds seemingly willy-nilly. Though the drivers obviously knew where they were going, we weren't sure how. There weren't many directional road signs. We did find one sign indicating a nearby city; it was such a rarity we took a picture. One can pretty much drive wherever you want.

We slept in the yurts and enjoyed the hospitality of their owners. Our jeep excursion included all of our meals as well. The owners prepared our breakfast of *buuz* (warm horse milk), *boortsog* (fried dough), *suutei tsai* (milk tea), and *kashk* (a thick dairy dish). We either had a sack lunch or stopped at a random restaurant in the middle of nowhere. Our dinner usually included yak meat, noodles, and vegetables along with the horse milk.

Jacky: We had to drink horse milk.

Ward: Yeah, warm horse milk. It's not so good. It had kind of a sour taste.

We washed up in the streams and used the outhouses provided by the yurt owners. An outhouse there was basically a hole in the ground with one board of the floor removed for access (mentioned earlier).

Some yurts offered horse rides for a little extra money. The Mongolians are excellent horsemen, so it was fun.

Ward: We were so far from anything. I don't think I could have found my way back to Ulaanbaatar. That was odd for me, because I normally have a strong sense of where I'm at.

Jacky: It was cool, though, because you could be riding in the Jeep, and all of a sudden, right next to you was a herd of wild horses running by.

Each day, we would go about forty miles, which took three hours. We traveled from Ulaanbaatar to Karakorum. One day, we ate lunch in the absolute middle of nowhere. There was a restaurant there, stocked by trucks that circled up fully loaded with soft drinks, vegetables, and everything they needed.

MORE ASPECTS OF CHINA

We knew pollution was a problem in urban areas of China, but we weren't prepared for the extreme level of contamination. None of the factory smokestacks had any cleaners on them, and the waterways along the side of the road were black. The discoloration wasn't from sewage, but from effluent released by the factories. We rode by the Three Gorges Dam along the

Yangtze River, where industrial waste flowed right into the ditches. We could tell the chemicals were toxic, just from the smell. At the end of the day, our faces were so dirty when we took off our glasses, we looked like raccoons. Our clothes got dingy and gray.

Many Chinese wear face masks to filter the air for breathing, but we chose not to. When you're cycling, you need every bit of oxygen you can get. By the end of a day of riding, though, our throats were sore.

The pollution was probably the worst in Beijing, although we were there in March when it is supposedly not that bad. We were told that in October and November, when all the wood and coal furnaces are running, the smog haze is so thick you can't tell whether it's a sunny day or not. We didn't go to Hong Kong, but they say that the pollution is so bad that if you run a mile it's like smoking two packs of cigarettes.

People there seemed resigned to dealing with the pollution. It was just part of everyday life. Even if they don't like it, the Chinese people don't have much of a say in how the government regulates, or doesn't regulate, industry.

> Ward: One of the things that I noticed was that there are so many people there that if one person loses their life to pollution, there's always another ready to take his or her place, at least economically speaking. I got the sense that while lives had value, people also acknowledged that as workers in the system, they were replaceable.

The Communist government has an interesting way of recruiting future members to the Communist party. Our firsthand experience came when we noticed certain young kids in Beijing wearing red arm bands. We asked why they wore them. It turned out the red arm bands were reserved for China's more intellectual children. The Communist government honored them by giving their families various luxuries. In turn, the young people are "strongly encouraged" to join the Communist party when they grow up.

The average person on the street, however, didn't have a sense of control or the creativity that goes with it. It was the land of copycats. Entertainment came from movies that had been copied. We bought a memory stick that was perfectly packaged, seemingly brand new, but it was half full with photos, etc., that we did not take. Nothing felt original.

This mindset of copying appeared to be the result of the education system. We heard from English-speaking people who were teaching English in China that they were only allowed to teach what was in the approved book. They were strongly discouraged from improvising or even teaching their students to work through problems on their own.

Ward: As a youth in China, you believe what's in the book. You don't question this.

Jacky: This was very disturbing to us. Some of the English teachers told us they asked students questions like, "What are your feelings after reading this poem?" The students didn't understand the question. They asked, "What's the right answer?" The teacher tried to explain that there wasn't a single right answer, and that it was only to get their thoughts about the subject or question. But that simply wasn't something they understood.

We could see why Chinese students test very well; they memorize everything in the book. But if you ask them to formulate their own opinions, many of them can't do it. The practical problems with this frame of mind came through to us loud and clear through stories from our Argentinian friend, Sebastian, who was helping to train Chinese commercial airplane pilots. He said it was scary, because if something went wrong midflight, a lot of these pilots were at a loss.

Sebastian said the Chinese were excellent pilots, as long as everything went by the book. "As Argentinians," said Sebastian, "sure, we read the book, but we fly by the seat of our pants. We get the airplane on the ground. For the Chinese, if it wasn't in the book, the airplane would fall out of the sky."

> Ward: We saw more evidence of this way of thinking when we visited the Three Gorges Dam. This six-hundred-foot tall dam on the Yangtze River is the largest dam in the world. However, it's built on a fault line. They never calculated the weight of the water that they were holding back in the dam, to consider if that additional weight could cause an earthquake. It was just like, "Who's doing the thinking around here?"
>
> It was pretty amazing to see, though. I like to see those large structures. The dam is about a mile and a quarter long and over six hundred feet tall. It's a lock system. They're able to raise large ships up to continue on navigating the Yangtze River. Amazing, but they had to displace a couple of million people to build it; they moved their towns up higher on the riverbanks.

Traffic on the Yangtze was continuous. It looked like a freeway of barges. We were stunned by the volume of traffic on the river, and the huge loads these barge-like boats carried. If they had put on ten more pounds, they would've sunk.

City streets, on the other hand, were sometimes surprisingly quiet. We rode past twenty-story high-rise apartment buildings that were entirely empty. It was like all the money from exports had landed here, and they didn't know what to do with it, so they built row after row of high rises. Even when we rode into small towns of two or three thousand people, we found twenty or thirty of these huge buildings, all vacant.

> Ward: In every town. If I saw one, I saw a thousand of these buildings. I said, "Jacky, there's a problem here. These buildings are brand new. How come they're all empty?"

We did learn later that the vacancies were at least in part a result of China's low-wage rates. They held their wages low to make their products more profitable on the world markets. It worked; they had huge profits. The problem was that the wages were so low in China that even two families living together couldn't afford to pay rent in these buildings.

> Jacky: What I understood was that the younger generation was starting to move out of the family home and move into their own places. The government expected more people to be looking for housing. But because of the cost, nobody could afford them so they stand vacant.

It was astonishing to go from one end of a city to the other. Bicycling only a few blocks away from these pristine facades took us to neighborhoods where people live in absolute poverty. After we were in Beijing, Diane Sawyer was there doing a newscast. We saw the places she was taken—from her luxurious hotel down a flower-lined promenade to the Olympic Stadium—and thought, "Oh, Diane, you are not seeing the real China."

We rode through all of Beijing and Shanghai, away from the tourist sites designed for Westerners. Just outside Tiananmen Square, we saw a new shopping district, but the buildings were all facades. There was nothing in them, though if you walked down the street, it looked quite upscale. Going into the alley behind the movie-set street, though, we were immediately immersed in squalor.

Even relatively new buildings looked like they had been around for decades. The pollution takes its toll, plus so many shortcuts are taken in the building process that things fall apart quickly. We rode past welders working on a freeway with no mask or goggles on. The welding arc is blinding; we had to wonder how good a job these guys were doing if they couldn't see.

Our sense was that the rapid-fire building was the Chinese government's way of showing their world dominance. That mentality, combined with an education system that doesn't encourage critical thinking, leads to problems in the long run.

The Communist government controls so much that the people feel helpless. We could see that. We could feel it in everyday transactions like going to the bank to exchange money, which required meeting with four different officials for paperwork and signatures. Your fate is always in someone else's hands.

GATHER ROUND

All over the world, when we met people individually or in groups, we managed some sort of give-and-take conversation, even with language barriers. People almost always tried to communicate with us. In China, though, like nowhere else, we often found ourselves not engaged but observed.

When we stopped in China, groups of people gathered around us and simply stared. One day, a group of welders from a nearby factory crowded around to watch us change a tire. Within five minutes of our stopping, twenty workers were standing around us.

> Ward: I couldn't believe that twenty people could stand there for fifteen or twenty minutes while the factory machines ran on. Maybe their jobs weren't that important, or maybe they had other people watching the machines. I don't know. We didn't go into the factory.

No matter what we did when we stopped, we attracted a group like this. Sometimes, we tried to sneak into town where nobody could see us and hide behind a building to eat, just for a little privacy. If they found us, we'd go, "The freak show is about to begin." We were the freaks on display.

The fascination with us as Westerners was understandable but uncomfortable. Over two weeks, in a city of over three million people, we saw one other Westerner. We never saw any people of color—no Indians, no Africans—just Chinese. We were clearly rare specimens, but it was a strangely impersonal experience, not like when the women in Rwanda wanted to touch Jacky's skin because they had never seen a white person before. That was affectionate. In China, we felt we were being watched.

O CAPTAIN! MY CAPTAIN!

We did find one place in Shanghai where we could relax for a while: Captain's Hostel. We needed to spend a little time while we waited for the US consulate to produce Jacky's new passport, and this was the spot to do it.

Captain Hostel, unlike a typical hostel, serves a number of long-term residents. One reason is the housing crisis we talked about earlier; it was simply too expensive to buy a house or rent an apartment, so people stayed at hostels. We met several people who stayed there instead of renting, including the Argentinian pilot, Sebastian, a schoolteacher named John, and a student/translator called Daniel. An older woman named Annie was staying there for months, and so was another Chinese girl, Jenn. They had four rooms with six or eight people in each room. It was like its own little community.

Our room was on the dorm floor; the rooms clustered around a common area in the middle. We met a lot of people there, because around five o'clock each day, people started showing up with beer and snacks. We'd enjoy our own little happy hour out there. Nobody sat in their rooms; they sat on benches in the common area. As we sat on the benches in a line it felt like we were waiting for the bus, so we were always joking about the bus being late, or how we had missed our bus. With the diverse group, you never knew who would come along or what story they might share.

Ward: It had all the makings of a sitcom. Kinda like *Cheers* but at a bus stop. We called it "Daniel's Bar." The only rule was that 50 percent of what we said had to be true.

One day, Jacky was doing laundry, and Daniel said to her, "Don't hang your clothes out in the common area." She asked, "Why?" He explained that he was drying his laundry out there and that some of his underwear went missing. That was odd, so we just hung our wet clothes to dry in our room and thought nothing of it.

A few nights later, we all decided to go out to a karaoke bar. There was one guy who was sitting in the common area who we didn't know, but instead of being rude, we invited him along. Karaoke in Shanghai isn't a public spectacle like it is in the United States; we had a private room just for our small group of eight. We sat on couches while waiters came to the room to serve drinks and food. Everything was going well, when a girl from Germany said, "My camera is gone!"

We figured it couldn't have gone far; nobody had left the room since we arrived. Even though we looked under every cushion, we couldn't find the camera anywhere. Eventually, security was called in. At this point, the place was a mess with pillows and cushions strewn everywhere. The room was dimly lit, so it was hard to tell what was going on. Security decided the cameras in the room were their best bet, so they left to check the recordings.

We were still going through gyrations, looking for the missing camera, when Jen said, "Okay, everybody take your clothes off. All you guys!" It was obvious from the women's light, pocket-less clothing that none of them was hiding a camera, so it was up to the men. The guys went along with the idea, starting by taking off their shirts. At first, the mystery man refused to join in. Finally, after a lot of pressure from the group he relented and all the men stripped down to their boxers and briefs.

Daniel looked over at the stranger and said, "Those are my underwear!"

We found the underwear thief at last! Not only that, but we found the camera in his vest pocket, too. The police showed up and took him to jail that night. The next day, they came to the hostel to see how long he had been staying there. He wasn't even staying there. He would just befriend someone and then steal their underwear and other stuff!

LIVING ROOMS

We had a lot of downtime in Shanghai, waiting for the passport, but luckily, we found a place we could be useful. We met a Chinese man from New Zealand who had inherited an apartment in the city and was renovating it. He was staying at the Captains Hostel because he wasn't done with the remodeling. Ward offered to help.

Not only did the job give Ward something to do—even if it mostly entailed scrubbing floors and cleaning up—it let him see how people in China actually live in their day-to-day lives. Walking into these apartments was like stepping back in time forty or fifty years. All the stoves were in the hallway, where everyone cooked and did dishes. The hallways had that peculiar smell about them. No place to vent any of the food smells. Also, the residents of this apartment building would peer out their doors to see a white man (Ward) scrubbing floors just outside their door. This continuous observation was very weird for Ward. The apartments didn't have their own bathrooms; you had to go down around a corner to find a cement trough with running water in it. One small room, maybe 140 square feet, held beds for six people.

The gentleman from New Zealand had changed to have his plumbing inside and also his cooking. His New Zealand salary could allow him to afford this. The changing middle class of China was struggling to even afford these small rustic apartments.

CHAPTER THIRTY

BORDER CROSSINGS: A MIXED BAG

Moving between countries was always tense, because there was so much to do, and so many things could go differently from what we had planned. As we mentioned earlier, it paid to arrive early in the day. We always wanted to get as far from the border as possible after crossing, because of the chaos that seemed part and parcel of the borders themselves. Often, though, the scene changed immediately; once we would cross the political boundary, the world was transformed. Borders were transfer points and there were times where people that were trying to transfer to another country would get stuck there due to problems with passports, not having the correct exit/entry papers, visa issues, etc. Many were without any money or shelter, so travelers on bicycles were vulnerable and could be easily preyed upon.

Also, we needed adequate time to get the right currency, start trying to understand another language (both verbal and body language), make sure we had the appropriate paperwork, learn the cultural "dos" and "don'ts" and find a place to set up camp.

Even with our best planning there were still times we encountered things we simply couldn't control.

WHEN A BICYCLE IS NOT A BICYCLE

Crossing from Chile to Peru was one of those times where we had to adjust on the fly and hope it all worked out. We got to the border in the morning, which was great, but the Peruvians demanded documentation showing that we owned the bicycles. They considered our bicycles to be similar to motorcycles, which required proof of ownership. Of course, we carried no such documentation.

On our side of the border, the Chileans said they didn't need documentation. Our bikes had no motors, so they weren't considered vehicles. Bicycles were no problem to them. But on the Peruvian side, proof was paramount. The argument continued and the frustration rose. Staying calm seemed to be the best idea, but Ward really wanted to explain that he thought this whole situation was idiotic.

After several hours of going back and forth between offices, we emerged with a piece of paper bearing seven different stamps. This paper certified that we were allowed to take our bicycles from Chile into Peru.

Ward: I joked that the only person left yet to stamp it was God.

We were warned that we must carry the paper with us at all times and not let anyone take it from us. So we did, but we never had to show it to anyone after that either.

POLAND TO SLOVAKIA

We had a similar experience crossing from Poland's friendly, pretty, flower-strewn neighborhoods to Slovakia's run-down buildings and empty streets.

> Jacky: The buildings were all gray cement. No one was out and about. There was no color. We saw people peering at us from their windows. It was eerie, going from a world of color to black and gray.

> Ward: Yeah, and we had just crossed a border is all. In Slovakia, all the light poles had speakers on them. That's how they broadcasted the daily news during the Cold War. The roads were horrible. We had entered a time warp only 200 yards into Slovakia.

When we left Slovakia and entered the Czech Republic, immediately we again saw flower gardens, the people were smiling, and the roads got better. Folks waved to us from their gardens. Leaving the oppression of Slovakia and entering the Czech Republic was reinvigorating. Political systems can really affect the population's attitude. During the Soviet occupation, Czechoslovakia was considered one country, but in reality Slovakia was always considered the redheaded stepchild. The break-up of the Soviet Union allowed each country to resume its individual identity.

NORWAY TO SWEDEN

One crossing that surprised us was the border between Norway and Sweden. We didn't expect to see much difference there. It was true that the scenery didn't change much at all (trees and more trees and then more trees), but when we hit Sweden, suddenly there was a huge grocery store with a parking lot full of Norwegian cars. There was a large price differential between the two countries that everyone drove to Sweden to buy their groceries. It was amusing. It was obvious that the Norwegians were very conservative. If we use beer as an indicator of price, a can of beer from the grocery store was three and a half to four dollars. The Swedish price for a similar beer was two and a half dollars. All of the groceries indicated that kind of price differential.

BOLIVIA TO BRAZIL

The differences in border crossings weren't always so amusing, though. Going from Bolivia into Brazil gave us a bit of a scare. The border station was just a little hut off a gravel road. The border patrolmen were sitting at a table under a tarp, not looking official at all. One of the guys tried on Jacky's sunglasses. We didn't know if we were going to ever get them back. We weren't sure just what was going to happen in this remote area. We were switching languages again, Spanish to Portuguese. After a short time, they sent us on our way. We didn't realize until later that they never gave us our entry papers and never even stamped our passports. We later found out how important it is to get all the proper documentation.

We headed down the road, when suddenly, a military truck came racing toward us. When they stopped us, several border patrol guards with machine guns got out and started poking through our stuff.

Jacky: I wasn't nervous because I knew we hadn't done anything wrong.

This crew went through all our bags and then motioned for us to move on. We figured we had gotten off lucky, when a few miles down the road we were stopped by another truck. Again, the border patrol with machine guns piled out and pulled us over. At this point, it was one hundred degrees out and we were hot and frustrated. We hadn't done anything!

It turned out that the road we were on was a known drug route. They were stopping us to make sure we weren't transporting drugs across the border. Our non-stamped passports could have been an issue at this juncture but, thank goodness, they never noticed.

> Ward: They definitely had the wrong people.

> Jacky: In hindsight, I see they easily could have planted some drugs on us and then demanded bribe money. Luckily at the time, that never crossed our minds.

Our return to Bolivia from Brazil also did not go as it should. As mentioned earlier, we were never given entry papers and it is imperative that you have these papers with you at all times. So, when we crossed back into Bolivia from Brazil, the border guard demanded our entry papers. No papers no exit. We pleaded with the guard that the rural entry checkpoint never gave us the entry papers. We could buy an entry paper for seven and a half dollars per person. We gave in and did that. Not very happy when we saw the border guard give us our paper and then pocket the money. Glad to get out with that being the only cost.

This is a little lengthier story but shows how even though we tried to have high safety standards, we could still get into dangerous situations and get scammed.

When we were traveling without our bicycles and had to rely on public transportation, border crossings could get even more dicey because we had to trust others to take us where we were going. To get to Ecuador from Peru, we had to take a bus to Tumbes. The border was still forty kilometers away and we were required to pass through customs by taxi.

We broke one of our rules that day, the rule that we would only get in taxis driven by certified taxi drivers.

> Jacky: It was Ward. He found a guy in jeans and a T-shirt in front of the gate. He didn't have a taxi badge. I told Ward this was breaking rule number one. But we went anyway.

> Ward: Okay, let it be documented. Ward failed.

We picked up our bags and started to head to his car. As suspected, it was not a taxi car. It was an old, rundown, black, smelly car.

> Jacky: Now I'm getting very uneasy. This has "Stop right now— BIRKIE—written all over it!" I sat in the back seat while Ward was in the front. I was sitting at the edge of my seat because I wanted to be on guard in case something happened.

The driver asked us if we wanted him to reserve bus tickets for us. They cost twenty-five dollars each. We didn't have that much money on us so we had to stop at an ATM. Was he going to try to steal our money? We kept a close eye on his movements. As we then headed down the road, he was befriending us, giving us travel tips, telling us how dangerous the areas were, and to only talk to him at the border. We started to trust him.

The border was chaotic and he did expedite the process, directing us to the correct window. As we were leaving, there was another guy yelling to us to get in his car. Instead, Ward and I climbed back into our original driver's car; he then told us to lock our doors. As we headed into the city on the Ecuador side, everything was crazy. There were people, carts, vendors, and vehicles everywhere. Our driver turned down a dirt road and then into a parking lot with a gate. What were we doing? The other vehicles in there were not taxis.

The car stopped and a friend of our driver came over. We were told this guy was going to buy our bus tickets for us and that we should give him the money. They wouldn't let Ward go along so we really didn't know if we were being scammed. He did return but wouldn't give us the tickets. Then Ward asked for our change and he said, "Come on, I helped you. You should give it to us." We picked up our bags and headed out with the taxi driver's friend. But, why was the area that we drove through that was so dangerous we had to lock our doors now safe to walk through with all of our bags? It made no sense.

We made it to the bus terminal, but we then needed to take a taxi to check in at the Ecuador border. (Yes, it is all very confusing and convoluted.) We were with the original taxi driver's friend at this time and believed he had a connection to the bus terminal. After taking this taxi to check in with the Ecuadorian border, we took the same taxi back to the bus terminal. The driver now told us he needed forty dollars more for an entrance fee. (Some countries charge an entrance fee to come into their country.) We gave him the money, and he then finally gave us our tickets. He left to pay the entrance fees and we never saw him again. We then found out that the bus tickets were only five dollars each (not twenty-five dollars) and there was no entrance fee! They scammed us out of eighty-five dollars.

However, at this point we were just thankful it wasn't worse! The rules and entry fees at the borders always differed, and they were rarely written in any place where we could read them. We had good luck trusting people to help us most of the time, but it didn't always work in our favor.

LAOS TO VIETNAM

As we were crossing from Laos to Vietnam, we faced a similar situation. The Vietnamese border guard told us that our Laotian money was useless in Vietnam. He, however, could exchange the money for us, which he did. He probably made a nice little profit on this scam, since we later found out that Vietnam had no problem with taking currency from Laos.

He was the least of our problems there, though. The much tougher challenge was the mud. After the mountainous border crossing, the Vietnam road deteriorated badly. There's a constant mist there, so the dirt road just turns to mush. We had to push our bikes through muddy ruts six to twelve inches deep up through this mountainous section. Thank goodness that only a few miles later we were back on hard surfaced roads.

CHINA TO SOUTH KOREA

We could never tell what rules would be enforced and what might be overlooked when making a crossing. Prior to our ferry crossing to South Korea, we had to fill out forms about everything we were carrying, so we dutifully reported our cooking knives under "knives, firearms, and explosives." We had the knives all ready to show them because we were sure this would arouse suspicion, but the Chinese Border police just took our paperwork without a second glance and waved us through. We were never questioned a bit and we were very surprised because we could have had explosives or firearms upon entering the ferry.

NORTH KOREA

We weren't at all surprised by the many requirements laid out for us entering the Korean Demilitarized Zone (DMZ). Even our clothing was specified. We needed to wear shoes, not sandals. Long-sleeved shirts were required. No bright colors were allowed. We had it all under control.

When we got on the bus, though, we realized Ward forgot our passports. How could he forget our passports after such careful preparation? Approaching the entrance to the DMZ, we saw armed military officers boarding the bus. We were all told to put our passports up by our faces. We didn't know what to do. Everybody was holding their passport up next to their face, and we didn't have ours. All we had was our little "Budweg Adventures" business type card with a picture of us on our bikes. We put those up by our faces, never believing this was adequate identification. But it was. They just said, "Okay," and moved on.

We were still nervous going into the DMZ. We were roughly two miles from the border, but we could see North Korea and they could see us. We were only allowed to take pictures of North Korea from a certain point in the viewing area. They would not allow us to view from the perimeter wall. We had the option to pay more to go into the neutral area right between the two countries, but we heard of people accidentally stepping over the line into North Korea and getting shot. We chose to keep our distance.

CHAPTER THIRTY-ONE

YOU DON'T EXPERIENCE THIS ON A TOUR BUS—ASIA EDITION

Learning about other cultures means being ready for anything.

THIS GUN SHOOTS BLANKS!

One evening in Laos started innocently enough, with a park visit and a nice meal at a little local restaurant. While we were settling our bill, a man came over to us and asked, in broken English, if we would like to have a beer with him. Sure, we'd like to have a beer with him. We joined him and another man at their table. It looked kind of comical, because the Laotians have a much smaller stature; Ward towered over them.

The men were fascinated by Ward. They were touching him, squeezing his arms and bear hugging his midsection, saying what a "big, strong man" he was. One of them even kissed Ward on the cheek.

It was a little strange, but we carried on being friendly, sharing pictures of our sons. When we took out their high school senior pictures, the men got very excited. "Oh, you make big, strong boys!" they said. They immediately got their phones out and started dialing.

We didn't know what was going on at first. They explained, "We're dialing the women."

They were calling women because they wanted them to come and have sex with Ward, to change their bloodlines. They had checked out the breeding stock and thought they could develop some stronger, taller men in their families with Ward's help.

> Ward: My thought was, well, I had had a vasectomy, so there wasn't much risk. Maybe we could use this as a fundraiser!

> Jacky: We just had to make sure we got out of town before they found out that Ward was fixed and shooting blanks.

Nothing came of this evening, but it makes a comical story of how different cultures might want to change their genetics.

SEOUL HAS A LOT OF "SOUL"

South Korea was notable for its incredibly friendly, helpful people. If we had been with a tour group, we never would have received the treatment we did. One day, we were biking down the road when a car pulled over and stopped in front of us and a young man came running back to give us a bag of chips and some very cold bottles of water. Another time, we were sitting on a bench just watching traffic and a car pulled up and the passenger got out and gave us a bag of donuts. Donuts were a regular part of the Korean diet. Then there was the time we were at a gas station, taking a break, when a guy came over and handed us bottles of water. South Koreans demonstrated a different kind of hospitality that we hadn't seen before in Asia.

One rainy day, we were huddled in a bus stop trying to stay dry, looking at our map, and trying to decide the best route to Seoul. We talked about how we didn't want to take a busy route; we wanted a route with fewer trucks and more scenery. A man waiting for the bus asked if he could help us. He showed us a scenic three-day route to Seoul that we could take. We gave him our business card and we were on our way.

Over the next few days, we started getting emails from him, saying that when we got to Seoul, he would like to host us. He wanted us to stay at his house Saturday night and go to church with him and his family. We tried to make it work, but we were flying from South Korea to Alaska on Sunday and had to get our bikes boxed and packed. We just didn't have the time. The man was undaunted, however. He offered to drive us and our boxed bikes to the airport in his pickup truck.

Not only did he save us from a forty-mile bus or taxi ride, but when he came to pick us up he gave us a special tour of the city, places we didn't have time to see. He took us out to a restaurant where he ordered seven different dishes so we could try varieties of Korean food we might not have had elsewhere. He wouldn't let us pay for anything. Then he sent all the leftovers with us.

He was such a giving man, and true to what we found in all of Korea. South Korea was second only to Argentina for hospitality.

CHAPTER THIRTY-TWO

LENDING A HELPING HAND

Helping in the world is very easy when you travel at 10 mph. Opportunities abound. Simple chance meetings were often enough to allow us to share our skills and ingenuity while we were building relationships with the world.

A SIGN OF SHORTNESS

Riding with Jeff in Peru, we came across a couple of Peruvian men trying to put up a large commercial sign on a post. They were struggling to get it in place. Their ladders and scaffolding weren't tall enough for them to reach, given their short stature. It was quite heavy. With two extra bodies and a lot of extra height, we could help.

We stopped and manhandled the sign into place in short order. They were very, very happy for the help. As we finished helping them, one of the men ran over to an ice cream stand and got ice cream cones for us. Our efforts to place the sign were not significant, but just a friendly interaction with others.

BOAT ON THE RUN

We mentioned before that Ward often carried things on his bike that he had picked up from roadside ditches. We couldn't always predict what purpose they would serve, but usually a need arose and Ward could help with something from his supply.

In Prince George, British Columbia, we were on a busy street riding along when a boat slid off the trailer pulled by a pickup truck, going in the opposite direction. The seventeen-foot fiberglass boat careened down the road until it skidded to a stop.

Upon seeing this peculiar sight, we turned around as fast as we could to see if we could help the driver. All the oncoming traffic was able to avoid the free boat. The straps holding the boat on his trailer had just dry rotted away. He needed to get his boat back up on the trailer and fasten it again, but it was heavy fiberglass. We tried to do it using the winch rope of the trailer, but it was rotten and it broke as well.

> Ward: Then I thought, "Oh, I've got some rope." I pulled it from my ditch stash and we were able to hook it up to the winch and winch the boat back onto the trailer. I think Jacky had to rethink her position on my ditch diving after that. She often thought I was wasting a lot of time picking things out of the ditch. She would even say, "What do you need that for?"

BREAKDOWN LANE

We were always eager to help fellow travelers any way we could. This often meant helping them get back on the road again after some sort of breakdown. Here are a few examples:

NEED SOME AIR?

In Argentina, we came across a car with a flat tire on the side of the road. It belonged to a man who had his wife and kids in the car but had no way to get air into his tire. We had several bicycle pumps, so we helped him out. We pumped up his tire and gave him one of our pumps in case he needed it again. (Yes, the volume of air from a bicycle pump is much smaller than a compressor, but it works.)

MOTOR HOME MAYHEM

On the Alaskan Highway, we repeatedly came upon motor homes stranded on the roadside with broken fan belts. Many times, the drivers were older folks who were struggling to fix the problem. We always stopped and offered a hand.

> Ward: On at least one occasion, I fixed the fan belt while Jacky got invited in for coffee. She always gets the best deal. I am lying under this massive motor home and it's dirty, oily, and I'm getting bit by mosquitos. In the meantime, Jacky is sitting on a comfortable couch or chair in a very clean and mosquito-free environment.

Another time, we came upon an elderly gentleman who was pulling a motor home trailer, but he couldn't get the truck's spare tire to come down because of a rusted cable. He and his wife were probably both in their mid-seventies.

> Ward: I was skinny and strong, so I slid under the back of the pickup and freed up the frozen cable and we got the tire down. He goes, "Geez, you saved our lives."

There was very little traffic on the Alaskan Highway, so these couples would have been lucky to find anyone else to help them. It makes us wonder if, even as we are telling stories about the people who helped us, there are people all over the world telling stories about the bicyclists who appeared out of nowhere and came to their rescue. Helping others helped the trip feel less self-serving, more like it was part of a circle of giving.

CHAPTER THIRTY-THREE

HAIR–RAISING MOMENTS

We wanted full immersion on this trip, and we got it. At times, though, being up close and personal was a little more than we had bargained for, especially where animals were concerned.

MONKEY BUSINESS: BIG, BAD BABOONS!

We had heard that once you go to the top of Yellow Mountain (which is part of the Huangshan Mountain Range in Southern Anhui Province), the views were so beautiful that you didn't need to see any other mountain in China. So we knew we had to go there. It started out quite pleasant, hiking up the path, encountering a few little monkeys. They seemed kind of cute.

As we went deeper into the forest, though, we noticed the monkeys didn't move to let us go by. They stood their ground. Also, they seemed to multiply. First, we only saw small ones, but suddenly several large ones jumped up into the path. Ten or more gathered, continuing to just stare at us.

Ward tried to shoo them away with his hands, but they were having none of that. Instead of scattering, they started hissing and snarling. We expected them to be afraid and run away from the big, scary humans but no such luck. Alone on the path, we had no choice but to retreat.

Jacky: Ward kept facing them and backing up slowly, but I started moving faster and faster back down the path. They just kept coming forward, toward us.

Ward: Lunging and lurching.

Jacky: Hissing, and snarling, and lunging at him. It was really scary.

We figured out afterwards that they weren't monkeys at all; they were baboons. The adults were big, three or four feet tall and sixty or seventy pounds. There was no way we would have been able to fight them off.

When we got back down to the bottom of the path, we asked the woman minding the little shop there about the baboons. We used a dictionary to show her the words for "monkey" and "attack." Her response was completely casual. Oh, yeah, this sort of thing happens all the time. She had sticks you could rent to help you scare them off.

Thus armed, we headed back into the fray but not without backup. We waited for a group to come by and planted ourselves in their midst. The baboons were still there, but this group had a guide; he had a stick and he knew how to use it to disperse the gathering crowd of baboons.

On the way down, we did the same thing; we waited for a group we could join. The baboons were not in the same place this time, but as we walked out through a picnic area, we saw them again. They were digging in the garbage cans and dumpsters and trying to grab people's food. Some park rangers were present and using their sticks to scare them away. But even the rangers looked frightened; we could see they were trying to keep their distance.

> Jacky: I think people have done this to themselves by feeding the baboons in the past. The animals have no fear of humans and they know we carry food. When the sign says "Don't feed the wild animals," DON'T!

BEARLY THERE

Depending on what region we were in, we had to look out for different kinds of animals. In Alaska, we were always conscious of the bear population, so we did things to lower the chances of a bear problem. As stated earlier, we hung our food in a tree, cooked away from our tent, and took our bike helmets into our tent at night, so that if we were attacked by a bear, we could at least protect our heads.

One night, we were camping alone in an open area of this campground, tucked in for the night, when we started hearing sounds outside the tent. We heard something lapping up water and sniffing around the tent. Then it started rubbing up against the tent. We were sure it was a bear.

For hours and hours, this beast circled the tent while we sat in there wearing our helmets, waiting for this animal to attack or go away. Finally, the sounds stopped and we were able to, somewhat comfortably, fall asleep.

In the morning, we woke up to find a stray dog walking around the area. We then realized our bear scare was actually a stray dog!

We felt silly, but a little further down the road, we met up with another biker who told us a similar story. He was camping and he thought he heard a bear in the campground. He had pushed the emergency button on his Spot satellite tracker to send an alert that he needed help. Then he saw it was just a dog, so he cancelled the call for help. It turned out that he was staying at the same campground that we had been at previously with that same stray dog. That dog was scaring everyone to death.

We did see black bears during our trip, mostly coming down the Alaskan Highway. We spotted eleven altogether. The last one was in Michigan, in our last month of the trip.

> Jacky: While bicycling in Michigan, we didn't expect to see any bear, but that bear surprised me so much that I slammed on my brakes and Ward ran right into the back of my bike. Ward said I needed to relax but, but, but the bear was only thirty feet away! I also scolded Ward for running into the back of my bike. Couldn't he see the bear?

> Ward: This was one of those times when I got upset that Jacky did not use her calm critical thinking attitude. Just for the fact that you are startled, don't do something unpredictable that can hurt others or yourself (life lesson).

CHAPTER THIRTY-FOUR

ARCTIC CIRCLE 66.6 DEGREES, YOU'RE INVITED!

Not to be confused with a "hell" ride (or maybe you should ask our friends) but 66.6 degrees is the latitude of the Arctic Circle.

CLOSEST OF FRIENDS—LITERALLY. CAN CLOSE FRIENDS REALLY GET CLOSER?

One of Ward's goals was to ride his bicycle to the Arctic Circle. We would have done it in Norway, but the timing didn't allow it, so we decided to try it on our tour through Alaska.

> Ward: I really wanted to go to the Arctic Circle. It was just one of my goals. (When you start a trip, you set mental goals. Mine were to ride to the Arctic Circle, go to the most southern city in the world, see the Great Wall of China, ride across the Golden Gate Bridge, and ride into Washington, D.C.)

> Jacky: I didn't have a great desire to ride to the Arctic Circle,

but that's because the initial plan involved only Ward and I biking it, alone...along the Dalton Highway, which is very hilly, all gravel, and rumored to involve grizzly bears. It didn't sound very appealing to me. We had no protection and we would be tenting.

I was, however, willing to drive a motor home or a vehicle. When I said that, Ward was all over it, because he wanted to invite a few friends along.

The Dalton Highway is the haul road for the Alaskan pipeline. There are very few roads in Alaska; this is the one that takes you from Fairbanks to Prudhoe Bay. It had a fair amount of truck traffic because it was the only road available supplying the oil fields of the north slope. This road was in some of the early episodes of the "Ice Road Truckers." According to many travel sites, the Dalton Highway is in the top ten most dangerous roads in America. The mud, steep grades, and avalanches give it this distinction. On our bikes using granny gear is not so bad. But Jacky had to use "granny gear" on the motor home as well.

Ward: I thought the route would be a tough sell to my friends. I said, "Do you want to go to the Arctic Circle? It'll be one of your worst experiences you'll ever have. It'll be cold, wet, and rainy. Your days will be spent fighting mosquitoes, black flies, and muddy roads."

Six friends said, "Sure!" (Frank Polari, Thunder Bay, Ontario, Canada; Joanne Snow, Madison, Wisconsin; Mark Pernitz, Madison, Wisconsin; Paul Scanlon and his daughter, Kelsey, from Rochester, Minnesota; Jeff Freidhof, Decorah, Iowa)

Some flew to Fairbanks with their own bikes; others rented

bikes there. We rented a thirty-foot motor home that was designed for six people, so with eight it was a little crowded, but we're among friends, right? Frank, our buddy (also met us in Rwanda and Thailand), joined us and brought a screened-in tent so we could spend time outside without the mosquitoes attacking us too badly.

The close quarters didn't give us much privacy. We joked with our friends that as the only married couple, we should be afforded special marital privileges at the Arctic Circle. Maybe they could all wait outside the motor home for twenty minutes. Our friend Mark, who is a lawyer, said, "What are you going to do with the extra eighteen minutes?"

Ward: That is a standing joke now. At first, I said I would smoke a cigarette. Now, we just laugh as we share the story and list of all the things we could do in eighteen minutes. And no, we were not granted the twenty minutes.

Jacky: We couldn't put them through the misery of standing outside that long. The mosquitoes were the size of quarters. Everyone was doing the mosquito dance as they were jumping around, waving their arms and legs and hitting themselves trying to conquer the mosquito invasion and shoo them away. We all had mosquito head nets on; everyone was always swarmed with mosquitoes the moment they stepped outside. Because there were eight of us in the motor home, we collectively decided to use outside toilets or nature when "Mother Nature" called. Jacky, Kelsey, and Joanne complained about this. They said that it wasn't fair because when they squatted, the mosquitos would just swarm around their bottoms. It was very difficult to do your business and simultaneously shoo the mosquitos away. Frank, in a rather philosophical way, contemplated on what would hurt more when swatting a mosquito that had landed on the end of his penis. The bite or the swat? Cycling, we found that there was a certain speed at which the mosquitoes wouldn't attack you. We called it Anti-Mosquito Speed, or AMS. This was great for mosquitos but the black flies could fly faster and also had a bigger bite. Climbing the hills of the Dalton Highway, one and a half miles at an 8 percent grade, you couldn't go fast enough to escape constant bombardment.

LAST BEER STOP?

It wasn't all grueling, though. We were all of the same mindset concerning the need to stop for refreshments—specifically beer—after a day's ride through heat, mountains, and dust. Just as we finished the 155-mile bike ride up the Dalton Highway to the Arctic Circle, we were told that the most northern bar in North America was only an additional sixty miles north. We had enough of our own beer supply that we bought from Walmart in Fairbanks that averaged fifty cents a can. The price at the bar for a can of beer ended up being more than six dollars. But, if you can, you have to experience the most northern bar in North America! Of course, we had to go there. (Years later, we did find out it wasn't the most northern bar in North America. We're glad we didn't know that then because it made for a great experience and a good story.)

The bar was in the town of Coldfoot, one of the camp towns set up for workers building the pipelines. The bar parking lot doubled as the town airport's runway, which was gravel. At one time, there was worker housing there, but that was no longer being used when we were there. Instead of seeing camps along the highway, we saw pumping stations that help move the oil from Prudhoe Bay to Valdez. Cyclists follow this route knowing they can stop at the pumping stations and find people, food, and water. They're not designed as rest stops, but that's how they're used. Many cyclists will start in Prudhoe Bay and venture to Argentina. We did many sections of this route only in reverse.

En route to the fabled northernmost watering hole, we passed by a stream that caught Ward's eye. He had to try the fishing.

> Ward: I said, "I think I'm going to stop here and fish. The rest of you guys ride on ahead. I'll just jump in the motor home when I'm done and meet you at the bar." The fishing was

great; I was catching Arctic grayling, which is from the trout family. I had five fresh fish in my hands after half an hour, so I was thrilled. And also nervous. I realized I was almost two hundred yards from the road, carrying fresh fish. I thought, "I'm bear meat." My little fillet knife didn't offer much protection against a grizzly.

Luckily, no bears caught the scent of dinner in the air, and I made it back to the motor home and then to the bar. I pulled out the charcoal grill and grilled up the fish in the parking lot that afternoon, right behind the motor home, for everyone to enjoy.

Our impromptu fish dinner that day brought a gentleman out of the bar to ask if we had any extra beer in our cache. The Coldfoot bar didn't allow any take-outs. That's in an attempt to help control the alcohol consumption of the oil workers in Prudoe Bay. (The heavy machinery and dangerous nature of oil drilling required a very high level of sobriety.) So, we took an inventory and determined that we had two spare cases of beer we had bought at the Fairbanks Walmart for fifteen dollars a case. We said we'd let him have two cases for thirty dollars. He paid us eighty. We tried to tell him we only paid thirty for both of them, but it was worth the extra to him just to be able to have the beer at home and not have to drive to Fairbanks to buy it. He said he had paid a hundred dollars for a case before. When you are thirsty, you are thirsty. We used the extra money for gas. Afternoon and into the evening itself became an odd concept in the Arctic, because the sun never set. We were there the fourteenth of June. The sun was always in the sky; we didn't know when to eat. Sleeping wasn't as much of a problem as it might have been, because we were always exhausted. We just slept when we were tired.

Jacky: I didn't actually bike to the Arctic Circle, but driving the motor home, I was in heaven. Being a dietitian, I enjoy cooking, and it gave me a chance to do that. I had not cooked regular meals for two years. I planned a menu for the whole trip. It was fun for me to sit and cook for these guys. They really appreciated it and the real hit was the breakfast burritos.

TEACH A BLIND MAN TO...SHOOT A GUN?

Our friend Frank, who is legally blind, was such a good sport on this trip. He had three goals, ride to the Arctic Circle, drive the motor home, and shoot a gun. We did our best to accommodate him.

We had two guns with us in the Arctic, to protect us from the bears, so it wasn't too hard to set up some targets to practice with. We found a safe, open area and set up a target. We let Frank have at it. Here was a blind guy shooting a gun in the Arctic Circle. He loved it.

To complete Frank's bucket list, we also let him drive the motor home when we were in Denali National Park. He drove us through a parking lot asking, "How am I doing? How am I doing?"

Frank was undaunted by his disability, which could have gotten him into some trouble. The first day of the trip, it became clear that we had to watch out for him. After Jacky filmed our launch preparations and interviewed us, everybody jumped on their bikes and headed north down the road. So did Frank, only he went the wrong way, south. He explained, "I couldn't see anybody!"

Jacky: I was yelling, "Frank, Frank, you're going the wrong way!"

The constant daylight made it hard to know when to stop for the night. We could be riding along and someone would say, "Maybe we should stop." Someone else would ask why, completely unaware of how many hours had passed. "Well, because it's midnight."

The long hours of daylight also gave road workers more time to get work done. On this one day we came upon some road workers. We stopped to chat because we saw so few people on the Dalton Highway. They were from the lower forty-eight and just working in Alaska for the extra monetary premium. A couple of the workers were in college and were also musicians. It did not take much coaxing of Frank to pull out his harmonica, and the two musicians started playing music. Oh yes, they were working and did not have instruments, but by taking their hands and a couple sticks to create a beat, we were jamming to a "Dalton Highway melody." You don't get that in the milepost book.

CHAPTER THIRTY-FIVE

MILEPOSTS: CYCLING THE AL-CAN HIGHWAY

The trip from Alaska down through Canada was one of our most challenging times. We rode the very remote Al-Can Highway, knowing all the while we shared the surrounding wilderness with all sorts of creatures: bears, bisons, wolves, and the most unliked...the nickel-size mosquitos.

We had heard of bears mauling women who were having their menstrual cycles, so we wondered how to handle that. Garbage stayed on our bikes for days sometimes, until we could find a dumpster to throw it in. We weren't sure it was wise to carry used menstrual products in those bags.

Jacky: I just couldn't imagine having to deal with that. There was one way I could avoid it, though, so I emailed my doctor back home at the Decorah hospital that I had previously worked at for ten years, and asked for a two-month birth control prescription. My doctor called it in to the pharmacy in Watson Lake, Yukon Territory, which was the next biggest town we were coming to. Watson Lake is a long way from nowhere and prices are high, but the price for a two-month supply totally floored me. Three hundred dollars!!

I left the pharmacy without them. I went back in. I went back out. I just couldn't make up my mind! This is a lot of money! Do I spend this huge amount? Finally, I decided I had to, and went in and bought them. It really helped, because I didn't have that worry with camping on the side of the road as that was a frequent occurrence. Without the birth control pills, it would have been super scary for me, and would have put Ward in danger, too.

Even though Alaska is part of the United States, it often felt like we were staying in a foreign country because it was so separated from the rest of the United States. As usual, we loved staying with the locals. We got to a little village called Midway around noon one day and happened upon a small store with a very inviting front porch. Several folks sat on the porch talking, so we joined right in.

Our midday stop was prompted by the possibility of catching fish in the nearby stream. The gentlemen who were sitting on the porch indicated the midday fishing was poor, but that early evening fishing would be much more fruitful. Even so, Ward decided to give the midday fishing a try. Jacky went along as she was on "bear watch" duty. Ward did not have any luck as predicted by the locals. However, they were willing to take him fishing that evening. This would mean that we were finished cycling for the day and would need a place to set up camp at the local store. The store owner offered us accommodations in a renovated school bus that sat behind the store. The bus reminded us of the type of buses used in the television show *M.A.S.H.* The owner's wife, unsure of his fishing ability, also said that if he didn't catch any fish, she would pull some halibut and salmon out from the freezer so we could all share an evening meal together. This became a "no brainer." Yes, we accept!

As Ward waited for evening to come to get his fishing lesson, he became anxious just sitting around, so he asked if there was anything to do around the store to help out. The owner said that if we wanted to, we could spray paint the old school bus that we'd be staying in. We very happily jumped at the opportunity to help out and paint the bus.

The evening fishing went the same as the afternoon fishing, no luck. We were then treated to a wonderful dinner of salmon and halibut. We found ourselves very fortunate to have this warm hospitality as our dinner conversation was about the Alaskan way, and how they handle people that aren't willing to fit in. They are apt to run you right out of town.

Ward: One of the stories was when the United States government had started restricting hunting at one of the nearby national parks. This was land where people hunted for moose and caribou for subsistence, until the government built up a hunting resort area and started flying in special guests to use the land instead of letting the locals access it. They flew wealthy guests in by helicopter to hunt, while denying a vital food source to the people who lived there. The locals didn't appreciate this change at all. So, they burned down this exclusive hunting resort.

Jacky: They burned it down three times!

Ward: This is part of daily life for them, to be able to go out and hunt food. They just said, "No. This isn't how it works here in Alaska." Finally, the US government officials just said, "Okay, fine," and opened up the land again for hunting.

We, on the other hand, were welcomed with open arms. We offered to pay for camping, but the owners at the Midway store wouldn't let us do that. Us painting the bus served as payment for camping.

Alaska was full of unexpected moments. We learned how kids carry guns to school for protection from moose, wolves, and bears, something you never see in the lower forty-eight. This was the wilderness.

They also told how the junk cars and trucks that we saw in people's yards on a daily basis weren't a sign of poverty but a testimony of true wealth. The Alaskans with lots of spare parts on hand are counted as rich, because they have everything they need on their front lawn and there is no need to trek to Fairbanks or Anchorage to get something as small as a bolt or a screw.

It was great to spend time with these people in Midway, because the distance between towns in Alaska and on the Alaskan Highway was huge. Some cities were up to four hundred miles apart. With so much time on the road we yearned to visit with other people. It's no wonder the whole place feels like a different country altogether. People told us that visitors often ask questions like they've wandered into a foreign land. "How do you say 'milk' up here?" and "What is your currency?" were common questions.

Ward: Those were some long, hot days of biking. I said to Jacky, "Normally, we do sixty miles a day, and that means taking over seven days to get to the next town; if we increase the mileage up to ninety miles a day, it'll only take five."

Jacky: I said we could do that as long as we could then have two days off the bike once we got to the town. I called it "civilization rejuvenation!" My most favorite and most exciting moments were when I saw power lines! That meant a town was not that far away. Once in a town, I took it all in. It was fun to go to the grocery store, actually use a laundromat, talk to others, and just relax and be settled for a day.

Ward: She did not like the long days but with twenty hours of sunlight and mosquitoes and wildlife it wasn't too hard to sell her on pushing hard to the next town. Sometimes she just needs that carrot out there to push forward, or a kick in the ass.

With the distances, we tried to stock up on enough food to get us to the next town. We bought four pounds of pasta, bread, cheese, and various seasoning packets to be made into sauces. Perishable items such as fresh meat, milk, and eggs were not part of our diet. Also, the cost of those items was quite prohibitive. However, we were able to carry cabbage and carrots, as they are a hardier vegetable and could withstand the heat and the constant rumble of the road. It was impossible to carry enough food on the bikes, so we had to get creative. As stated earlier, sometimes when we saw motor homes stopped on the side of the road at a lookout point or in a campground, we struck up a conversation with the travelers and asked if we could buy some food from them. We always tried to pay, even if it was just for a can of beans or a loaf of bread, but almost everybody just gave us the food.

Even when we thought we had reached a town that had food, we would often be wrong. We used a milepost book that told us what was available coming up the road, and we'd get excited when it looked like a store was nearby. Very often, though, it turned out to be closed. We felt we were in luck one day when we found a bakery/restaurant open. When we went inside to buy a loaf of bread, they would not sell it to us. They said they only make enough bread for their restaurant. If we bought a sandwich, then we would get the two pieces of bread that came with it. We couldn't afford their very high prices and declined. A bison burger was fifteen dollars. Maybe we'll get lucky up the road. All we wanted was a loaf of bread!

We could wait for food but not water. Luckily, there were streams all over and we had a purifying system for drinking water. We were using a system called Pristine. Two drops of this and one drop of this and you had potable water. We didn't need Giardia, Cryptosporidium or any bacteria or viruses giving us problems.

The improved road conditions and the high fuel cost had a devastating effect on the stores. It's contradictory to think that the better road conditions would cause stores to close, but what it did was to allow vehicles to make less needed stops. The early days of the Alaskan Highway had roads that were very rough gravel, but today only a few sections remain in that condition. The improved roads make travel much quicker. The motor homes that are on the road can now make it from town to town pretty easily, so they don't need to stop as often as they used to. Also, the few remaining stores that were open saw a dramatic increase in bathroom usage. The store owners found that all the extra bathroom usage taxed their septic systems and the regulations to get new systems were very stringent and expensive. Store owners were forced to close because their septic systems could not keep up and they couldn't afford to fix them. Therefore, travelers had to purchase something from the store before they could use the bathroom. In regard to the high price of diesel fuel, it caused less vacationers. It was also the only fuel source that served to run the generators for the stores' electrical needs, which became cost prohibitive.

CHAPTER THIRTY-SIX

GRAND CANYON: WHEN YOU THINK YOU HAVE IT ALL FIGURED OUT

From the outside, it always looked like our trip was ad hoc; that we'd find a place on the fly and pitch a tent. But we typically always had some sort of calculated plan. With the stringent rules of camping at the bottom of the Grand Canyon, very deliberate planning needed to be done.

We wanted to go down into the canyon and see it from all angles, but getting a reservation at Phantom Ranch to camp at the bottom isn't that easy. Would-be campers had to apply six months in advance, and even if you called that early, it was unlikely that you would get a spot. On the other hand, we had heard that if you arrived at the Grand Canyon without a reservation, you could get in a rotating queue for a daily permit if you were willing to go back day after day to see if your number came up.

We arrived four days early. The next morning we went to the

Ranger's Office to get in line to register for camping permits. We were given number eleven for that day. Then we worked our way down to number seven the next day. Then three the following day. We knew the next day was going to be our turn to get a permit.

> Ward: All this time, I was talking with the permit lady, saying I needed two nights for six people because our friends from Madison and Thunder Bay would be joining us.

> Jacky: On the fourth day, we figured we were going to get the permit, so Ward went to the Ranger's Office alone. He ended up seeing the same woman that he saw the previous mornings and got the permit. We found out later that Ward had made a mistake, or the permit lady made a mistake.

Kay and Harry from Madison and AnnaMarie and Denise from Thunder Bay joined us for the nine-mile hike to the bottom. We took the South Kaibab route down, because it's less crowded; however, it was more rugged and rustic, which made it more difficult as we were carrying our packs and all our camping gear, cooking gear, food, and beverages besides water. It wasn't like the popular Bright Angel trail, which has steps most of the way down. Where we were, if you stepped wrong, you could go right over the edge to a tragic death or very severe injury. We were glad to have walking poles to help keep our balance.

You carry all your food in and all of your trash out of the canyon. This made our calculated packing tricky; we didn't want to have a lot of cans and garbage to haul back out with us. Boxed wine, however, seemed like a no-brainer because the collapsible bladder (without the box) just gets smaller as you drink the wine. Of course, we had to have beer, too, and there may have been a bottle of whiskey and some margaritas tucked away as well.

Climbing down into the canyon was the hardest part of the trip because of the weight. It's like climbing downstairs; you're always putting the brakes on, bracing yourself. Your calves and quads aren't used to that braking action. This type of training does not occur on the bike.

October is prime time to do this, because it's cooler. Other times of the year, it can get up to one hundred degrees down in the canyon. The temperature on our hike probably only got into the eighties. Perfect.

Most people don't ever see the base of the Grand Canyon. A very, very small percentage ever hike to the bottom. It was well worth the effort though. When you get to the bottom, you cross a footbridge over the Colorado River before getting to the campsites. You could only get down there one of two ways: ride a mule or hike.

> Ward: You could tell the people who had hiked down and back up. They all had this kind of shuffle walk in their legs. Our calves were so tight that it looked like the walk of the zombies.

We made it down, though, and set up our cozy campsite—two tents for six people. Later that first evening while we were cooking dinner, the campground ranger came by. He needed to see our camping permit. No problem; it was hanging right outside our tent, visible at all times just like we were instructed. The ranger was friendly, and we joked around with him, calling him "Ranger Rick" and generally having a good time.

The next day, we hiked six miles up to Ribbon Falls, which was refreshing to do without packs on. The walking helped unkink those sore muscles from the day before. It was a little bit of a challenge, as we had to cross some small streams, but we just took our shoes off to walk through it so they'd be dry for the hike out the canyon the following day.

Back at the campsite, we were quite pleased with ourselves, cooking up dinner and celebrating our hiking prowess. It only made sense to drain the wine, whiskey, and beer rather than lug all that liquid back to the top of the south rim. Water was the only liquid we needed for the following day. Along came Ranger Rick again, so we offered him a drink. No, he didn't want that. He was back to validate our permit for that night. We said, "Sure, it's on the tent." However, when he inspected it, he stated it was not valid for that evening. Our permit was only for one night, not two.

Ward: I go, "Oh." Then everyone's looking at me.

Jacky: I said, "No, we had it for two nights. We paid such and such amount." And he's like, "No, that's only for one night. You're lucky there's one space available down here tonight or I would make you pack up and hike out now."

Ward: It was dark and we were tired. Mentally and physically, we weren't ready for the climb out.

Ranger Rick wasn't so nice to us after that. He was adamant that he would have the office check on us on the way out to be sure we paid for the second night. We were just glad we didn't have to get a move on right at that moment. There was no way we were prepared to cope with carrying our gear and navigating the trails at that point, especially in the dark.

It wasn't much easier the next day. As a consequence of crossing the waterways barefoot the day before, Jacky's toes had gotten badly infected.

Jacky: Every toe hurt. Even the weight of a sheet on top of them was really painful. "How am I going to hike out?" Plus, our muscles were so sore we could hardly walk. Luckily, we had our hiking poles with us. Still, it was a pretty miserable hike out.

Ward: Even Denise, who is a bodybuilder and was always telling us how tough she was, said, "I don't want to play this game anymore." It was rough. Our friend, Kay, laughed and said to her, "You don't look so intimidating now."

Halfway up at the Bright Angel campground we all rested and even a few shorts naps were enjoyed. We were beat and we had pushed our limits to the max.

As brutal as it was to hike out with the lingering effects of consuming all of our adult beverages, with very sore muscles and infected toes, the canyon itself was truly one of the wonders of the world. We can honestly say that, because we've seen so many beautiful places.

Ward: I had seen the Grand Canyon while flying over it, but actually seeing it...just standing on the edge...it kind of brings me to tears because it was just such a grand sight. I was going, "Wow, millions of years of water going through here. How does this happen?" The colors were truly amazing.

Jacky: We got up one morning while we were camping on the rim to view the sunrise. The colors were surreal. Prettier than any photograph of the canyon that I have ever seen. The Grand Canyon, one of the Seven Wonders of the World, is a must-see.

CHAPTER THIRTY-SEVEN

PEDALING FOR PENCILS

When we started our trip, people frequently asked us if we were riding for a cause, such as a cancer charity. We didn't start out with a cause, and although cancer causes were meaningful to us, we wanted to support something that was directly related to our experience. As we went along, we thought more and more about how we could share our incredible experience with others. We were having such an extraordinary journey, we felt like we wanted to give back somehow.

When we got to Chile, the perfect program fell into place. We were staying with John and Anne Walker, a couple originally from Iowa. As we were sitting with John one day out in his flower garden, we were describing our idea for a program. As we told him we wanted to name it Pedaling For Pencils, he suggested adding Write to Remember. Anne is a schoolteacher, so she arranged for us to present a few programs at her school to tell the kids about our trip. After each talk, we gave out pencils for the students to write their own stories and dreams. That's how Pedaling for Pencils: Write to Remember was born.

Pedaling for Pencils had several layers: We talked about how we wrote things down to plan our trip and make our dreams come true, as well as to remember the trip after we did it. We emphasized to the students that with simple tools like a pencil and a piece of paper, they could achieve their goals, too. They could write poems, draw pictures, solve math problems, or write music. Whatever inspired them could be strengthened by putting pencil to page.

We took Pedaling for Pencils to schools in several countries. One memorable program was in New Zealand, where Rotarians Lynn and Barry Williams hosted us for a few days and organized a series of school visits for us. We went to ten schools in a four-day period to share our message with kids. So many kids heard our story and received pencils that we actually bought the town out of pencils. We had to go to a neighboring town to buy more. Barry came running in at the end of one program to deliver the new batch of pencils. What a great problem!

Barry arranged for us to speak at all grade levels, but the most engaged students were probably the youngest. Some of the smaller grade school kids were completely charmed by our stories. They came up to us afterwards and asked, "Can you sign my pencil?" It's not easy to write your name on a pencil, but these children were so eager to share a memory with us, we did our best. Once, when we went to a library between talks to work on our website, a young boy came in and said, "I was at your talk! I saw your bikes outside. Look, I'm riding my bike!"

Another special time was when we were in New Orleans. Ward's cousin, Russ Carll, lived there and lined up three different schools for us to present at. He came to each presentation with us. By the third school, he said, "I think I could give this talk." This is the second time that we were able to meet up with Russ and his wife Angela. The first time was in Loire Valley, France, when they rented two Gites and invited friends and family to come and enjoy this time with them. It was very special and we feel very blessed to have had those experiences and memories with them, as since our trip ended, Russ has passed away from cancer.

In South America, we got the chance to see some of the students' written work. After Machu Picchu, we spoke with a school group and asked them to write down what they dreamed about. We kept those written dreams and mailed them back home to Decorah.

The students wrote about their aspirations as rural people of Peru; the overriding theme was that they hoped to work in tourism, where there were more opportunities than in the rest of their economy. Students' responses to the "dreams" assignment were different in different places, though. In New Zealand, we received more answers along the lines of, "I want to write a book." Or, "I want to be a doctor or a farmer."

The kids themselves, however, were essentially the same everywhere. Kids are kids no matter whether they live in Peru or Chile or New Zealand or Asia or Decorah, Iowa. We asked them what they did after school; they told us they hung out with their friends. What did they do when they hung out? They played soccer, played with their pet, or listened to music. Everywhere we went, the children had the same answers.

South Korea was one of the few exceptions. Starting fairly young, the South Korean students said they wanted to learn English. They were less focused on entertainment and play and more motivated to do well in school. Once they got to high school age, especially, the South Korean students were quite serious and diligent about their studies. They all said, "Well, if we want to get into a college, we have to study." There was no more PlayStation or just looking at your Facebook.

Pedaling for Pencils opened a lot of doors for us to meet kids and learn about education in different parts of the world.

Jacky: To date, we've given out over five thousand pencils. Kids are so happy to receive them, even though we didn't have special pencils made with our names on them or anything. We would buy them as we needed them, so we wouldn't have to carry them. The pencils are a symbol to dream!

Ward: The special pencils were very expensive and not practical for us to carry. Rotary was going to sponsor us and get us pencils, but they ended up costing twenty-five cents apiece. In other places, we could get them for three to five cents apiece.

We didn't need them monogrammed and just having them shipped to us would have been impractical.

In countries where we couldn't speak the language, we stopped and asked kids on their way to school if they could teach us the word for gift. Then we said, "Here is a gift for you," and handed them a pencil as they headed to school. It made us feel good, and it was a lot of fun. It put a smile on their face. In those situations, we had to be sure we had enough pencils for all the kids that were in front of us.

CHAPTER THIRTY-EIGHT

COSTS AND STATISTICS OF THE TRIP

Three years of travel, by the numbers:

MILES BICYCLED: 33,523

Our trip covered more miles than this, but these are the miles we traveled on the bikes. All the air, ferry, bus, and train miles add another forty thousand miles to our adventure.

We had a daily budget of fifty dollars per day for the two of us. In Europe, it was difficult to maintain that budget. If we camped for free, we stayed within budget.

FOOD COSTS: $18,249

The cost for food varied widely around the world. Norway, Denmark, British Columbia, and the Yukon were very expensive, so we prepared most of our own food. We cooked almost everywhere except in Peru, Bolivia, Ecuador, Colombia, Thailand, Cambodia, Laos, Vietnam, China, Mongolia, and South

Korea. This was for two reasons. One, the food was so cheap there you could get a meal for a dollar or two and it would be enough for us to share. Second, camping in these countries was limited and not always safe. We didn't cook if we weren't camping. Cooking in the hostel or hotel was available in some of the places but not all.

BEVERAGE COSTS: $9,401

After a long day on the bicycle, we both enjoy a beer or two or a glass of wine. It relieves the tensions of the road and helps to numb some of the pain of working that hard. Our fifty-dollar-per-day budget was sorely tried in Northern Europe. There, we had a beer once every couple of days and certainly no wine. In British Columbia, they also taxed their alcohol so much it was cost prohibitive. Poland and Slovakia embrace beer and have minimal tax, so it was very cheap and we could enjoy that end-of-the-day beverage without worry. Wines in Italy, France, Spain, Chile, and Argentina were inexpensive and very good. But in a lot of the world the beer was nothing special, and the wine was "so-so" as well. In China, in most areas they only sold the "Great Wall of China" wine, which was not good at all. We didn't see any other wines on the shelves and it was our supposition that they were forming a restrictive import monopoly of sorts for their wine.

At the onset of our trip in Europe we saw everyone buying bottled water so we thought their water was unsafe to drink. So, we also started to buy it. It was very expensive at one Euro ($1.62) for a sixteen-ounce bottle. Later, when we were mentioning this to a gentleman, he laughed and said, "That's only because they are picky with the taste of their water." For a few weeks, we were spending our money foolishly on bottled water!

Beverages also included coffee in the morning when we were not camping and couldn't make it for ourselves or while we were riding and very cold and needed a stop to warm up. In Europe, they sell mostly expressos, which don't offer a large quantity of warmth, so we learned to ask for an American coffee with hot water added to it; that was more of what we wanted and were used to.

HEALTH INSURANCE: $22,500

Even while we were away from our base in Decorah, it was critically important to maintain our health insurance. We did upgrade the insurance to include travelers' insurance. This was the only constant payment we had during our three-year trip (that same insurance coverage for a three-year span now would cost $36,000).

AIRLINE TICKETS: APPROXIMATELY $13,800

Our airline tickets did add up, but the amount we paid seems reasonable. As we stated at the beginning, we vowed to come home for important family events. We never missed one of our boys' Marine Corps deployment leaves. When we were in Alaska, Ross was afraid to give us a date for his leave, because it kept changing. We were a little sly and followed his Facebook postings. He was arranging a date to get together with his friends once back in Iowa. We knew we were safe if we went home over that time period. It worked out and we were able to see him before he left for Iraq.

FLIGHTS TAKEN:

- June 2007: Minneapolis to Frankfurt (start of trip)
- November 2007: Madrid to Rwanda—roundtrip (Rotary Service work)
- December 2007: Lisbon to Minneapolis (returned to Iowa for son John's wedding)
- January 2008: Minneapolis to Costa Rica (Work time for Trek Travel)
- January 2008: Panama City to Bocas del Toro, Panama— roundtrip (mission trip for our church)
- February 2008: Panama City to Sao Paulo, Brazil
- February 2008: Sao Paulo to Ushuia, Argentina
- April 2008: Santiago, Chile to San Diego, California— roundtrip (son Ross's graduation from Marine Corps boot camp)
- September 2008: Bogotá, Columbia to South Carolina (pre-deployment leave for son John)
- October 2008: Minneapolis to Los Angeles
- October 2008: Los Angeles to Auckland, New Zealand
- December 2008: New Zealand to Sydney, Australia
- January 2009: Melbourne, Australia to Bangkok, Thailand
- June 2009: Incheon, South Korea to Anchorage, Alaska
- October 2009: San Francisco to Minneapolis—roundtrip (pre-deployment leave for son Ross)
- November 2009: Dallas to Minneapolis—roundtrip (Thanksgiving with our families in Iowa and Wisconsin)
- January 2010: Orlando, Florida to Minneapolis—roundtrip (funeral of Uncle Maury)
- May 2010: Boston to Minneapolis—roundtrip (wedding of niece)

DONATIONS TO ORPHANAGES AND PEDALING FOR PENCILS: $2,800

These donations included rice and sugar that we purchased in Rwanda to take to the Kigali orphanage. We also paid for the paint necessary to paint the orphanage school in Peru. We gave donations to other orphanages such as one in Hue, Vietnam, and another in Phonsavan, Laos. Besides giving to orphanages, we bought thousands of pencils to give out to children all over the world through our Pedaling for Pencils program.

CAMPING AND HOTELS: $16,595

Staying in campgrounds proved to be the safest and most economical way to travel. The campgrounds of Europe had many different levels of service and wide price differences. In Slovenia, we paid thirty-five dollars just to set up our tent. That only left us fifteen dollars for food and beverages that day and everything was expensive there. In Denmark and Norway, it cost over fifty dollars to stay at a hostel/campground and that, again, was just to put up our tent. However, Slovakia was very reasonable at six dollars per night and the food was very cheap as well. In Slovakia, our daily budget of fifty dollars covered two days.

When we had to return to the US or fly to another continent, it meant we had to fly out of a major city. Therefore, we couldn't camp and had to stay in a hotel. At those times, the hotel or hostel frequently cost over one hundred dollars. Those costs for lodging were very painful to pay. Most people wouldn't think favorably on this, but when we would have a layover at an airport that was an overnight, we were thrilled. That meant we could sleep at the airport and have a night of free lodging!

Passing through New York City, for instance, we used a hotel discount site called Mobissimo to find our best and least expensive option. It was the Comfort Inn Central Park, for eighty dollars a night, which is a steal in New York City.

Our least expensive hotel was in Anta, Peru. It only cost four dollars per night for this filthy place, described earlier.

All in all, the combination of free camping, paid camping, hostels, hotels, and staying at peoples' homes allowed us to rest as we saw the world. Looking back, we could have probably tried harder to do more free camping and more home stays. It was at those times that we had additional experiences with the people and the culture that were so enriching.

We did use "Warm Showers" quite a bit during our last year of circumnavigating the United States. Warm Showers is a hospitality organization for bicyclists. People offering their homes in this organization provide different amenities depending on what they signed up for on the Warm Showers site. Most provide sleeping space inside, while some may want you to camp in the lawn instead. Many will provide meals and let you do your laundry. Through Warm Showers, we met many friendly and intriguing bicyclists, each of them with their own very interesting and inspiring stories to tell.

The Rotary Club also helped us out. Ward, a Rotarian of an international organization, would contact members of Rotary Clubs and ask if anyone could host us for a night. They almost always came through. In fact, after staying a night and them learning of our route, they would call ahead to Rotary members in those towns we planned to stay in to line up additional home stays. It was very comfortable staying with them, as we were all members of this international club. It was like a brotherhood.

Being members of the Elks Lodge also proved to be beneficial. Once we were in the United States, we were able to utilize this organization. We would go into the lodge, have a drink at the bar, visit with the locals and ask if the Elks had space in their lot for us to put up our tent. (It is not uncommon for people to stay with motor homes, etc.) Not all of them had grass to place a tent so this was not always an option. But once the locals got to know us and were more comfortable with us, we were frequently asked to stay at their houses. We made many friends through the Elks.

MAINTENANCE COSTS: $3,000

We went through twenty-four tires, forty spokes, twenty-five inner tubes, five rims, three cassettes, six chains, six pairs of cycling shorts, five pairs of gloves, and one pair of cycling shoes.

We ended up fixing one hundred flat tires during the trip. We had a system to help keep track. Whenever we'd have a flat tire, we would write the date and number of the flat on the new inner tube itself or on its fresh patch.

> Ward: I would never put a fifth patch on a tube. If it had four patches on it that was enough. We figured with five patches the probability of a leak was much higher.

> Jacky: Can you believe we changed one hundred flat tires?

> Ward: We? You only changed one. Does that count as we?

Jacky: Well, when "we" clean the house together and you wash one dish, does that count as "we?" You seem to think so!

In reality, we were a tire-changing team. Ward started by taking off the wheel and removing the tube and tire, and then he would inspect the tire to determine the cause of the flat. Jacky got out the new tube and pump, and together we searched out the hole on the flat tube. Once the problem spot was identified, Ward replaced the tube and tire and Jacky patched the old tube. So, yes, we did change tires together.

Side bar with photo: Okay, sometimes we had some help from the locals.

One major cost occurred when we accepted the Schwinn Bicycles as part of their marketing campaign (stated earlier in the book). It turned out the hybrid-style bike named World Traveler seemed to have been designed to ride around the block and not around the world. When the drive train and wheels started to fail within the first two weeks because of the extra weight and rigorous riding conditions, it was apparent that $1,800 in upgrades were needed. We were fortunate that our friend Travis, now owner of Decorah Bicycles, made it very easy for us to upgrade our bikes by shipping the necessary parts to us in Australia, where we otherwise would have had a $3,000 bill.

TOTAL COST: $85,000

CHAPTER THIRTY-NINE

"RESEARCH"

For all of the necessary expenses on our trip, there were plenty of opportunities for entertainment as well. One of the surprises was a "sponsorship" that came from a friend in Decorah. He gave us two hundred dollars but not to buy food or bike parts. We weren't even to use it for beer or wine. No, he had something very different in mind. He wanted Ward to research sex and sexuality across the world. This research required general observation and maybe even going behind some closed doors.

Ward: I said, "Jacky, I have to do this. I've been sponsored!"

My research always started on the street. I looked for those situations that appeared to be very genuine—a man being attracted to a woman and vice versa. And then I looked at those that seemed to be driven by an exchange of money. Each country had its nuances.

In Norway, Sweden, and Denmark, sunbathing topless was just part of the culture. It was not unusual to bike past a beach and see women very comfortably and visibly lying topless on their towels. When we were away from the beach, though, they were more conservative, with men and women dressing more modestly. Also, men and women did not show many signs of public affection. In Latin America, however, touching and signs of affection in public were common. Central European countries had a conservative approach to sex as well; their gentlemen's clubs were very few and served as the front for brothels.

To get the best information, I went to a brothel in Gerona, Spain. If you are going to get the facts, then you should go straight to the source, right?

Upon entering what I first thought was a strip club, I ordered a fifteen-dollar Heineken, and within a few minutes a young lady approached me and asked if I wanted to go upstairs. I said, "No," and continued to drink my beer. Only a few moments later, another lady approached me and asked if I wanted to go upstairs. Again, I said, "No." I originally thought this was going to be similar to an American gentlemen's club where there was a floor show. Then a third lady approached me and asked if I wanted to go upstairs. Normally, our rule was, "If they ask three times, then you accept." Did the same rules apply? Nope! But now as it was the third time, I had to ask what was the going rate to go upstairs. I was amazed that it was only twenty-five Euros to have sex (thirty-seven dollars and fifty cents or two and a half beers). This was for sure a time to refuse hospitality. I finished my beer and got out of there as quickly as I could.

Later that evening, Jacky was interested in the results of my research. I told her that I was not very comfortable in that environment. That it was a front for a brothel. After explaining the details of the establishment, I told her that the going rate for sex was only twenty-five Euros. I probably should not have told her that because now when we want to be intimate, I get that whisper in my ear, "Twenty-five Euros, please."

GET A ROOM

Motels in Chile, South America, presented a unique situation. When we wanted to rent a motel room, we were often asked how many hours we wanted the room for. We indicated the whole night, but this was not the norm. Rooms were rented by the hour. Chile was very open about these types of motels— they were called "love motels." They often had a large heart as the entrance sign. These hotels were interspersed throughout the country, both in the metro and rural areas of Chile. We thought that people staying in these rooms were having sex for money or having a quick fling. With frequent customers, we questioned how clean the room was. It didn't seem to fit our morals. We did find out that these rooms were rented for sex but for guests to have sexual privacy, not necessarily for money, although there was some prostitution. South Korea had some similar type hotels and again we were asked how many hours we wanted to rent it for. The rooms came with sex gels, condoms, and all the primping tools you could ever want—the necessary perfumes, cosmetics, blow dryer, curling iron, and hairspray to put yourself back together after a mid-afternoon rendezvous. We were not sure that these were issues of prostitution but more the concept of having a mistress.

SELLING SEX

The Argentinians sure liked their lingerie. Even small towns in Argentina had numerous lingerie shops. They were all over the place. It was just part of the culture and something we didn't see in other countries.

The Peruvians showed their sexuality in a completely different way. The signs for gasoline included a poster of a bikini-clad woman; it also included the price of the fuel. It seemed odd that these women were not of Peruvian descent but had Northern European features including blonde hair.

It was interesting, and often disturbing, to see how sex was treated in different cultures. In Southeast Asia, economics was a big factor. Local men could not always compete with Westerners for girlfriends because the Westerners had a lot more money. These older Westerners—many in their forties and fifties—could take very young girls out for dinners, movies, drinks, and shopping. The typical Asian man's resources were nowhere close to providing those luxuries for a lady. It felt weird to see such a young girl with such an older man.

Ward: I'm going, "There's no way she's attracted to him." It was rather repulsive.

Jacky: I felt sorry for the girl and that she had to stoop to that level for a better life.

In Cambodia, we saw a number of "ladies of the night," but they were predominantly outside the bars, not at designated strip joints. However, money still played into it. Also, to our surprise in Phnom Penh, Cambodia, many gas stations had strictly female service attendants and, more surprisingly, were dressed very similarly to waitresses at our "American Hooters" restaurants. They had more business than any other gas stations. Their marketing techniques were working.

In Thailand, we were told that there were high government officials that were kingpins in the sex trafficking. It seemed so far askew from what we are used to in our western culture. We know that it occurs in the US but it's not so blatantly obvious.

DRINK UP

Another thing we had to research was beer. People were always saying, "Oh, if you get to this country, I'll buy a beer for you." We took them up on it. We set up a "Buy Ward a Beer" PayPal icon on our website where people could send us some money to buy Ward a beer. We took a picture of Ward with the beer, showing what kind it was and what country we were in. It was a neat and fun way for people to sponsor us.

> Jacky: Everyone in Decorah knows Ward likes beer. Sometimes, though, we got messages through PayPal saying, "Ward, this is not for you. It's for Jacky. She needs a glass of wine."

People loved to hear from us on the road. It was a friendly way for them to sponsor us, and PayPal made it easy. Lots of people sent extra money, for instance, to sponsor a day's food, beverages, and camping. It was a nice connection between us and people **who** wanted to follow and support our trip. We had around three thousand dollars come through the PayPal account, which may not seem like a lot over three years, but it sure helped.

> Ward: I ranked the beers on a scale of one to five as I went along. The best was at the Hofbräuhaus in Munich. I gave it a five. It may have been a situational rating, though, because our son Ross was with us, which made it really special.

At the Hofbräuhaus, the waitresses were a little more robust and could carry three to six one-liter steins in each hand. The beer was oh, so good! I like lager beer that's not too hoppy, not like craft beer. It shouldn't be snobby, but pure. Germany had some of the best, most pure-tasting beer.

The Southern Argentinian beer, Quilmes, and the Chilean, Austral, were very good as well, but they actually trace their lineage back to German brewmasters who escaped Germany after World War II. I could always find a German ancestry to the best beers. (At that time, our trip was not inclusive of Belgium and other countries that are well known for their beer.)

The worst beer, on the other hand, was one I had to pour out. Nobody could believe I would ever do that, but it was in Rwanda, and it was banana beer. I just couldn't drink it; it was sweet and syrupy.

The percentage of alcohol in the beers was wildly different depending on where we were. In China, the beer called "Snow" has 1.9 percent alcohol. It tasted like alcohol-flavored water. Snow beer is one of the most-consumed beers in the world, only because there are so many Chinese and this is their beer of choice.

Lithuania had a choice of alcohol content, 9 percent, 12 percent, and 14 percent beer, though you apparently had to earn your stripes to get a taste of the high-test stuff.

Ward: I went up to the bartender and pointed to the 14 percent. He wouldn't serve it to me. He gave me a glass of 9 percent. The locals, though, came in with empty two-liter bottles that the bartender gladly filled up with 14 percent. I guess I needed to prove myself.

As mentioned, our website had an icon that featured a beer mug that followers could click on to buy Ward a beer. When they clicked on it, the beer mug turned upside down and emptied. With this, and the pictures of beers enjoyed all around the world, it was like saying "cheers" to all our friends as we traveled.

CHAPTER FORTY

LESSONS LEARNED

We knew we would ask a lot of questions on our trip, but two we never expected to ask, or ask so often, were, "Are there bugs on my face?" and "Is there sugar in it?"

The first question came from our diligence with sunscreen. Biking for three years means applying lots and lots of sunscreen. The residue from these lotions, unfortunately, made our faces a bit sticky. When we whizzed along, little gnats got stuck to our faces.

> Ward: Jacky was always asking me, "Are there bugs on my face?"

> Jacky: He wouldn't always tell me and I'd go into a store and go to the bathroom just speckled with bugs. Gross and embarrassing!

The other question came up a lot in Brazil where sugarcane was so abundant. They seem to put sugar in everything from coffee to avocado shakes to making a Caipirinha cocktail.

CAIPIRINHA COCKTAIL RECIPE

2 oz Cachaça

1/2 to 2 tsp sugar

1/2 lime

Squeeze lime and mix with sugar in glass.

Add ice and cachaça.

(Cachaca is similar to rum but instead of making it with molasses, it's made with the juices of pure sugarcane.)

AVOCADO SHAKE RECIPE

1/2 avocado

1-1/2 cups milk

1/2 cup ice

3 Tbsp sugar

(Some add sweetened condensed milk.)

In Vietnam, your cup of coffee is half coffee and half sweetened condensed milk.

> Jacky: I don't put sugar in my coffee. In Brazil and Vietnam, I couldn't get just plain black coffee, even when I asked for it! They put sugar in everything and I am not a sweet lover.

> Ward: She kept saying, "I want something without sugar!" (I agreed with her. She doesn't need sugar in her coffee because she is already sweet enough.)

UNEXPECTED LESSONS LEARNED

One lesson we learned, everywhere we went, was that we

should not try to instill our standards on others. We were wrong to assume that they would be happier living like we do, because it just wasn't true. As long as they had food, shelter, and safety, people all over the world were just as happy as we were. We seem to have it all in the United States, with our material things; we think others need it, but they don't.

For instance, one day we were biking down the road in Peru and came across two kids having a great time playing in a pile of dirt. We said, "Look at how happy they are. Why do we think that they would be happier living like us?"

In Laos, we saw two little boys, maybe two or three years old, playing with a pair of plastic grocery sacks. They filled the sacks up with water and poured them over each other's heads. They stood there naked, dumping water on each other, for about half an hour. They were having a blast. Their enjoyment was just so pure we had to take a picture.

We also learned how important it is to pay attention to our intuition. If we felt that a place wasn't safe, even if the reason wasn't obvious, it was worth changing plans. One campground was very packed with campers and people just picnicking for the day as it was a holiday. We ended up having to set up camp in a more remote area. We had many people still around us until dusk, when they went home. At the time, it felt very eerie.

Jacky: I lay in our tent and listened to cars on a desolate road behind us slowly passing by. Would they see our tent and stop to bother us or would they not see our tent? Did we run the risk of repeating Sweden's near miss?

Ward might have been fine with it, but I had a really bad feeling about it. We packed up all our stuff and moved to be closer to some other campers in the campground. (I should have also trusted my intuition the day we got into the scammer's taxicab in Peru.)

We found that most people wanted to help us, but we were aware that some only wanted to help themselves. We just had to learn how to evaluate situations based on a combination of gut feelings and the evidence of how they behaved toward us.

Ward: We found that first impressions could be very misleading when we were dealing with a different culture. Things that looked like a bad situation at first could easily turn out to be quite nice, if we were careful not to jump to conclusions based on our own background.

It could be hard to tell how any situation would turn out. In Mongolia, as we mentioned earlier, we were kind of nervous about taking an old Russian Jeep into the wilderness, but it turned out to be a great three days.

Other times, we entered areas that looked so poverty stricken it made us worried. Maybe we were being judgmental about the poverty or the lack of infrastructure. Yet, some of our best memories came from camping out in the yard of a rundown farmhouse. What looked dubious at first glance often turned out to be a wonderful experience.

People themselves could be a puzzle if we didn't understand their culture. Coming into some Eastern Bloc countries, we thought the people were very unfriendly because none of them smiled or waved. However, if you got to know them, they were warm and friendly people underneath those sullen faces that were trained to be like that while they were under Russian communistic rule.

NEW RULES OF THE ROAD

Several themes became like new rules for us as we traveled. Some of them we still use today. One theme that struck us over and over again is that we were the only ones responsible for making things happen. Now we say, "If you want it to happen, make it happen."

We also learned that it's best not to try to talk if you're more than ten feet apart. This became clear in Argentina, when the winds were so strong. The wind and traffic makes all verbal communication garbled.

Our ten-foot rule merely states, "Do not talk to me unless you are within ten feet."

Jacky: Ward was normally biking in front of me. I'd be telling or asking him something and he wouldn't respond. I would think he was ignoring me, so either I'd yell it again or start to get a little miffed. In reality, he never heard me! After clarifying that problem, we established the ten-foot rule.

Ward: One day, Jacky was riding behind me all day long and she wasn't saying very much—normally she's pretty chatty on the bike—I looked back and saw she was eleven feet behind me. I wasn't sure if she stayed that far back just so she wouldn't have to talk to me.

Jacky: He'll never know.

We still use the ten-foot rule in our house today. We might yell up the stairs or through the house, and the only reply we get back is, "Ten feet!" Better to wait until we're in the same room than spend the day shouting across the house and misunderstanding what is being said. We've come to the conclusion that this rule could be implemented in almost every situation.

Another rule is, "Don't ask for directions to a place more than twenty miles away," because nobody knows them. This was a pervasive problem; it didn't happen only in small, isolated communities. If people did travel more than twenty miles away, they often couldn't give us the directions we needed. They would give us directions using major highways and interstates, as that is the route they take in a vehicle. They would not give us directions using secondary roads. We often had to remind them that we were traveling by bicycle. That didn't seem to help as they (and most people) don't know the names of the secondary roads more than twenty miles away.

When asking locals the distance a town was away, they would often tell us in minutes of driving. It was difficult to convert that to kilometers as we didn't know the speed that they travel. Therefore, we would ask how far it was in kilometers. They were typically off in their estimates. We soon learned that however many kilometers they quoted us, we needed to double it. But whenever we would ask a fellow bicyclist the distance to a town, they were very precise in their kilometers. When telling people of our journey they could comprehend riding our bikes from California to Phoenix, but it was incomprehensible to ride our bikes from the Arctic Circle to Key West, Florida. We believe this is because most people in the United States don't travel much and aren't very knowledgeable about world geography.

Ward: For instance, people asked where we started in the United States and I'd say, "The Arctic Circle." I'd just get blank stares in return. If I mentioned starting one leg of the trip in San Diego, though, people got it.

Jacky: After explaining to people the countries and continents that we bicycled through over the first two years, we found it didn't even register. All they heard was what we had done and what we were going to do in the United States. Traveling through five other continents was even more incomprehensible to them than biking down from Alaska.

In regards to photos, download your photos constantly! Make CD disks of them and mail them home. If you have cloud-based storage, upload your photos to that. We used FTP (file transfer protocol) to upload our photos.

We also advise people to restrict their use of internet cafes.

Currently, they aren't as prevalent as they were during the span of our trip. But for us they were our source of communication to others and our way of downloading our photos. We were using memory sticks to store many of our photos on. Therefore, the memory sticks were inserted into many different computers. One memory stick got infected with viruses and we lost many very special pictures. After that, we purchased our own small laptop that we carried with us.

We talked before about border crossings and crossing them early in the day versus later. Another tip is how to handle that country's currency. It is best to spend down the currency that you have before crossing the border. The rates of exchange at borders are never in your favor, especially after crossing the border. Some countries won't even exchange another country's currency. It's not always easy to know how much money it is going to take to get to the border. Try to calculate how much you will need for food, housing, etc. so you don't have much currency left that you have to spend down.

SOUNDING JOY

After our trip, we can honestly say that we've "heard it all." The unique noises of each country provided the soundtrack to our journey.

QUIT WAKING ME UP!

We got to know countries not only by their people and the sights but also by sound. In Peru, for instance, the truck horns were so loud around the clock that they woke up Ward, whom is a deep sleeper. It was the same in Bolivia, Vietnam, and

Cambodia. We could be sleeping quite soundly when suddenly we'd be woken up by the horns honking.

In Costa Rica, it was the chickens. Every morning, we heard the roosters crowing. We had never heard so many chickens and roosters crowing in the morning in any other place.

Brazil featured gorillas groaning in the early mornings while we were camping along the tributary to the Amazon. Australia nearly drove us crazy with bird calls. We never found out what kind of bird it was, but it was incredibly loud. Every morning at 5:30 they'd start in. Also in Australia, we'd hear the thumps of the wallabies and kangaroos and even sometimes, the screech of the Tasmanian devil making his own soundtrack.

In Lithuania, we heard incredible yowling outside our tent—two cats were procreating less than two feet away and only stopped when dogs began barking.

Music, of course, set the scene in many countries. In Argentina, we often heard music from girls' sixteenth birthday celebrations that went on until six o'clock in the morning. Even the Argentinian weddings would last until six o'clock in the morning.

Ward: One night, I had slept quite well only to hear the music still going at half past five in the morning. I got up and went to experience the end of the party. The party was then winding down, so I assisted the wedding party in taking down the decorations and cleaning up. (I'm wondering what they were thinking when they saw a tall "gringo" show up to help clean up.)

The Patagonia winds were our constant nemesis. We heard it in our ears constantly. It just never stopped. It was relentless. No reprieve. It wore on us, and soon we began to hate it! All night long we would listen to the noise of the tent shuddering in the never-ending wind. Even in the hostels the sound of the wind was very hostile! We tried to beat it by getting up at four o'clock in the morning, but that didn't work because it never quit! The wind was a hurricane of sound.

As much as we loved getting to know the sounds of each place, it was quite a relief when things were silent for a few moments in our tent at the end of the day.

CHAPTER FORTY-ONE

OUR JOURNEY
ENDS..."NOT!"

An interesting thing happens when you travel: you find out who you are when no one else knows you. Stepping outside our normal roles was hard at the very beginning of the trip. It was strange to feel that we were no longer defined as a hospital dietitian and a bike shop owner. Nobody knew anything about us. We were just "the travelers." The loss of identity was a very weird feeling.

We slowly became a bit more reserved in our approach to people, because we learned that they were judging us solely on our mode of transportation, not our professions or who we were as individuals. To them, we were the bikers. We tried to remain reserved and quiet until people got used to us and were comfortable with us.

With thirty-two different languages to decode, we didn't always have the opportunity to talk meaningfully with folks or explain who we were. If we got across to them that we were married and had kids, that was a pretty big accomplishment.

We did have a business card to hand out, with our names and our mission statement on it, but it didn't tell people a whole lot about us and many people didn't know English anyway. In the beginning when we met people, we were tempted to start our conversation by mentioning our occupations, because otherwise we were nobodies. But in reality, we had no jobs or location to ground us. All we had was a post office box and a lot of experience.

> Jacky: It was a strange feeling. I almost felt lost. Like there was a part of me missing. My identity was gone, or redefined.

Ironically, now that we're back home, we're still known as "the travelers" here, too. We have a home and are working again, but our trip and our travels are still the most interesting things about us. That's what people want to hear about.

> Jacky: People approach us and ask, "Are you guys the ones that biked around the world?" And others ask, "Where's your next trip?"

> Ward: Even my Rotary classification has changed. I'm working as a contractor, but that's not how they describe me. I now get introduced as the adventurer.

It's a challenge to redefine ourselves now that we're back. Within two days of returning, we went from total freedom to regular jobs and home ownership. We'd had a lot of ideas about what we would do when we returned—a speaking tour, a bestselling book, etc.—but none of that materialized out of thin air. Plus, we had consumed our discretionary funds, so we had to work. Day-to-day life took over.

But also, right when we returned in 2010, many people treated us as celebrities and actually called us that. It was an uncomfortable feeling. We appreciated their admiration, but we had always stressed to people we met on the road that we were two normal people, just as they were, that were traveling to learn about other cultures. There was nothing special about us other than maybe how willing we were to go out of our comfort zone. We wanted to convey that same thought and feeling back home.

WHO WERE YOU?

On the other hand, our trip gave us the opportunity to explore our identities from a different perspective: that of our ancestors.

> Ward: I wanted to have some connection to my great grandparents, who came from Poland. I wanted to get a sense of the landscape and why my family moved from there to a spot about forty-five miles outside our town in Decorah, Iowa. I discovered that the landscape was identical to the farmland I grew up on. I was like, "Whoa."

It was a wonderful journey crossing from Lithuania to Poland. We could see how similar the landscape was to Northeast Iowa. It made sense that farmers from Poland would choose to settle in Iowa. It's unfortunate we never found their gravestones in Zlotow.

HOMELESS FOR THE HOLIDAYS

We didn't follow a lot of holiday traditions on the road, but we did try to recognize our birthdays and major holidays. We include this section to show that sometimes these occasions were wonderful experiences and other times they were just another day. It all depended on where we were, but we always tried to make the best of it.

Ward's fiftieth birthday fell on the day we crossed from Lithuania to Poland.

> Ward: I said to Jacky, "This is about as good as it gets, because I'm home. I've come to my home country."
>
> With the help of PayPal, I received $250 in birthday gifts. Everyone said I should buy a beer. A pint of beer cost fifty cents, so that would have been 500 beers. That was more birthday than I could take.

Ward's second birthday on the road was in Cuenca, Ecuador. We met up with our Pastor Bryan from Decorah, who knew Cuenca quite well and toured us around. We went for a big hike in Las Cajas National Park just outside of Quenca. The varied eco-systems would remind you of the movie *The Lord of the Rings*. Jacky was unable to join because of her sprained ankle.

Birthday number three happened back in the United States, in Coos Bay, Oregon. It was pretty uneventful, just a day riding along the West Coast.

Jacky's first birthday away was in Chile. We stayed at a tiny camping area and went to eat in their restaurant, but it was nothing special and actually disappointing. The next day, though, we had a great meal to celebrate.

> Jacky: We were told about a restaurant that served salmon,

and salmon's my favorite food. We had a beautiful dinner with wine and great conversation with the owners. That was probably the best meal I had on the whole trip.

Birthday two for Jacky came in Vietnam (as we mentioned before). It started off by us stopping at a little restaurant in the morning for a bite to eat. We had just passed into Vietnam the day before and didn't know much of the language yet. A few young girls sat with Jacky and taught her how to say the basic words in Vietnamese. Later that day, we stopped at a family kiosk. We were sitting outside drinking our soda and having our snack and the owners invited us into their house. It just happened that it was one of their daughters' birthday. Through gestures and writing down birthdates we were able to discern that it was each of our birthdays that day.

Jacky: Since I was so far from home, it was pretty special to me.

Jacky's third birthday came in Summerfield, Florida. We invited some new friends over for dinner that we met through the bike shop that Ward was temporarily working at. It was so fun to host a dinner party again. We hadn't done it in almost three years!

Birthdays are something we celebrate pretty big, normally, so we felt a little bit of a void, not having family and friends around to mark the occasions. We found that Americans celebrate birthdays a lot more than people in many other places. Nobody in Poland is impressed that it's your birthday. So, we tried to make them special between us. We missed these times back home.

Christmases were especially hard, because we were used

to making it such a special time with family, friends, and church. December of 2008 when we were in Australia it was particularly rough, just spending the day by ourselves. We spent Christmas in Barron Heads. We were told many Australians spend their Christmas at the beach and some have Santa bikinis, etc. We thought this would be a fun and memorable Christmas. However, the weather was cooler—around sixty degrees Fahrenheit. Therefore, beaches that normally would be full were empty. Everything in the nearby town was closed and not much activity of any sort was going on. Luckily, some other campers invited us over for Christmas dinner, but it was still hard being away from our sons and family.

Christmas in Florida may have been even worse, because after attending Christmas day mass at a nearby church, we were sitting in a hotel room in Tallahassee and the entire city was closed down. Earlier in the day, we bought some special snacks and beverages and shared them together that afternoon. Once we were done, we just sat in the hotel room and watched TV. We kept thinking about what our family back home was doing. The freedom of the road is a wonderful thing, but we also knew what we were missing.

IN SICKNESS AND IN HEALTH

People often ask us what we did when we were sick or injured. Thankfully, we didn't get hurt or ill very often or very seriously. Astonishingly, over three years, there were only three incidents that stopped us in our tracks. Jacky sprained her ankle when she tangled with some dogs and crashed her bike in Ecuador, Ward suffered through days of not moving when he caught the desert flu, and Jacky had to hide in the dark and quiet for a couple of days when altitude sickness struck when biking through the Peruvian Andes.

It's amazing that these were the only real health problems we faced. We had some stomach issues from eating different foods in new places, but nothing serious and nothing a little Imodium couldn't cure. However, we didn't baby ourselves in regards to food. We tried to eat at local vendors as much as we could. We feel it helped us a lot in tolerating different foods and conditions. We think we owe our good health to our plan, which also called for limiting our daily riding and resting when our health called for it.

TOGETHERNESS

Lots of couples say to us, "We would never survive being together 24/7!" They wonder how three years of constant contact affected our relationship. Although there were challenges, we feel our relationship was strengthened by the way we faced them.

One thing we learned was that it was important to solve our problems right away. Letting conflicts fester only made them worse. One ongoing miscommunication was about pace:

Ward: I sort of suspected that Jacky wasn't trying hard enough. I'd tell her to catch up to me and ride my draft, but she'd still lag behind. It was frustrating. I was always thinking I was going to let her pull so I could rest but she would not do that either. I thought she was slacking.

Jacky: I was back there thinking, "I'd love to be in the draft!" If I could have, why wouldn't I? Drafting saves 30 percent of your energy. He didn't understand until later that I was pushing as hard as I could.

We learned not to make assumptions like that about each other's perspective. Better to talk it out right away and understand what we were up against. Then we could figure out how to improve the situation.

> Jacky: We had to deal with our problems right away. We didn't have another room to go in to cool off. We just had our one tent with sleeping bags that were zipped together. So, it was best to talk it out and solve the problem at that time.

All of that togetherness, though, didn't mean we had a whole lot of privacy. We were often camping in people's yards and in campgrounds that were packed with other people. We also stayed at Rotarians' houses quite often. Not surprisingly, we had different takes on how to deal with this.

> Ward: All of the guys I talked to before the trip mentioned one goal I had to pursue: have sex in every country. Of course! Why wouldn't you?

> Jacky: First off, I didn't know about this goal. Second, I wasn't comfortable doing that in other people's houses. It just felt disrespectful. Third, we were only in Croatia for three hours!

> Ward: She's too nice. It's a family trait.

Solutions included sleeping bags that zipped together for nights in the tent, but even Ward admits it was a hard goal to reach, especially when our stay in some countries was so short.

Jacky: Although we were together the majority of the time, I did find some "me" time when Ward would go to Rotary meetings, fishing, or biking with the locals. He never seemed to need "me" time.

WOULDA, COULDA, SHOULDA

So much went right on this trip, whether by luck, planning, or just the generosity of others. Still, we look back and see some things we would do differently if we did it again. Here's a partial list of what we would change:

1. Take fewer tools but more bolts.
2. Visit more historical sites.
3. Do more research on interchangeable biking-to-hiking equipment.
4. Eat more local cuisines from restaurants, especially in Europe.
5. Raise more money so we could do number four.
6. Keep in closer contact with our sons and family.
7. Allow more time for wandering.
8. Leave more adjustment time for our return.

COMING HOME

Arriving back in the United States was a happy and proud moment for us. When the airport speakers announced, "Welcome home, Americans," we were truly touched. It brought tears to our eyes.

Ward: Now I knew the rules. In the United States, I could be whoever I wanted to be. I had that freedom to claim any identity I wanted to create. I wasn't stuck returning to my old role.

Jacky: For me, it was comforting, a familiar feeling, but I felt a bit like we were still on the road.

We jumped right into a remodeling job that was two and a half hours away.

Jacky: I was looking forward to getting together with my friends and family to see what they were up to, share stories and pictures, and have a drink together. But that didn't happen. By going right back to work, I never felt like I actually returned. It was like I was still on the road. I was still away from everybody. I never had the return that I was so looking forward to. It was a hard adjustment for me.

Plus, the house we had purchased—over the internet—was the oldest stick-built house in Decorah. As our son John said, it "needed a lot of love."

Ward: It was a golfer's dream. All the floors slanted to one corner. Hole in one!

The house featured low sagging ceilings, a stone basement, and an old clawfoot bathtub. Many mice had inhabited it before us. We had our work cut out for us. On the other hand, Decorah Bank and Trust helped us buy it even though we didn't have jobs yet. Our reputation apparently made us seem like a low risk.

Interestingly, it wasn't the big things that we noticed so much. It was the little, everyday differences. It was so special to have sinks with running water, and a refrigerator and freezer for storing food.

Jacky: I couldn't stop stocking up! When I went to the grocery store, I was like a kid in a candy shop. Also, it was super to have Tater Tots casserole and salsa again, foods I craved on the road.

WHAT'S NEXT?

We were glad to be home once again, but our love of travel has never really stopped. We frequently get the itch to be on the bike, to move through time and space, and experience life at 10 mph again. After so long in one place, we've got to get going again, like sailors who need to be out on the water.

Our traveling days are definitely not over. When this book comes out, we will have returned from a trip to India in 2013, a trip to Turkey/Greece/Bulgaria in 2014, a trip to Brazil/Argentina/Uraguai in 2015 (Ward only), a trip to Africa which included climbing Mt. Kilimanjaro and then cycling in Europe for Jacky's fiftieth birthday in 2016, touring the Balkin countries for Ward's sixtieth birthday (B-Day celebration in Budapest) in 2017, and biking through Kyrgyzstan and Kazakhstan in 2019.

Success is not always measured by how much money you have, your job, or your material possessions. Success comes from inside. Being happy with where you are at, where you are going, how you are helping and treating others, and being happy with life's adventures so far.

Jacky: This may be my final chapter of this book but not for our adventure and travel. With this trip came an open mind, an open desire. A flexibility to deal with the unknown that creates a sense of excitement and ability to lower your expectations. Being able to problem solve when a curveball is thrown at you. To appreciate your guardian angels and to be thankful for friends, family, and God because we never could have done this trip without them. We love the freedom of biking and knowing that we have everything we need...and that we can make it even without current-day technology. With the unknown comes a surge of adrenaline. Never knowing what's up ahead and having my partner by my side.

Ward: Writing my final chapter has come as a very difficult thing to do. I want to give you the essence of seeing the world at 10 mph. Do I tell you how I found myself? Do I try to make some prophetic statement that will change the world or positively affect you? Or do I share with you how 1,106 days of seeing the world slowly created an addictive force that I may never cure. Experience the world!!!

Let's start with, "Was I trying to find myself?" I was not "lost." I had already had the mandatory two midlife crises. I was living on the theme that if you say you will do something...DO IT! "Don't be a blow bag." Also, I wasn't lost. I was just going on a path I had not been on before. I was going to make the journey that I had said that I was going to do. (Thanks, Jacky, for the prenuptial.)

Prophetic statements came from the truly wise. Our journey gave us wisdom, but there are so many other people who are much, much wiser. Listen to them.

As I speak of an addictive force, I have become addicted to the smell of the world, the unique taste of different foods, the wind, rain, and sun on my face, the unknown and unbelievable hospitalities, the cultural differences and the cultural similarities.

The most addictive force has been relying on my own skills to figure things out. You might say I developed a confidence that I can figure things out no matter what the situation is. (Arrogance or naivety...maybe the same for both.)

As I reflect on the three years of travel, I saw my confidence levels rise in all of these areas: language, finding language, getting money, procuring food, and most importantly finding our way (with paper maps and sometimes without). I know my confidence of seeing the world will diminish someday. Physical strength, eyesight, and all the normal aging processes will make our future bike travels more challenging, but until then I will want to continue to see the world at 10 mph.

The world is yours. Maybe we'll see you on the road.

APPENDIX

EQUIPMENT

Clothing besides the obvious (we had to pack for all seasons, it's important to be able to layer):

- Dress shirt for attending more formal meetings
- Rotary jersey (as we attended Rotary meetings in various countries and also gave presentations at times)
- Bike shoe covers (booties)
- Wool socks (one pair)
- Medium heavy tights (one pair)
- Bike shorts (two pairs) and any other older shorts that will wear out quickly
- Flip flops for the shower
- Shoes to wear when not on the bike also suitable for hiking
- Long-sleeve polypropylene or warmer top
- Bike jersey or other tops that can be used both for biking and with shorts/pants
- Zip-off pants so you can have both shorts and pants in one
- Scrunchy skirt (don't need to worry about wrinkles) in case you need to be dressier (match with one of your biking tops that's not a jersey)
- Head band and warmer hat

- Medium heavy pair of gloves
- Bike gloves
- Windbreaker jacket with zip-off sleeves to be a vest
- Arm warmers

BIKE SPECIFICS

- Soma steel frames in case we needed to weld them
- Thirty-six spoke wheels for strength
- Eight speed shifters
- Xt rear derailleur
- SPD dual-sided pedals
- Tires 26 x 1.50 or larger for all road types

BIKE EQUIPMENT

- Duct tape and zip ties (constantly used)
- Front and rear back racks made of cro-moly steel
- Front and back waterproof panniers
- Large waterproof Ziplock bags to keep clothes additionally dry and sorted
- Top bag for miscellaneous frequently needed items
- At least two water bottle cages (extra water bottle cages can be used to soak dried beans while you ride so they are ready to cook at the end of the day)
- Tubes
- Tire patch kit (we never put more than four patches on; when we would put five patches on, too often one of the patches would leak)
- Spokes to fix our broken wheels and also to toast our bread over our stove
- Lube—normally petroleum, but sunscreen does work as well

TOOLS

- Screwdriver
- Adjustable wrench
- Cassette remover
- Spoke wrench
- Extra brake pads, disk or rubber
- Bike pump
- Miscellaneous bolts and screws for the bike

ACKNOWLEDGMENTS

As we stated in the beginning of our book, we couldn't have done this trip without the wonderful support from our friends and families. You all added a special element to our trip.

(If we have misspelled a name or forgotten someone, we are deeply sorry.)

PEOPLE WHO JOINED US OR WHOM WE MET UP WITH ON THE ROAD

- Frank Pollari (three different times: Asia, Rwanda, Arctic Circle)
- Jeff Freidhof (two different times: Peru, Arctic Circle)
- Ben Garrett and Christina German (New Zealand)
- AnnaMarie Dannhart (two different times: Asia, Grand Canyon)
- Denise St. Marie (Grand Canyon)
- Kay and Harry Lum (Grand Canyon)
- Joanne Snow (Arctic Circle)
- Paul and Kelsey Scanlon (Arctic Circle)
- Mark Pernitz (Arctic Circle)

- Sue Zbornick (Sydney, Australia)
- Denise and Eric Clement (Reno, Nevada)
- Doug and Sue Burks (Summerfield, Florida)
- Greg and Sue Franken (Summerfield, Florida)
- John and Molly Budweg (Alaska; fishing trip)
- Aaron Milburger (Boston, Massachusetts; biked with us to Portland, Maine)
- Maggie and Den Olson (Copenhagen, Denmark)
- Laura Budweg and Mark Nystrom (Loire Valley, France)
- Russ, Angela, and Marshall Carll (Loire Valley, France)
- Connie Spreen and Dan, Axel and Sander Peterman (San Jose, Costa Rica)
- Jim and Jane Kirchner (San Jose, Costa Rica)
- Kelly Reagan and his children (Orlando, Florida)
- Dale and Maddie Putnam (Orlando, Florida)
- Shana and Andrew Dibble (Orlando, Florida)
- Craig and Sarah Chiles and their children (Orlando, Florida)
- Dan Spilde (Daytona Florida for the Daytona 500)
- Lee Hackman (Daytona Florida for the Daytona 500)
- Marc Folkedahl (Daytona Florida for the Daytona 500)
- Eric Clement (Daytona Florida for the Daytona 500)
- Larry and Chrissy Peters (Navajo Truck Stop, New Mexico)
- Ralph and Louise Laingren (Key West, Florida)
- Decorah Lutheran Mission Trip: met in Bocas de Torro, Panama
  - Pastor Bryan Robertson
  - Bernie Ramlo
  - Robert Pietan
  - Glenn Barth

FRIENDS AND RELATIVES WHOM WE STAYED WITH WHILE ON THE ROAD

(In addition to this list, we stayed with many Rotarians and Elk members that also showed unbelievable hospitality.)

- Judy Smith (Litchfield Park, Arizona)
- Wilson and Mariza Daltou (Tangerra de Serra, Matto Grosso, Brazil)
- Fabio Carvalho and Larissa (San Carlos, Brazil)
- Barry and Lynn Williams (Paeroa, New Zealand)
- Cindy Klein (Issaquah, Washington)
- Russ Carll's nephew (Seattle)
- Dick and Barb Freudenthal (Portland, Oregon)
- Maury and Maria Peters (Chula Vista, California)
- Russ and Angela Carll (New Orleans, Louisiana)
- Aaron Budweg (San Francisco, California)
- Lisa and Wayne Koch (Boston, Massachusetts)
- Dave and Alice Mathison (Vancouver, British Columbia)
- Malte and Kristi Bruggeman (Houston, Texas)
- Darrell and Betty Branhagen (DeSoto, Texas)
- Kathy Krob (Anderson, South Carolina)
- Jerome, Barb O'Kones's brother (Chapel Hill, North Carolina)
- Greta Budweg and Susan French (Ashburn, Virginia)
- Mark Ploegstara (Princeton, New Jersey)
- Dave and Annette Swick (Monacle Lake, Michigan)
- Tim Staton (Copenhagen, Denmark)
- Martin and Sabina Haus and Brunhild Peters (Aschaffenburg, Germany)
- Maureen Larson (Lillihammer, Norway)
- Ralph and Louise (Vasteras, Sweden)
- John and Ann Walker (Santiago, Chile)
- Claudia Manhal (Ames, Iowa)

- Aaron Budweg (Eldora, Iowa)
- Clark Budweg (New Hampton, Iowa)
- Larry and Chris Peters (Cedar Falls, Iowa)
- Greg Budweg (Minneapolis, Minnesota)
- Paul and Judy Scanlon (Rochester, Minnesota)
- Doug and Gina Mello (Punta Morales, Costa Rica)
- Tom and Theresa Bockman (Punta Morales, Costa Rica)
- Dale and Jody Ellickson (Punta Morales, Costa Rica)

THANK YOU to all of you for sharing our trip with us and helping to create great memories and wonderful relationships.

CPSIA information can be obtained
at www.ICGtesting.com
Printed in the USA
LVHW111046110820
662876LV00005B/88/J